"Augustine's legacy for sex in the West his texts, eminently the *Confessions*, are duced, so as to yield to and inspire de: can indeed. Its triple authorship produ makes seduction about play itself rather than about accomplishing the deed. Can seduction substitute for sex? It can, if sex is about pleasure, the pleasure of the text, a pleasure in the seduction of words forming the body of the text, its flesh. The textual dynamics enacting ultimately the love of God are sexual in their seductive effects, producing pleasure in play that keeps desire alive with desiring what it longs for and cannot quite possess—except in the play itself that is realized textually. This desire is expressed in praise that excites passion for the divine other, the one addressed as 'you.' But to enjoy it, you must abandon all resistance and risk endless joy without reserve.

"The motivations of the whole tradition of Western literature, including the discourses of theology and philosophy, can hardly be grasped without taking into account the dynamics of desire deciphered in this book that seduces the saint. He is made to confess his seductiveness. It is a ravishing read!"—William Franke, author of *Poetry and Apocalypse: Theological Disclosures of Poetic Language*

"*Both seduced by Augustine's text and seducing it in return, as they themselves confess, the authors offer a provocative and enticingly fresh guide through Augustine's Confessions. . . .* a deeply insightful set of studies, well theorized and thoroughly interdisciplinary."—Patricia Cox Miller, Syracuse University

Seducing Augustine

VIRGINIA BURRUS
MARK D. JORDAN
KARMEN MACKENDRICK

Seducing Augustine

Bodies, Desires, Confessions

Fordham University Press
New York | 2010

Library of Congress Cataloging-in-Publication Data

Burrus, Virginia.
    Seducing Augustine : bodies, desires, confessions / Virginia Burrus, Mark D. Jordan, and Karmen MacKendrick.—1st ed.
        p.   cm.
    Includes bibliographical references and index.
    ISBN 978-0-8232-3193-5 (cloth : alk. paper)—ISBN 978-0-8232-3194-2 (pbk. : alk. paper)—ISBN 978-0-8232-3195-9 (ebook : alk. paper)
    I. Augustine, Saint, Bishop of Hippo. Confessiones.   2. Sex—Religious aspects—Christianity.   I. Jordan, Mark D.   II. MacKendrick, Karmen, 1962–   III. Title.
    BR65.A62B85   2010
    270.2092—dc22

                                                                              2009054043

Printed in the United States of America
12 11 10   5 4 3 2 1

First edition

One, two, three—but where is the fourth . . . ? (Plato, *Timaeus*)
for Daniel Boyarin, who hosted this party

Contents

Preface

This triple-authored book began as a twinkle in someone else's eye. In the summer of 2005, acting in his capacity as director of the University of California's Center for the Study of Sexual Culture, Daniel Boyarin invited the three of us to deliver lectures on the topic of Augustine and sexuality at a symposium that was to be held in Berkeley in the spring of 2006. Both Daniel's generous invitation and our enthusiastic acceptances were themselves the outgrowth of a conversation that had begun in the fall of 2004, when all four of us met (some of us for the first time) at a colloquium at Drew University. (Traces of this exchange, to which others added much, are preserved in Virginia Burrus and Catherine Keller, eds., *Toward a Theology of Eros: Transfiguring Passion at the Limits of Discipline* [New York: Fordham University Press, 2006]). Sparks of debate as well as agreement warmed that initial engagement, as we found ourselves returning to two well-traversed texts—Plato's *Symposium* and Augustine's *Confessions*—to consider afresh the complex convergences of desire and discipline. Not surprisingly, such themes once again drew us when we met in Berkeley for the symposium that had by then been alluringly dubbed "Sex in the City of God: Erotic Augustine." The richness of the conversation on this occasion owed much to the generous and insightful responses offered by Carla Freccero and Ramona Naddaff, as well as Boyarin himself, and the pleasure of intellectual exchanges continuing in the wake of that symposium rendered the thought of a joint publication on eroticism in Augustine's *Confessions* sorely tempting, despite our daunting awareness that the world is scarcely in need of more books—least of all more books about Augustine, one might well add. In the end, we gave way to temptation, without, however, utterly ceasing to resist: it would be "a little book," we told ourselves. And so it has proved.

We are grateful for the support of Drew University's Presidential Initiatives Fund, which allowed us to meet together and further test some of our ideas with colleagues at Drew, including (but not limited to) Louis Hamilton, Stephen Moore, and Traci West. Other opportunities to present our work individually to fellow scholars were also extremely valuable, and we thank our various hosts and interlocutors without here naming them all specifically—a concession to the danger of tripling the usual burden on readers' patience that we hope will be forgiven. In the end, however, all three of us remain rather stubbornly textual creatures; arguably, that orientation unites us as much as our shared obsessions with eroticism and Christian traditions. So we read and we wrote; we swapped texts and exchanged questions and hunches; and we occasionally borrowed and lent sentences and paragraphs. But we were also respectful of each other's interpretive and writerly particularities, even idiosyncrasies. (For those of you who are curious—and cannot guess—Virginia was the primary drafter of Chapters 1 and 4, Mark of Chapter 2, and Karmen of Chapter 3. Other mysteries will remain veiled.) This means that we decided to allow certain differences to remain. For example, each of the first three chapters touches upon the decisive turning point in *Confessions* when Augustine chooses not merely Christianity but also, more specifically, an ascetic version of it, figured in the text as a woman called Continence. One might suggest that for Chapter 1, this scene is a sensuously teasing seduction; for Chapter 2, a crashing denial of bodily pleasure; for Chapter 3, an erotically complex performance of willed submission. In Chapter 4, moreover, the figure of Continence returns in the guise of the "heaven of heavens," a disembodied eternity that must finally be rejoined to terrestrial temporality. These readings cannot be simply merged, and yet each is important, we feel, and each is the product of a particular kind of seductive engagement of the text to which a given writer at a given moment was attracted. At the same time, the accumulation of interpretations mimes Augustine's own propensity to revisit and revise his own texts and thoughts, an iterative process to which we have been collectively drawn. What success we have had in coordinating our readings and harmonizing our voices has been greatly enhanced by the sharply insightful and deeply generous responses to our manuscript offered by Jim Wetzel and Catherine Conybeare, as well as by the support of our friend and editor Helen Tartar and the hardworking staff at Fordham University Press. No one who knows these unusually good and smart people will be the least bit astonished by our testimony, nor will they be surprised to know that we failed to take advantage of *all* of the good advice we were given!

It must finally be acknowledged that each of us is trained in a different discipline, yet we have all tended to resist discipline as well. A loose weave of philosophy, theology, literary criticism, and history provides an intellectual space for this book that we can share—differently.

Seducing Augustine

Introduction
Pleasurable Temptations

Augustine can safely be credited with a dubious sexual reputation. This is true for at least two reasons. On one hand, his most famous work—the elusively autobiographical *Confessions*—pivots on a conversion that has as much to do with the chastening of desire as with the correcting of belief. Augustine reaches his breaking point, as he tells it, in a private garden in Milan. There, jarred by a series of unexpected textual encounters, the man who has for at least twelve years been begging, "Give me chastity and continence, but not yet," suddenly discovers that the "not yet" has already arrived. "I sought neither wife nor any worldly hope," he announces, marveling at his own instantaneous transformation (*Confessions* 8.7.17, 8.12.30).[1] The moment has already arrived yet time notoriously flees, and much of the performative work of the *Confessions* is directed toward narrowing the gap between the relentless vicissitudes of temporal desire and the much-desired peace of eternal bliss.[2] For we discover, perhaps to our surprise, that the latter does not simply supersede the former. A decade after the decisive moment in the garden, Augustine is *still* chanting, "O love, who always burns and is never extinguished, charity, my God, set me on fire! You command continence; give what you command, and command what you will!" (10.29.40). The breaking point in the garden is, then, a moment *ever* to be seized: continence is always threatening to depart, always also on the verge of coming again. Ultimately, and paradoxically, it is by intensifying and sustaining the passion to undo passion—by begging, indeed very nearly commanding God to overpower his own desire—that Augustine begins to seduce eternity. Delicately suspended between shameful acts of dissipation frantically repeated and repeatedly renounced and the elusive lure of endless pleasures ever longed for and never quite reached, his *Confessions* is an irreducibly erotic text, but by no means a simple one. For many readers, it may seem to offer at once too much desire and too much renunciation.

On the other hand, Augustine is often accused, with rather less textual specificity but considerably more doctrinal force, of having single-handedly ruined sex for the western world. Ute Ranke-Heinemann, for example, refers to him with bracing decisiveness as "the man who fused Christianity together with hatred of sex and pleasure" and thereby "paved the way not just for the centuries, but for the millennia, that followed."[3] Augustine's innovative concept of "original sin" (as it is traditionally labeled) lies at the heart of the problem, underlining the pervasiveness of sexual perversion while dictating that only an indefinitely deferred grace can bring healing. In the meantime, he suggests, the violence and volatility of desire—reminders of humanity's flawed condition—are to be mitigated by disciplines of monasticism or monogamy. Procreative sex with one's marital partner is the safest kind, but danger lurks even there; neither can those living celibately expect to evade the temptation to lust. Humans are inescapably sexual, yet sexuality after the Fall is inevitably perverse and thus haunted by sin and shame. Adam and Eve *might* have had guilt-free sex in Paradise, but they ran out of time. There will be no more guilt in heaven, but unfortunately there will be no more time for sex either: although resurrected bodies will keep their fleshly genitals, these will serve purely decorative purposes. Once again, and now more severely from the vantage point of such an encompassing theological program, we are confronted with what may seem an excess of both desire and renunciation in Augustine's thought.

How do we proceed from such a seemingly infelicitous starting point? As it happens, it is precisely his dubious sexual reputation and propensity for excessiveness that attract us to the late fourth-century African church father and tempt us to undertake this reading of his *Confessions*. Because we are drawn by the very ambivalence that Augustine's thought evokes, we have little interest in simply accusing or defending him. We will certainly resist him at many points (struggling to render the proverbial "strong reading"), yet we like to imagine that he will have his way with us at least as often as we with him. As Geoffrey Harpham argues, "Resistance to temptation is *both* imperative and impossible."[4] The dynamic of temptation and resistance so well analyzed by Harpham will be crucial to our reading of Augustine. That reading will circle around four sets of seductively intertwined themes—secrecy and exposure, asceticism and eroticism, constraint and freedom, and time and eternity.

Here we must register the significant legacy of Margaret Miles's 1992 *Desire and Delight: A New Reading of Augustine's Confessions*. In this work, Miles argues that the *Confessions* is helpfully understood as "a text of pleasure," in Roland Barthes's terms. She is not the first to note affinities between Barthes's theory of textual erotics and certain ancient Christian understandings of the relationship of language to desire,[5] and she does not engage Barthes's work closely or extensively. In fact, aside from a few free-floating invocations of such recognizably Barthian phrases as "pleasure of the text" and "text of pleasure,"[6] Miles's explicit references to the French theorist are confined to two cited passages from his 1973 *The Pleasure of the Text*.[7] Nonetheless, insights gleaned from Barthes permeate her reading and shape some of its strongest claims about the seductiveness of Augustine's *Confessions*. Proposing that the *Confessions* is centrally concerned with the theoretical problem of "how to get—and keep—the greatest degree of pleasure," Miles emphasizes that the text itself also effectively evokes—and sustains—the reader's pleasure. She notes that one "is quickly seduced into passionate relationship" by the *Confessions*; it stimulates "a responsive kaleidoscope of feeling—gratification, denial, frustration, discomfort, and satisfaction."[8] The first nine books in particular "reproduce the strains, anxiety, and energy of the life they narrate," Miles suggests, as Augustine skillfully sustains "unresolved contradictions that disturb a reader, keeping her awake, irritated, engaged."[9] "Unresolved contradictions in a text create a pleasurable tension," she repeats; "they function to invite the reader into the text as a conversation partner, opponent, supporter, and co-author." She continues: "Augustine was acutely aware of the role of dis-ease, disequilibrium, and tension in producing pleasure." In narrating his own sexual history, further-more, he "shows remarkable skill in engaging readers' erotic curiosity only to refuse to satisfy it."[10] ("The text you write must prove to me *that it desires me*," Barthes may be heard to murmur insistently in the background. "I am interested in language, because it seduces and wounds me."[11])

Tension between resistance and submission, order and chaos, is inherent to the paradoxically painful pleasure prolonged within the textual seduction of Augustine's *Confessions*, Miles suggests. Such a possibility, however, appears to be as alarming as it is alluring: can resistance not break free of its dance with desire—specifically, with the desire to *submit*? Miles urges that "one must somehow manage to see simultaneously the problems and dangers of Augustine's thought—the authoritarianism, the exclusionary strategies—*and* its extraordinary power and beauty." She adds the warning that "if one reads in the *Confessions* only its powerful beauty, one is susceptible to its many seductions, its prohibitions, its silences, its politics, and institutional allegiances"; included in what is excluded by the dangerously attractive text, she further notes, are "women and the natural worlds of bodies and senses."[12] Reading both women and the sentient body back into the text becomes a significant part of Miles's agenda. Strikingly—and crucially—for her this ultimately requires breaking away from the "many seductions" of the *Confessions*. The desire of the text is at once too phallic and too disembodied to be safely engaged. "The *Confessions* tempts the reader to read without a body, especially a female body," warns Miles. "A gendered reading . . . reveals the absence of a female subject position in the text; it also makes visible Augustine's extensive use of male sexuality as a primary and pervasive model for human life."[13] It is not enough that the temptation to read without a body—or, alternately, with a merely metaphorical male one—be *resisted*: it must be actively *opposed*. Indeed, Miles argues, the "dynamic of temptation and resistance" is itself part of the "danger of his construction of spirituality."[14]

Thus, having begun by reveling in her delight in Augustine's text, Miles ends by firmly disentangling herself from the tentacles of her own desire. She wants both to be seduced (by some aspects of the text) and not to be seduced (by others); however, since resistance to seduction is all too easily encompassed *within* seduction (does "no" *really* mean . . . "no"?), she must finally exit the textual play altogether. Lamenting both the sexual repressions and the political oppressions mobilized within the *Confessions*, she evades its "problems and dangers" by killing her own readerly joy, an act that she ultimately attributes to—one might also fairly say, *blames on*—the erotic failures of Augustine's text.[15] Pointing out that the later books of the *Confessions* attempt to resolve the very tensions, contradictions, and gaps that make its earlier books so pleasurable to read, she charges that they offer a pseudo-pleasure masked as "true"—or, perhaps better, as *truth* itself. Thus, Miles acknowledges enjoyment of the "disorderly narration" of Books 1 through 9 but must, regretfully, leave joy behind upon arriving at the "contemplative exposition" of Books 10 through 13.[16]

Interestingly, one of only two lines of Barthes that she cites in this work—and she cites the line twice—is this: "The text of pleasure is not necessarily the text that recounts pleasures."[17] The first time, the line appears as a chapter epigraph, in a context that indicates that Miles's argument coincides with Barthes's: the pleasure of a text like *Confessions* exceeds, and is not necessarily linked to, its description or narration of pleasures.[18] Indeed, in Barthes's view, to "take pleasure in a *reported* pleasure" is extremely difficult.[19] The second time she cites the line, Miles seems to bend—almost to reverse—Barthes's sense, suggesting that Augustine's text ceases to seduce precisely when it ceases to recount or report sensual pleasures, despite the pleasure that he himself appears to experience in its writing.[20] "Clearly author's pleasure and reader's pleasure do not coincide," she asserts with regard to the last four books of the *Confessions*, claiming to speak on behalf of "generation after generation of readers" (in this, apparently excluding the perversely philosophical ones pleased *only* by the later books). "The *Confessions* does not reproduce Augustine's pleasure in his reader," she repeats, echoing (though not citing) Barthes's own statement that the writer's pleasure does "not at all" guarantee the reader's pleasure.[21] Not merely *not pleased*, Miles pronounces herself positively "harassed" by the author's increasing, and increasingly one-sided, excitement. This sense of harassment arises, paradoxically, less from his oppressively domineering will—though she *does* note the more confident and dogmatic tone of the later books—than from his disappointingly docile flesh: "The young Augustine's sexual body—insistent, demanding, aggressive—is present in the later books only in diluted, emaciated, furtive form, as wet dream, hastily expelled from

Augustine's 'real self.' "[22] No longer tempted by the once-seductive textual body, Miles is, she confesses, "profoundly sad"[23]—and understandably so. In the triumph of resistance lies its own undoing: where desire is negated, there is nothing left to resist.

Except, perhaps, the negation of desire.

Yet Miles's dilemma cannot simply be dismissed: how *can* the pleasure of this particular text be sustained, in the wake of what are by now not new but relatively long-standing criticisms of sexism, heterosexism, and their accompanying sexual repressions—criticisms with which we are (it goes almost without saying) deeply sympathetic? As Barthes notes, "The pleasure of the text does not prefer one ideology to another." Indeed, bliss "can erupt, across the centuries, out of certain texts that were nonetheless written to the glory of the dreariest, of the most sinister philosophy."[24] The possible coincidence of pleasure with political values would thus seem arbitrary, at best; that pleasure and politics should diverge and thereby come into conflict, at least as likely. However, Miles's own reading demonstrates, and Barthes also acknowledges, that a text may in fact cease to please when "I do not like the demand." In such a case, it "prattles"; it is "frigid"; it "bores."[25] It may be that we as readers defend ourselves against unwanted demands (against ideology per se?) by refusing the pleasure of the text, choosing to be bored rather than excited by its attempted seductions. Ironically, at such a point, pleasure and politics may begin to align themselves *too* exactly.

We should note, however, that boredom is both more and less than the absence of pleasure. Indeed, "boredom is not far from bliss," Barthes suggests cryptically; "it is bliss seen from the shores of pleasure."[26] What could that mean? The differences between the frequently converging concepts of pleasure (*plaisir*) and bliss (*jouissance*) here begin to matter: for Barthes, the former is associated with plenitude, continuity, comfort, and euphoria, the latter with loss, disjunction, discomfort, and ecstasy; eros arises at the intersecting borders of both. Boredom, then, is would-be bliss misrecognized as merely failed pleasure, we might say: in boredom (as Barthes understands it), pleasure may interrupt its own complacency to reach toward bliss, for "what pleasure wants is the site of a loss, the seam, the cut, the deflation, the *dissolve* which seizes the subject in the midst of bliss."[27] Moreover, a text that offered no provocation or irritation, no shadow of "dominant ideology" would be not only "frigid" but "sterile."[28] What is sterile cannot be rendered fertile, but what is frigid may yet be seduced. And we seduce by abandoning ourselves to seduction. As Jean Baudrillard notes, "To be seduced is to challenge the other to be seduced in turn."[29]

Precisely where the *Confessions* both offers and provokes greatest resistance, we will not, then, denounce Augustine (far less excuse him!) but rather divert and pervert him—turning him aside from his *truth*, as Baudrillard describes the movement of seduction,[30] so as also to be turned aside from our own self-certainties (or so we may hope). That is to say, we will opt to sustain the play of seduction as long as possible. We will do so, furthermore, in the name of politics as well as pleasure. If one accepts (both for example and for the sake of argument) that the *Confessions* supplies no positive "female subject position" yet seems everywhere to assume a "male sexuality," does the text not nonetheless (even thereby) seduce our readerly "femininity," emergent at that queer site where deep resistance meets deep responsiveness in a bursting-forth of joy that (momentarily) both reverses and undoes the binary between text and reader, masculinity and femininity, activity and passivity? Put otherwise, is every absence or gap in a text as subtle and complex as the *Confessions* not potentially a lure or incitement, overflowing with possibility, every attempt at domination an opportunity to assert oneself in turn? Baudrillard suggests that seduction "implies a reversible, indeterminate order."[31] For his part, Barthes notes with regard to the erotics of reading that "there is not, behind the text, someone active (the writer) and out front someone passive (the reader); there is not a subject and an object. The text supersedes grammatical attitudes."[32] As we will discover, seduction not only destabilizes gender and other hierarchies of "position" (including the grammatical) via its logic of reversibility but also (and by a similar logic) disarms moral codes: it offers no firm and immovable place from which to deliver judgment or enforce norms, but only the fluid and reversible play of temptation and resistance, persuasion and acquiescence, in which desire is both drawn and countered by desire. Yet is this not a possible aim of politics as well as pleasure—to subvert "the authoritarianism, the exclusionary strategies," as Miles names the "dangers" conveyed by the text?

Such a hermeneutics of seduction—sustained through all thirteen books of Augustine's *Confessions*—will lead us to some quite different conclusions than the ones Miles reached in 1992; but, after all, we stand in a quite different intellectual moment. Rather than attempt to expose Augustine's sexual history—"Augustine suffered from an addiction to sex"; "he has been frightened and damaged by the painful abrasiveness of his early experience"[33]—we will explore how the *Confessions* conjoins the erotic with the secret, the imaginary, and the fictional, rendering Augustine's actual sex life not only inherently unknowable but also very nearly irrelevant. (Of course, one *does* continue to wonder: but that is just the point.) Rather than decry the absence of the sexual body from the last four books of the text— "Augustine's body . . . is in hiding . . . as flesh made word"[34]—we will explore the complex and intensely ambivalent relationship between seductive flesh and persuasive words that pervades all of its books, and more. (The present absence of one body—His Body—may be seen to haunt Augustine's entire corpus with longing.) Rather than struggle to escape the control of the text—"as a disobedient reader, I have allowed my sensitivities to highlight features of the *Confessions* . . . more revealing than Augustine might have wanted them to be"[35]—we will engage the painful pleasure of willed submission that lies at the erotic heart not only of the *Confessions* but of Augustine's broader understanding of sin and salvation. (If perfect obedience is necessarily impossible, then disobedience is a happy inevitability.) Rather than mourn his fateful otherworldliness—"Augustine's formulation of the spiritual life as a withdrawal from attachment to the world of senses and objects has played a role in creating the present condition of the earth, a planet in ecological and nuclear crisis"[36]—we will unfold the bottomless depths of beauty that Augustine discovers within creation, extending desire endlessly precisely by refusing satisfaction. (Eternity is in the potent joy of the moment—which can never quite be grasped.)

Although our exploration of Augustine's erotic theory and practice will center on his *Confessions* (397–401), it will at several crucial points spill beyond that text—most notably, into the early books of *On Christian Teaching* (396–426) roughly contemporaneous with the *Confessions* and the later books of *City of God* (413–27), written some twenty years after the *Confessions*. For some readers, this latter stretch in particular may raise the question of how to negotiate change and continuity in Augustine's thought—a much-vexed topic, as it happens. Interpretation of his "conversion" in 386 is all the more difficult precisely because it carries so much narrative weight in the *Confessions*: To what extent was it a conversion to Platonism rather than Christianity? Why does it go unmentioned in works written closer to the event? Many have placed more emphasis on the turn that Augustine's thought took a decade or so later—that is, around the time that he began to write the *Confessions*—but, again, assessment of this narrative line is complicated by the fact that Augustine himself insinuates it, this time in his *Retractations* (426–27).[37] Recently, Carol Harrison has argued strongly against overplaying the 396 turn and in favor of taking the 386 "conversion" more seriously as setting the course for Augustine's later intellectual project, suggesting that "the defining features of his mature theology were in place from this moment onwards."[38] More recently still, David Hunter has noted the significance of a shift taking place later than 396, more specifically, around 410, with regard to Augustine's increasingly positive understanding of the body and sexuality.[39]

While we find such interventions significant and instructive, our approach to the temporal challenge of reading across Augustine's textual corpus will be less linear, not least because Augustine's own writings (both individually and collectively) seem consistently to subvert the linearity that they also narratively inscribe. As M. B. Pranger has framed the issue broadly, "the historian of antiquity and the Middle Ages faces the problem of literary immobility." Our sources do not share our own historiographic assumptions that time "is the intrinsic regulator of progress and the guarantee of linearity and plot"; on the contrary, they draw us into a world at once dauntingly remote and strangely familiar in which "time is bent, so to speak, and made curvilinear, so that it obeys the patterns and rituals of retardation and repetition."[40] To the extent that Augustine's thought advances, it typically does so by looping back on itself, as the writer engages in a seemingly endless iterative process of self-amplification and self-correction. Thus our own readings of the *Confessions* will not infrequently circle through other texts, both within and beyond the Augustinian corpus. This they do not so as to *represent* (in the guise of a historical argument) the complex temporal shuttlings of Augustine's developing thought, but rather so as to *prolong* the ongoing intertextual assemblage of what Barthes calls a "circular memory."[41]

We will, finally, eschew widespread scholarly convention by choosing *not* to include a recitation of Augustine's biography in this very brief introduction. Such a recitation not only would lodge us all too securely within a linear temporality but also would inevitably rest heavily on the very text that remains to be interpreted in the pages that follow. Augustine's views on desire in the *Confessions* cannot helpfully be "explained" by reference to relationships in his life that we know only through their polished recounting in the *Confessions*—where they serve (among other purposes) to perform and convey his views on desire, as we will see. Even if we felt confident in the biographical data themselves, we would have little confidence in the hermeneutical resort to biography. The relation between a human life, the literary corpus attached to it as author, and the worlds of thought and imagination potentially evoked by that textual body is complex and mysterious, to say the least. The Augustine that readers will discover here is the one who has seduced us—and he has not seduced each of us in exactly the same way—by provoking us to seduce him. Or was it the other way around?

1

Secrets and Lies

I've a great admiration for Augustine, of course, and the feeling that I don't know him enough; I will never know him enough. That's one more reason to ask for forgiveness of him. But on the other hand, I try, not to pervert him, but to "mis-lead" him, so to speak, into places where he couldn't and wouldn't go.

> Jacques Derrida, "Composing 'Circumfession'"

To be seduced is to be turned from one's truth. To seduce is to lead the other from his/her truth. This truth then becomes a secret that escapes him/her.

> Jean Baudrillard, *Seduction*

And how do they know whether I tell the truth . . . ?

> Augustine, *Confessions* 10.3.3

In Book 2 of his *Confessions*, Augustine embarks on an account of the misadventures of his sixteenth year. Recalling his own "impurities," "corruptions," and "wicked ways"—and thereby, as he puts it, "gathering myself from the scattered state in which I fell to pieces"—he archives a wasted youth: "I dared to grow wild in diverse and shadowed loves" (2.1.1). Nothing mattered to him at the time but "to love and be loved," he professes. "I was hurled and spilled out, and I flowed and boiled over in the midst of my fornications" (2.2.2). In the act of recollection, Augustine thus skillfully performs his own dissipation, but what, if anything, has he actually disclosed? He tells us that he fell apart, he ran wild, he overflowed. The metaphors increase and multiply: they themselves fall apart, run wild, overflow. Yet the teasing text, while seeming to spill all, remains veiled in its very metaphoricity.[1] As he elsewhere explains, in figural speech "things withdrawn, as it were, may be desired more ardently and, being desired, may be discovered with greater pleasure" (*Against Lying* 24).[2]

Sometimes his confessions even hide their secrets boldly, under bald-faced lies. He does not shrink from admitting it: as a teenager, when shameful deeds failed him, he simply made them up, lest he have nothing to brag about to his friends. "Afraid of being reviled I grew viler, and when I had no ruinous act to admit that could put me on a level with these abandoned youths, I pretended that I had done what I had not done" (*Confessions* 2.3.7). Augustine misled his audience when he was sixteen—unremarkably, perhaps. We might pause to ask whether he is doing it still. We might pause to ask, in other words, how well *any* of us knows Augustine. Certainly, each of us seems to know him differently. One scholar sees a man with a notable, even surprising, preference for stable monogamy, remaining faithful to his partner for the full thirteen years of their relationship—"which was considerably more than his own father, Patricius, had ever done for his mother, Monica."[3] Another discovers a somewhat pathetic "sex addict" who is finally forced to choose abstinence in order to restore much-needed equilibrium to his life.[4] Yet another detects a writer with a "penchant for figurative language" and a "tendency toward hyperbole" evidenced in an often "lurid" and possibly "deceptive" use of sexual images and metaphors.[5] Indeed, it would seem that the author of the *Confessions* all too easily deceives his readers, above all by tempting them to imagine that they can know him. He artfully misleads his readers, not least by inciting their curiosity about sex. Why does he do this? Or rather: why do we let him? If we continue to be drawn, he will eventually elude us, causing us to stray into shadows where every object slips the grasp. Allowing ourselves to be thus diverted, thus dispersed and scattered, can we also hope to mislead *him*? Might it even be to pervert him, after all? Perhaps this is what he has been wanting all along.

For Augustine's confessions are seductions.[6] Ostensibly addressed to God, they beat gently against our ears, enticing us to listen in. They deliberately lead us astray; they actively lead us on. "One cannot seduce others, if one has not oneself been seduced," notes Jean Baudrillard.[7] Augustine is infinitely seducible, as he so boldly confesses (2.3), and his seducibility draws us. He seduces more by what he does *not* show and tell of his own seductions than by what he does, however. Although he repeatedly speaks of spilling himself out, the pornographic "money shot" remains outside our angle of vision. Indeed, Augustine's sexual pleasure is as secret—thus as unrepresentable—as a woman's is reputed to be: it is even possible that he is faking the whole thing.[8] But why would he do that? For the joy that inheres in the sheer intimacy of confessing to another, of confessing oneself *as* other, perhaps—as he himself hints. If so, he is not *completely* faking it. The sexual content of the confession may begin to seem nearly irrelevant, having already, by the time we read it, been doubled and displaced by a confessional performance in which Augustine has, yes, spilled himself out. Yet it is a different spilling than the one we were expecting. Repeatedly, he redirects our attention, diverting us from the course of anticipated revelations.

Augustine's confessions turn us aside from the straight and narrow path of revealed truth, then. Arguably, all confessional discourse does so. As Jacques Derrida notes, the truth of a confessional declaration or avowal "is not a truth to be known or . . . revealed." It "does not consist only in lifting a veil."[9] It is, rather, a truth to be "made" or "done" (*facere*), as Augustine famously puts it, proclaiming to his God, "I want to make truth in my heart before you in confession, and in my book before many witnesses" (10.1.1).[10] This "made" truth lies close to fiction while suspending the distinction between "the fictional, the invented, the dreamt event, the fantasized event . . . and the event presented as 'real.'"[11] Indeed, because it remains unverifiable to the extent that the soul's intentions are never fully knowable, the truth of confession is also haunted by the possibility of the lie: as Derrida puts it, "we are always already in the process of excusing ourselves, or even asking forgiveness, precisely in this ambiguous and perjurous mode."[12] If for Augustine lying is as tragically inevitable, and as devastatingly destructive, as sin itself, "it is not, however, the same thing to hide truth as to offer a lie" (*Against Lying* 23).[13]

Close to fiction, haunted by perjury, resisting revelation—perhaps the secret of confession is . . . its very secrecy. "Everything that can be revealed lies outside the secret," writes Baudrillard;[14] conversely, the secret lies outside what can be revealed. Confession's secreted "truth"—if truth is the right term at all—remains buried even in its uncovering. The very attempt to achieve self-transparency augments the sense of opacity, hiddenness, elusiveness. There is always more to confess; one never gets to the bottom of it. As J. M. Coetzee notes, "behind each true, final position lurks another position truer and more final."[15] Or rather, the pursuit of final truth begins to undo itself in confession. In the words of Michel Foucault, "Truth and sacrifice, the truth about ourselves and the sacrifice of ourselves, are deeply and closely connected."[16] A more profound knowing is also a more profound unknowing, as kataphasis and apophasis continually fold into one another. Thus, in the process of confessing, Augustine becomes not an answer but a question to himself, and also to us (4.4.9; 10.33.50). The mystery deepens even as his words overflow. Just so, in the secret, writes Elliot Wolfson, "to unveil the veil . . . is to veil the unveiling."[17]

In the paradoxical un/veiling of the secret, confession of seduction doubles back on the "original" event that it both displaces and repeats. For all seduction, like all confession, has a special relationship to the secret, as we have already begun to see. "It is by way of this play of veils . . . that seduction occurs," suggests Baudrillard. "This is where seduction is at play and not in the tearing away of the veil in the name of some manifestation of truth or desire."[18] Veils unveiled reveal more veils: confession is never more seductive than when a seduction is confessed. Drawn, as if irresistibly, this chapter will explore several passages in Augustine's *Confessions* that display such a doubled un/veiling. His erotic secrets, as we shall see, cannot be exposed, but they *can* be re/covered, and the play of veils does not cease to thrill. Fornications are secreted within a tale of gratuitous theft: rotting flesh arrives as a useless yet pleasurable gift. A woman's body shrouds its impenetrable otherness in a deceptively simple text: there is no end to the un/veiling of her mysteries. The object of love is stolen by death before we can see him: only the unseen God can withstand the devastating force of human passion, and only the unseen God can draw human desire infinitely.[19]

"An Exceedingly Unfriendly Friendship"

"Close to our vineyard there was a pear tree laden with fruit" (2.4.9). Thus begins an account that is among the best known in the *Confessions*. Here, in Book 2, in exchange for the narrative of sexual transgressions that he has initially led us to expect, Augustine tells us the story of an adolescent theft—a petty theft at that, as he himself emphasizes, involving a group of restless boys and some worthless pears that were discarded and thrown to pigs almost as soon as they were stolen. If we are paying attention, we may feel robbed of the juicier repast that he initially seems to promise—a full disclosure of the entanglements of love and lust that captured his sixteenth year. For, as Margaret Miles puts it, "Augustine frustrates the reader's prurient interest in his youthful sexual exploits" by offering a meticulous analysis of a minor transgression that "takes the place of any concrete description of his sexual activity." She goes on to observe that "he will repeatedly use this textual strategy." That he should make a habit of such strategic displacement apparently puzzles her, however: "Why does Augustine repeatedly stimulate, only to frustrate, the reader's erotic interest?" Answering her own question, Miles suggests that Augustine systematically fails to describe sexual acts because "he refuses to provide this potential temptation to his readers." In addition, she adds, he wants to downplay the element of sexual pleasure by foregrounding instead the distinctly unpleasant force of "compulsive attachment" that he discerns in sexual acts.[20]

Such an explanation cannot be simply wrong, but it does seem inadequate. For by refusing to gratify his readers' expectations of an exposé, Augustine does not necessarily lead them away from temptation. On the contrary, his tactics of iteration and displacement seem well calculated to prolong and intensify temptation—as Miles herself acknowledges. If Augustine repeatedly stimulates without satisfying desire, this may suggest less an act of compulsion than one of compelling (self-)control, in other words; nor should we overlook the fact that bait-and-switch is the bread-and-butter of the art of erotic suspense. "This is what occurs in the most banal games of seduction," observes Baudrillard: "I shy away. . . . There is above all a strategy of displacement (*se-ducere*: to take aside, to divert from one's path) that implies a distortion of sex's truth." The truth of sex—its "quick, banal end, the orgasm"—is no substitute for the secret of seduction without end, in Baudrillard's view.[21] Thus it is that readers of Book 2 may not even pause to register frustration as such: Augustine's bait-and-switch tactic works surprisingly well. The theft of the pears, as he recalls it, seems to bring pleasure as sharp and disturbing—and also as inconclusive—as a teenager's sexual encounters might be imagined to be.

The theft is disturbing in part because it appears senseless: Augustine's motivations remain a mystery even to himself, and thus they, too, seduce. He is not hungry, and the pears are not tasty. The pleasure of the crime, he emphasizes repeatedly, cannot therefore lie in possession or consumption. What, then? It is the act of disobedience that thrills him—that is, the simple, shameful fact of having done something he should not have done. Initially he proposes that such a gratuitous crime lies beyond perversion: it lacks "even that sham and shadowy beauty with which vices deceive us" (2.6.12). However, he subsequently discovers in his disobedience a vicious and perverse imitation of virtue, after all: "Was I, being a captive, mimicking a maimed freedom through the dim likeness of omnipotence by getting away with something forbidden?" he wonders aloud (2.6.14). The point is not that to play God is a sin but rather that to sin is to play God—a much more interesting proposition. Even when he rebels, his very perversions imitate and thus confess the goodness of his creator. Or—*especially* when he rebels?

But there is still more hidden within this theft than the pleasure of disobedience, the joy arising from the mimicry of divine freedom (about which we will have more to say in Chapter 3). As Augustine searches his memories, he avows: "I would not have done it alone; I most certainly would not have done it alone." What delighted him was "the crime as committed in the company of others who shared in the sin." He acknowledges that "the theft gave us a thrill" and repeats: "I would not have done that deed alone; in no way would I have done it alone. . . . To do it alone would have aroused no desire whatever in me, nor would I have done it." He seems sure of himself on this point. "Let the others only say, 'Come on, let's go and do it!' and I am ashamed to hold back from the shameless act," he confesses. He concludes that it is friendship—albeit "an exceedingly unfriendly friendship"—that seduces his mind and draws him to behave shamelessly (2.9.17).[22]

Given the mutual exposure already entailed in a sin committed in the company of friends, confession might here seem redundant. "It would seem to be as superfluous an act as stealing what one already has," as Lyell Asher puts it.[23] It does, however, have the effect of extending both the pleasure and the circle of intimacy. In this case, it also inscribes itself in a book that others may *take and read*. Augustine's theft is archived for humanity, and so is his confession. It is deliberately made part of a memory and a history of confessions. As he puts it, "I need not tell all this to you, my God, but in your presence I tell it to my own race, to those other humans, however few, who may perhaps pick up this book" (2.3.5). But his confession of theft also enfolds its own memory and history, for Augustine is not the first to have tasted forbidden fruit.[24]

If the episode of the pears is not only archived but also archivally produced—produced, above all, from the archives of scripture—how are we to judge its claims to veracity? Augustine has already confessed that he invented accounts of sexual transgression in order to be able to confess them to his friends. This confession of a lie, occurring in the midst of his confessions of fornication, complicates our assessment of the latter, which we may begin to suspect are so many empty boasts—especially since all we get, when we search for plausible details, is a story about stealing pears. Is even the theft a fiction, or at least a quasi-fiction, a nearly mechanical archival production that will repeat itself down the centuries? Where is the "truth of sex" in these *Confessions*?

The truth is that we cannot know the truth about sex. The secret is that it must remain secret. This is because Augustine may be making it all up, and also because he is not doing so. He is following a script and also creating one that others will follow; indeed, he is doing so rather self-consciously. It is, moreover, a script traversed by blank spaces, silent gaps. Unlike (thus also like) Adam, Augustine claims not to remember whether he actually tasted the flesh of the forbidden fruit. He confesses that he tasted the thrill of freedom. He tasted the pleasures of friendship. Indeed he "loved" them both. But the flesh of the pears may or may not have passed his lips—he is not sure, he cannot recall, but the main point, it seems, is that *it does not matter*. The pears *could* have been the objects of his love (*amor, cupiditas*), but in fact they were not (2.8.16). His text will not quite appropriate the scriptural event of the consumption of the flesh of the fruit, nor will it quite refuse it. It equivocates, it covers over clarity—just as his confessions more generally equivocate regarding the sensual pleasures of sexual acts, which remain secreted in his text, at once repeatedly avowed and ever undisclosed. Untouchable, out of our reach, refusing pornographic representation (refusing to be written as fornications after all)—and thereby continuing to seduce. For pornography, as Baudrillard observes, is the "end of the secret."[25]

Augustine prefers to confess the pleasures of relationality. He prefers to convert lust into love, to promise fornications while in fact delivering friendships. Yet the translation of lust into love—the effective switching of the bait—only serves to erode the distinction between lust and love—to remind us of the lust secreted *within* love. We may imagine that we catch him with a bit of pear in his mouth—or a beautiful body in his bed. But he has already caught himself lusting for friendship, for sociality. He has already confessed his desire. It is in the theft of the pears, related just after he has told of his father's report of seeing the stirrings of desire in his adolescent body, that Augustine detects the beginnings of the lust for love that will lead him astray repeatedly. If the confession of the theft of the pears inscribes misguided love as the original sin, it also hints that the perversion of sin is the secret of salvation.

"A Pact of Libidinous Love"

"There are, in the *Confessions*, seductive female figures; there are no seductive women," Miles observes.[26] This statement itself seduces—first with the promised attractions of female figures, then with the negated figure of seductive women. It also raises questions about the relation of the figural to the literal and of the seductive to the feminine. That seduction is conventionally associated with femininity may partly account for women's particular susceptibility to figuration, in Augustine's text and more generally: the figural conveys hiddenness, manifesting the endless capacity of language to turn itself aside from its own truth; "it is not a lie but a mystery," as Augustine puts it elsewhere (*Against Lying* 24). By the same logic, women's veiling within the figural may be understood to contribute to their seductiveness. Yet Miles seems inclined to identify the figural as the source not of shimmering mystery but of flat reduction, complaining that Augustine's "understanding and literary treatment of actual women is limited by the female figures that inhabit his psyche: the good mother and the sexual object."[27] Setting aside the problem of the accessibility of Augustine's (or anyone else's) psyche, we may agree that "actual women" exceed the limits of objectified female figures produced within a masculinist imaginary; indeed, as Luce Irigaray has taught us, the feminine itself emerges as a kind of excluded excess of discourse.[28] However, what exceeds discourse also seduces from within discourse. If in *Confessions* there are no actual seductive women, then we are seduced by the women who are not actually there—by the women who beckon from somewhere *else*.

We are seduced, above all, by one particular woman. Every reader of *Confessions* knows who she is, though no reader learns her name. We first hear of her in Book 4, where Augustine opens his description of his life in Carthage from age nineteen to age twenty-eight by declaring his sinfulness in characteristically titillating terms: "we were seduced and we seduced, we were deceived and we deceived, amidst diverse desires" (*Confessions* 4.1.1). Once again, he switches the bait, however. Seduction, deception, and desire turn out to relate primarily to the spheres of rhetoric, religion, and reputation—not sex.[29] And oddly enough, the following note, which *does* relate to sex, is tucked into the middle of a description of his professional endeavors: "In those years I had someone (*unam*), not recognized by that union that is called lawful, but one whom a restless desire, lacking prudence (*vagus ardor inops prudentiae*), had tracked down, to whose bed I was nonetheless also faithful" (4.2.2).

Intriguingly, the woman in Augustine's bed is not only nameless but is also lacking all nominal designation. Translators and interpreters are quick to fill the gap, dubbing her Augustine's "mistress," "concubine," "common-law wife," or "partner," among other labels, each of these choices obviously reflecting an attempt to map a somewhat ambiguous late-fourth-century social relationship onto one familiar to current readers. However, even were such historical concerns not in play—concerns that are often also overtly moralizing—it would be extremely difficult, if not impossible, to duplicate in English the teasing elusiveness of Augustine's Latin, and it is this elusiveness that largely accounts for the seductiveness of his initial mention of his—of his *what*? For that is just the point: he does not call her mistress or concubine, any more than he calls her wife; rather, he manages not to call her *anything*.[30] Their bond, as he represents it, is not the kind that can be called by name, deriving from no law. Rather, it is the kind called into being by a burning desire, or *ardor*.

Augustine's desire, as he himself describes it, may seem immoderate, but it is difficult to find anything in it that is *wrong*. After all, it draws him inexorably to one to whom he keeps the faith of a shared bed, which is even more than marriage requires of a man—and considerably less than a self-proclaimed reputation for seduction implies of him. Indeed, it is possible to detect a sarcastic note in his reference to the "union that is *called* lawful (*quod legitimum vocatur*)," hinting that he is reluctant to grant marriage any clear-cut moral privilege.[31] Nonetheless, he is obviously also ambivalent about his all-too-ardent love, and his ambivalence infuses his brief account with otherwise unaccountable excitement. He continues: "In her I could prove by my own example what the difference is between the constraint of a marital agreement that is contracted for the sake of descendents (*foederatum esset generandi gratia*) and the pact of libidinous love (*pactum libidinosi amoris*), where an offspring may be born even against our wish, although once born it compels one to love it" (4.2.2).[32] If ardor is excessive with respect to the law, which provides for the generation of heirs, a desirous love is excessive with respect to the will to generate heirs. Yet fecundity also exceeds desire: one need not plan families to have them; one need not want children to love them. This Augustine proves "in her."

But what exactly does he prove? And why is it so hard to know what to call her? She is not yet either subject or object, arguably not even the object of Augustine's desire. Admittedly, Miles is not unusual, nor is she unreasonable, in suggesting that Augustine reduces her to just that—a "sexual object." Elsewhere, however, Miles hints that the unnamed woman eludes even the grasp of objectification: "Without using far too much imagination, we cannot reconstruct a fully fleshed character. . . . It would be presumptuous for an historian to attempt to reconstruct it. Too much imagination, projection, and speculation would be required."[33] It is by hiding from her readers that she seduces, then, tempting them to imagine "too much." She tantalizes precisely because she is no more than a trace[34]—the trace of Augustine's desire, which itself proves excessive in relation to the laws that produce both marital subjects and linguistic objects.

If she is the trace of his desire, his desire is also her trace. And by Book 6, when she is mentioned for the second and last time in *Confessions*, that trace has become a bloody track of grief. Now thirty, Augustine finds himself tempted by "the union that is called lawful": to his mother Monica's delight and his friend Alypius's dismay, he becomes engaged to a respectable young woman—or rather to a respectable young *girl*, for his bride-to-be is still two years too young to wed (6.13.23). "In the meantime my sins were multiplying," he writes, just when we might have thought they were decreasing, "for the one with whom I was accustomed to share a bed was torn from my side (*latere*), on the grounds that she was a hindrance to the marriage, and my heart, where she cleaved (*adhaerebat*), was cut and wounded and it was trailing (*trahebat*) blood" (6.15.25). This image is not only shockingly graphic but also allusively scriptural, as Danuta Shanzer has shown.[35] The "one" is torn from his side like Eve from Adam, in a violent replay of Genesis 2.21–22—"he took one of his ribs"—that is also a perverse reversal of Genesis 2.24: "therefore, a man leaves his father and mother and cleaves (*adhaerebit*) to his wife, and they become one flesh."[36] In a slightly later treatise, *On the Good of Marriage* (401), Augustine presents the bond between Adam and Eve in Paradise explicitly as a model for marriage: "The first natural bond of human society is husband and wife. And God did not make them singly and join them as if from alien births but created the one from the other, further signifying the power of their conjunction in the side (*latere*) from which she was drawn (*detracta*) and formed" (I.I).[37] In the *Confessions*, however, the primeval bond is implicitly the model for his relationship with the one who evokes his libidinous love. As Shanzer frames the implications of *Confessions* 6.15.25 for our understanding of the anonymous woman, "If Adam and Eve were married in Eden, then so, in a sense, was she married to Augustine."[38] In a lost paradise, the constraints of marriage have become strangely entangled with the excesses of desire, it would seem.

She keeps the faith of their pact, as Augustine goes on to relate. Does she not here, momentarily, break the surface of subjectivity, or very nearly so? "And she returned to Africa, vowing to you not to know another man, leaving with me my natural son whom I had from her." Augustine, unlike Adam, proves "no imitator of woman (*nec feminae imitator*)" with respect to chastity, however. It would have been better if he had, he feels. "Not a lover of marriage but a slave to desire," he is more faithful to the bed than to the woman, it seems, and now he must find another (*aliam*) to fill the empty space. Still, his heart aches not for an other but for the one: "Nor was that wound of mine made by the prior amputation cured, but after the sharpest burning and pain it festered, and it continued to hurt, as if the pain had become duller but more hopeless" (6.15.25). God closes the flesh around Adam's excised rib, but Augustine's cut will not heal.

Both the woman's self-willed chastity and his unwilling promiscuity, her austere virtue and his multiplying sins, are measures of their common grief, then, as each mimics and parodies *fides*, after the fall. After the fall comes the tragic sundering of will so painfully exposed when they are parted, leaving her cut off from her desire and him from his love. Still, Augustine can remember what it was like to cleave to another in a "*pactum libidinosi amoris.*" It is this seductive memory that continues to mislead him, drawing him along the well-worn path of sexual habit: as he imagines it, "the escort of long-standing custom" is conducting him relentlessly "to the kingdom of uxoriousness" (6.15.25). Whereas marriage initially seems to be positioned ambiguously in comparison with his own relationship in Book 4, he is now unmistakably critical of its anticipated conveniences and comforts, not least of which is steady access to a sexual partner to whom his wounded heart will not cleave.

Fortunately, before he actually weds his youthful fiancée, Augustine is led astray yet again. This time he is seduced not by an *actual woman* but by a card-carrying *female figure*—Continence, to put a name to her. She is not the only female figure who is trying to seduce him at this point, however. Certain nameless "old girlfriends" (*antiquae amicae*) have also showed up, uninvited. He imagines them enticing him thus: "They tugged at my fleshly garment and whispered, 'Are you going to send us away?,' adding, 'From that moment unto eternity we will not be with you' and 'From that moment unto eternity this and that will not be permitted you.'" "This and that," it would appear, cover a multitude of sins so sordid and shameful that Augustine cannot name or describe them; indeed, he cannot even bear—or dare—to give them his full attention. Yet seduction does not initially require or desire full attention, perhaps: his temptations, wisely, do not confront him in the open; rather, "it was as if they were muttering behind my back and furtively plucking at me as I retreated, so that I would look back" (8.11.26). It is at this point that Augustine turns desperately toward Continence, who seems to stand on the far side of a boundary, alluringly just out of reach. He is impressed by her "chaste dignity": she is smilingly cheerful without being silly, seductive without any hint of impropriety, "coaxing me to come and to set aside doubt, and reaching her devout hands toward me to receive and embrace me." Married to the Lord himself, she is the mother of many children. Her arms are already full of "boys and girls, many youths, and of every age, both grave widows and elderly virgins." Regardless of whether their births were planned or unplanned, she loves them all. Is she also the lover of many men? She flirts with Augustine teasingly, leaving him blushing, for the memories of "this and that" are still on his mind (8.11.27).

The competing seductions of sensual pleasures and holy Continence staged at the end of Book 8 replay the proverbial seductions of Folly and Wisdom that Augustine has already introduced in Book 3, which chronicles the famously dissolute period of his student years in Carthage.[39] "To love and be loved was sweet to me," he recalls, "more so if I also enjoyed the body of the lover" (3.1.1). He passes quickly from the body of the lover, and the confusion of emotions that its enjoyment aroused, to the wonders of philosophy, however, as he takes to heart Cicero's advice "to love and seek and pursue and hold fast and strongly embrace wisdom itself, wherever found" (3.4.8). Turning to the Bible, he almost discovers the wisdom he desires, but unfortunately he does not recognize it—or her—for who it—or she—is. "And behold, what I saw was something neither open to the proud nor bared to children, but humble in approach, exalted in ascent, and veiled in mysteries." Failing to appreciate the seductiveness of such hidden beauty, he perceives only lack of style. Spurning the apparent lowliness of Scripture, "my sharp wit did not penetrate her interior," he avers (3.5.9). Instead, "I came across that bold woman, lacking prudence, in the riddle of Solomon . . . and she seduced me" (3.6.11).

Repeatedly, he succumbs to the wrong female figure. But by the end of Book 8 he will finally get it right, choosing Continence (8.12.30)—and thus proving an *imitator feminae* after all. Choosing Continence, he is choosing Wisdom. He is also choosing Scripture, who is the final female in this series of figural displacements.[40] By Book 11, her veiled mysteries, previously disdained, have begun to draw him powerfully indeed. "Open to me the pages of your book," he begs his God. "Open your door to my knocking" (11.2.4). The metaphor of opening gives way to an "indistinctness of surface and depth,"[41] as Baudrillard describes the seductions of the feminine. "Behold the depth of your words, the surface of which is, see, before us, enticing the little ones: but behold the depth, my God, behold the depth!" Thus Augustine addresses Scripture, adding: "It is a horror to look into it, a horror of honor and a trembling of love" (12.14.17). Indeed, Scripture is an invisible abyss of multiplying signification visibly evident in the play of letters on the page: "from these words can be understood things that vary and yet are all true" (12.18.27). No one should imagine himself to be in sole possession of Scripture's multifaceted and promiscuously disseminated truth, for "all lovers of truth" share her in common (12.25.34). She suits her style to her readers, moreover. For fledgling exegetes, she is a laplike nest (12.27.37). For others, her words are "a dark thicket" in which hidden fruits are fleetingly glimpsed and joyfully pursued (12.28.38).

What does it mean to take not an actual woman but a female figure as your spouse? Indeed, to take a female figure of figuration, a female figure whose femininity is itself, moreover, figural—a terrifying depth, a cradling nest, an enticing thicket, and so on. In exchange for carnal sex with the one (an act he never actually describes) we are offered passionate reading with a diverse multitude (an act he never actually completes): even grammatically speaking, Scripture (*scripturae*) is a multiplicity, not unlike the pleasures, his "old girlfriends." Can she, however, prove sufficiently versatile to match the "this and that" of Augustine's polymorphous desire? Can she offer him the joy of a beloved body? If she very nearly can, it is only because this elaborately fleshed-out literary figure is textually entangled with the absent and longed-for flesh of the one woman Augustine actually loves. Banished, she is drawn back into the text through the female figure who overflows it— Wisdom/Continence/Scripture. In the process, the tidy allegory of Wisdom and Folly is undone. For when "discourse *seduces itself*," as Baudrillard puts it, it subverts its own drive to produce a transparent truth or meaning.[42] To the extent that Folly is an unambiguous sign for the lure of Manichaean heresy, Wisdom an obvious cipher for the attraction of catholic Christianity, they are figures of seduction but they are not seductive. It is in their turning aside from their own truths that they seduce, as the distance between pleasure and continence, concubinage and marriage, the bodily and the figural, very nearly disappears. She seduces—they seduce—because they are—she is—veiled in mysteries.

"The Friendship of Mortal Things"

Augustine brags frequently about the diversity and multiplicity of his desires. We should not, then, expect them to be confined to rotten fruit and female figures. In fact, with the exception of his mother, his *Confessions* has much more to say about his relationships with men than with women. Some of his intimate male companions are made known by name—Nebridius and Alypius, for example. But the one for whom he expresses the most intense love remains as nameless as the woman with whom he lives for so many years—nameless, but not without designation, for Augustine refers to him confidently as "my friend."

Augustine introduces this friendship in Book 4, soon after first mentioning the woman. The contrast between the two accounts is notable. His reference to *her* is concise and constrained. The very excess of desire is conveyed with extreme economy, as thirteen years of cohabitation are made to fit with deceptive modesty into one dense paragraph, indeed into one densely complex sentence. His description of his feelings about his *friend*, however, is verbose and performatively passionate, even showy, almost parodic—very nearly camp. An intimacy that lasted less than a year before death cut it short leaves much still to be felt and expressed, it seems: it takes up most of the book. Yet we learn no more about the boyfriend than about her. Much as *she* will later emerge flickeringly to view as she takes a vow of chastity, *he* is glimpsed briefly as he accepts the seal of baptism, rebuking Augustine's disdain "with a wondrous and unexpected independence" (4.4.8). In each case it is in acknowledging a ritualized gesture of differentiation that Augustine is able to perceive, and also to begin to exceed, the limits of his own love. But only in painful hindsight—only after it is already too late, perhaps. And it is always too late, in the case of his friend.

For Augustine chooses to write about his friend from the vantage point of his death. The gaping abyss of loss lures a plenitude of verbalized grief. The very excess of his own grief fascinates and horrifies Augustine. It seduces him into grieving even more—or perhaps better put, into distending his memories of grief still further, for all of this is of course written many years after the fact. Indeed, belatedness haunts the narrative. Augustine and his friend grew up in the same town, were of the same age and knew each other from childhood, yet their intimacy was not kindled until Augustine returned from Carthage to teach rhetoric in Thagaste. Even then, he professes, theirs was not a "true friendship," for that could be the result only of a divine "gluing" that would secure "those cleaving to one another by means of the love diffused through our hearts by the holy spirit." The blessings of paradisiacal *caritas* are apparently denied this couple because of their Manichaean beliefs, then. Nonetheless, "the fervor of similar studies" swiftly ripened a relationship that was, as he puts it, "sweet to us." Indeed, it was a delight to him "above all delights of this my life" (4.4.7). Yet it was extinguished almost as quickly as it was ignited, as a fever that had seemingly abated returned to rob his friend of life—or rather, to grant him eternal life, leaving Augustine to contemplate his own feverish state. Even the death was belated: if only his friend had died while still submissive to Augustine's Manichaean teachings, rather than rejecting them so painfully by embracing Christian rites initially performed without his will. Looking back, Augustine sees that death freed his friend from the tyrannical "madness" of his friendship, leaving Augustine himself both exposed and in full flight from his own self-exposure (4.4.8).

What is grief? Augustine describes its symptoms skillfully, but he cannot make sense of the immensity of his own pain. "I became a great question to myself," he observes. A world without his friend yields no pleasure at all. "Only weeping was sweet to me," he recalls, "and it succeeded my friend in the affections of my soul" (4.4.9). He marvels at the tenacity with which he cleaves to his own mourning. "How is it that sweet fruit is plucked from the bitterness of life—to lament and to weep and to sigh and to complain?" (4.5.10) Unable to answer his own question, he contents himself with confessing his condition: "I was miserable, and every soul bound by the friendship of mortal things is miserable; it is torn to pieces when it loses them, and then feels a misery with which it is already miserable even before it loses them." "The friendship of mortal things" thus dooms one to grief; in fact, one is always already grieving, in anticipation of unavoidable loss. And now Augustine does, after all, begin to answer his question: grief is sweet in the face of loss because it appears to be the one thing that cannot be lost; thus it mimics immortality. His is not like the legendary friendship of Pylades and Orestes, either of whom preferred death to life without the other. He prefers life. Clinging to his grief even more passionately than to the dearly departed, Augustine protests the transience of creation. Prolonging his mourning, he tries to halt the march of time, and in so doing he also resists the rub of difference. Tears are a frozen mirror in which he preserves the image of his friend as he used to be, before he died—or perhaps, before he broke ranks with his teacher. He can imagine them as two halves of one soul, virtually indistinguishable (4.6.11).

Or he can replace his friend with other virtually indistinguishable friends, and pretend that *they* will live forever. "Having loved one who would die as if he would not die," he finds himself prolonging the "great fiction and long lie" (*ingens fabula et longum mendacium*): friends might die, "but the fiction did not die." The fiction of immortality lives on because Augustine cannot bear to relinquish the pleasures of friendship: "to speak and to laugh with one another, to yield to each other willingly; to read pleasant books together, to joke and to be serious together; sometimes to disagree without rancor, as one would with oneself, with the rare discord itself seasoning the more usual accord; to teach or to learn things from one another, to long impatiently for those who are absent, to welcome those who arrive with joy"; such acts and gestures "set our hearts aflame like kindling and make one out of many." "This is what is loved in friends," he concludes. It is no surprise that we mourn the loss of such precious gifts, no surprise that we want to believe that they will never forsake us (4.8.13–4.9.14).

This is why the friendship is not a true one, then—why it is a fiction and a lie. The point is not that God denies the bliss of true love to doctrinal deviants. It is not even that Augustine's swiftness to replace his friend (as he later tries to replace the woman) suggests a failure truly to know and love the other as other. The point is that Augustine does not know how to love the immortal creator as such, and he is therefore equally incapable of loving *any* mortal creature, whether man, woman, or pear.[43] "Happy is the one who loves you, and the friend in you, and the enemy for your sake," he proclaims to God. "For that one alone loses no dear one, to whom all are dear in the one who is not lost. And who is that but our God, God who made heaven and earth and fills them, because in filling them he made them?" (4.9.14). Augustine's well-known insistence that we must "love all things in God" may sound merely banal to our overly familiar ears. Yet it conveys a perhaps still often underappreciated proposal, namely, that by embracing "the friendship of mortal things" both promiscuously and unpossessively, we are not bound but freed in love.[44] Such a freeing love is, by definition, simultaneously love of creatures and love of that in which they transcend themselves, for indeed one can only love creatures "in God," just as one can only love God in the beauty of creation. It is in the mutual, though nonsymmetrical, transcendence of God and creation that the primal seduction plays itself out.

Yet there is a fine line separating the extremes of a love in which the difference between creation and creator has collapsed from those of a love that is endlessly seduced by their mutual transcendence. A grasping attachment that confuses what is mortal with what is immortal may mimic a divinely promiscuous love in its zeal never to accept loss of a desired object. A "true friendship," however, is truly promiscuous, accepting mortal mutability, difference, and multiplicity as the conditions of erotic self-transcendence in the infinite unfolding of a divine love. Thus it is that Augustine's eloquent description of the pleasures of friendship—his powerful depiction of the spiraling joys of mutual love—is so strangely shot through with ambivalence. For these pleasures and joys may seduce us into denying the very transience that is the source of their sweetness, by obscuring the seductions of the eternal God in which they rest. Augustine's youthful friendship with his unnamed friend marks an almost—but not quite—great love. Its failure begins before the friend's death, when Augustine proves unable to accept the loss of shared belief, an inability that reflects simultaneously his theological misperceptions and his refusal of change and difference. The erotic failure, which is also a theological failure, is confirmed both by his grief and by the cessation of his grief, each of which enact a denial of creaturely transience, an attempt to hold mortality at bay. It has been suggested that Augustine's grief at the departure of the unnamed woman is "short-circuited," whereas his grief for his unnamed friend allows time to do its appropriate work in achieving acceptance of the loss.[45] Yet Augustine himself seems quite concerned to demonstrate the perversity of his extravagant grieving for his friend precisely insofar as it refuses acceptance of loss.

A more mature Augustine, faced with the loss of another lover, finds grief a less effective distraction from itself and loss less easily filled.

Is there, then, nothing but failure secreted in the love of this special friend, cloaked in its "great fiction and long lie"? What, if anything, might Augustine be hiding in this particular corner of his prayer closet? The spectacularly anachronistic question of his sexual orientation has for the most part produced disappointingly uninteresting answers. "The evidence that Augustine engaged in same-sex sexual activity is missing or underwhelming," notes Alan Soble.[46] Indeed, Augustine's unselfconscious passion for the friendship of men, together with his tendency to render such relationships ascetic, seems unremarkable in its late ancient Mediterranean setting.

However, two features of Augustine's eschatology, as it surfaces in Book 4, do seem to grant his love for his unnamed friend a particular gendered inflection. At the very beginning of his account he has offered a scripturally larded definition of divinely ordained friendship: "it is not true friendship, unless you bind (*agglutinas*) those cleaving (*haerentes*) to one another with the love that is poured in our hearts through the holy spirit, who is given to us" (4.4.7). The second half of this line is clearly a citation of Romans 5.5, but the first half echoes the language of binding or cleaving found in Genesis 2.24: "and he will *cleave* to his wife"—*adhaerebit* in the Vulgate, *conglutinabitur* in the Septuagint-based Latin translation also known and cited by Augustine (e.g., *Literal Commentary* 9.1.1). Splitting the biblical text by doubling the translations, as it were, he is able to read his friendship both with and against the union of Adam and Eve: he and his friend do cleave to one another; however, they are not divinely bound in the *caritas* that suffuses the hearts of those who have been granted the holy spirit. The impediment of shared heresy distracts from another possible problem, namely, sexual difference. For here as elsewhere, Augustine's attraction to the notion of a primal sociality among humans deriving from the bond between Adam and Eve draws him to a marital ideal that is in tension with his own experiences of love between men. As we have seen, his *On the Good of Marriage* opens by identifying "the power of friendship" as "the great and natural good" of humanity, exemplified in "the first natural bond (*copula*)" of human society"—that is, "husband and wife" (1.1). In the *Literal Commentary on Genesis* (401–415), he wrestles directly with the tension produced by such a near-conflation of marriage and friendship: only the need for procreation can account for the sex of man's original friend, he proposes, since "for companionship and conversation, how much more suitable it is for two friends (*amici*) to dwell equally than for a man and a woman" (9.5.9).[47] Augustine's evolving exegesis of Genesis 2 as the charter document for both human sociality and heterosexual marriage ensures that male-male friendship, however frequently described and indeed paradigmatic for his broader understanding of the bond of friendship, is pushed off the map of theological articulation, rendered virtually unnamable.[48]

And thereby, perhaps, rendered all the more seductive—a hunch that seems confirmed by the appearance, at the end of his account of his grief for his friend, of the figure of Christ—unusual in the *Confessions*, as we shall see in the next chapter. Augustine has just urged: "If bodies please you, then praise God for them. . . . If souls please you, let them be loved in God" (4.12.18). Unveiled as the most desirable of ensouled and enfleshed spouses, Christ teaches us how to love divinely, exercising his own sublime powers of attraction. "He calls us to return from here to him, in that secret place from which he came forth to us, in that first virginal womb where the human creature was wed to him, mortal flesh, that it might not always be mortal; and from there as if he were a bridegroom coming forth from his chamber he exulted as a giant to run his course." These images are not novel (see Psalm 18.6/19.5) but they *are* strikingly presented, as the virgin's womb is equated with the psalmist's bridal chamber, and incarnation is seen to be an instrument of divine enclosure as well as disclosure, of secrecy as well as revelation. A marvelously gigantic groom, this cosmic Christ comes forth so as to draw us in, and he draws us in by withdrawing just as he has come, ascending just as he has descended, always leaving a teasing trace. "And he pulled back from our eyes that we might return to our own hearts and find him; for he withdrew, and behold he is still here" (4.12.19). For Augustine, submission to the seductions of Christ is the only resolution for the erotic dilemma presented by the beauty of creation and the createdness of beauty, as Christ both manifests divinity in fleshly beauty and holds himself aloof from it. Like Augustine's friend, he is always already dead and gone but therefore all the more alive and present in desire.

Submitting to Seduction

There are many ways to read Augustine's *Confessions*, but if we want to read it for seduction, then we must stop looking for revelations. This is not only or even primarily because we cannot really know the truth about Augustine's sex life. It is also because knowing this, even if we could, would be of merely modest enjoyment or use. From the perspective of Augustine's own confessional theology, the seduction of the secret ultimately eclipses the desire for truth—as it must, if we are to attain salvation.

In his *Confessions*, Augustine seeks to draw us into a seduction. He seduces us first by performing his own seducibility; he repeats the trick, again and again. He submits to his readers in advance, not so that we might enjoy the illusory triumph of *finding him out* but in the hope that we will be seduced into *seducing him*. Misreading him, misleading him, even perverting him, so will we too be misread, mislead, perverted—and finally converted. By what or whom? By everything and everyone and thus, ultimately, by God.

For even Augustine is not promiscuous *enough*, not scattered *enough*: monogamy is his great temptation. His loves and friendships are not carnal *enough*: he is prone to imagine them sublimely immortal. His shame is that he does not have more shameful loves to confess. He should perhaps just make them up, for acts of imagination count too: indeed, what we are capable of imagining may make all the difference. *All* things are good, and *all* things are transient—the "things" that are fleshly, like a piece of fruit or a lover's body, and those that are not, like freedom or friendship. *All* things are to be enjoyed and none is to be possessed. *All* things are lovable. The beauty of even a markedly inferior pear, its taste on the tongue; the thrill of spontaneity; the comfort of companionship and the pleasure of touch; the wondrous abundance, indeed the rotting excess, of divine creation. So many more pears than anyone could possibly want, so many more friends. So much more piggish desire than any pears—or lovers—could possibly satisfy.

Augustine seduces us with untold tales of seductions that must remain hidden. A boy's experience of the joy of sex is covered over with his unaccountable enjoyment of the theft of pears. A young man's passionate desire for an unnamed woman veils itself in reticence, even as his all too voluble grief for a deceased man obscures the scene of their love. These secret places are shadowed with pain even as they shimmer with delight. As Augustine seems to suggest, we are never nearer to the gathering embrace of divinity than when we have wandered the farthest, never closer to letting go than when trying vainly to grasp it *all*. The secret is to submit to seduction—always to give oneself more. Will a divine seduction finally draw us away from the flesh altogether? This seems to be both Augustine's hope and his fear. But seduction is, necessarily, reversible; as Christology teaches, we withdraw from the flesh so as to be drawn back to it. "But how do you ascend, since you are up high and you can turn your face to heaven? Descend so that you may ascend, and ascend to God" (4.12.19).

2

The Word, His Body

[For the Roman gods] to prescribe that men represent them on stage, not in their impassibility, but as prodigiously corrupt natures—adulterers, agents of incest, thieves and perjurers . . . to prescribe this, I say, resulted from what these gods staked . . . on *becoming incarnate*. Incarnation all the same under the appearances of the histrionic body.

Pierre Klossowski, *Le Bain de Diane*

Aurelius Augustinus, in whom the world of myths died, in whom awakened all the first givens of our most recent problematic, suffered bitterly the impressions of his pagan adolescence.

Pierre Klossowski, *Origines cultuelles et mythiques d'un certain comportement*

. . . deceiving by innumerable lies my pedagogue, my teachers, my parents because of my love of gaming, my passion for watching frivolous spectacles, and my eagerness to imitate comic sketches.

Augustine, *Confessions* I.19.30

*A*fter he had been seduced three times over by Christian speeches, Augustine wrote two books about words and bodies. *Confessions* was the second of them, a sequel better than the original. Persuaded to affirm the truth of Christianity, then to reform his life for baptism's sake, and finally to accept a sequence of ordinations, Augustine the bishop began rather with the already familiar analogy in Christian rhetoric that aligns models for human words with hypotheses or fantasies about the divine Word, the incarnate God. Before *Confessions*, he began to write a book entitled *De doctrina Christiana*, which can be translated as *On Christian Teaching* only so long as "teaching" calls to mind a public act of persuasion rather than a list of inert tenets. Indeed, the earlier text is often read as a manual of scriptural exegesis or of homiletics, though also as an instance of Christian ambivalence toward pagan rhetorical art. It is better to read it under its grounding analogy: incarnation is divinely chosen because it is the most seductive speech. Its power is invoked in scripture and preaching, which anticipate an art for Christian words that can at its best imitate the persuasion of divine flesh.[1]

What Augustine began to write about words and bodies in *On Christian Teaching* seems not to have satisfied him. He composed the first part of it shortly after his consecration as bishop. Perhaps he even circulated its first two Books in roughly finished form, together with the prologue.[2] But he chose not to finish the work. Book 3 breaks off in mid-thought, about two-thirds of the way through the whole text as we now have it.[3] Augustine stopped writing *On Christian Teaching* and began writing his *Confessions*. We might even imagine that he stopped the one in order to begin the other.[4] Augustine resumed writing *On Christian Teaching* only thirty years later, as he tells it, in the course of a retrospective review of his authorship (see *Retractations* 2.4). He concluded then a different work, pushed by other concerns to perform another belated castigation of his earlier self.[5] Fortunately, before that revenge on his middle age, Augustine had already pursued questions about words and bodies from *On Christian Teaching* into *Confessions*, his second and better answer to them. The two texts are linked efforts to retell seductively the motive of his own seduction.

The Morality of Signs

Augustine's *On Christian Teaching* promises some lessons or precepts for "treating" the Christian scriptures (*praecepta quaedam tractandarum scripturarum*, preface 1.1).[6] Augustine's *praecepta* do not pretend to be either method or system because he recognizes an old difficulty in rhetorical art. If not from the frustrations of his daily teaching, Augustine could learn from Cicero's Crassus that the advice of rhetorical manualists was often shrugged off as unhelpful for real composition (*De oratore* 1.32.145–46). The city's art of rhetoric could not be captured by didactic methods and comprehensive systems; how much less could the art for applying Christian words persuasively to bodies. Augustine's "precepts" and "ways" are tentative helps that rely on illumination by the Holy Spirit (pref.5.10). Even Augustine's title emphasizes an anti-manualist motive: "*doctrina*" means "what is taught," "what is espoused."[7] The title *On Christian Teaching* calls up the learning, the believing community that encircles scriptural understanding, as it subordinates the meaning of the scriptures to the lived ends of Christian proclamation. Scriptural texts are not puzzles in a void. They are texts passed down within a community for the use of its *doctores*, its teachers, in hastening the community toward its end.

Augustine's title resonates in his preface, which defends the transmission of divine wisdom through human lineages of readers and teachers. He tries especially to forestall the objection that precepts are unnecessary because the scriptures can be grasped through divine inspiration, by some assurance of presence. His defense relies already on the analogy between human words and the incarnate divine Word, though he will not enunciate it for a few more pages. To reach human beings, the divine Word takes on their flesh. Just so, thought takes on human word-sounds in order to be spoken and heard, takes on word-characters to be written and read. Teaching about God can be reliably committed to texts only if there is a human community to teach reading—both of natural languages and of divine rhetoric in scriptures. To put the proportion perhaps too naively: What the assumed human person is to the Son in the Trinity, so the spoken or written word is to the inner word of thought, and so the believing community is to the transmission of once incarnate teaching—*doctrina Christiana* in a double sense, Christian by transmitted content and by transmitting form.[8] But so far as incarnation is understood on analogy to the need for spoken words, it marks at once nearness and distance: the teaching has indeed been given, but only from another and after much labor of learning the "common," artificial language.

Augustine foretells this extended analogy in his title and his prefatory defense of the project. He then builds it into the definitions, arguments, and structure of the work as he first conceived it. We can sample only a few of these constructions, beginning with the definitional distinction between signs (*signa*) and things (*res*). *Res*, "things," means not so much substances as end-points in referring chains. "Things" do not signify something else, with appropriate qualifications for anomalous scriptural cases. In relation to a sign, *res* also means the subject matter and content, the message, the point. So the distinction doubles when Augustine characteristically differentiates things to be enjoyed (*frui*) from things to be used (*uti*). A sign is useful for getting to its thing, which can be enjoyed (at least conditionally) in the act of understanding, of reading. Augustine quickly pushes the distinction to its limiting case: only the Trinitarian God is to be enjoyed simply speaking. Everything else, every thing and sign, is to be used—sometimes lovingly—so far as it leads to the enjoyment of God. The system of signs, rightly used, tends toward a singular enjoyment, but only through a series of refused seductions to stop early—a series of refused fetishes that would rather substitute the present artifact for the still absent archetype.

Signs are either natural or "given," intended (2.1.2). Natural signs, best illustrated by causal connections, signify without intending to do so. Smoke does not intend to communicate the presence of fire, though it is a sign of fire. Given signs, in contrast, are those that "living beings give one another to exhibit, as much as they can, the motions of their souls, or things sensed, or things understood" (2.2.3). Given signs are further divided into the fitting or immediate (*propria*) and the transferred (*translata*; 2.10.15). "Transferred signs occur when the things that we signify by proper words are themselves taken over to signify something else" (2.10.15). The example Augustine gives is the use of "ox" to refer, in Christian iconography, to the evangelist Luke. When he comes actually to deal with translated signs in scripture, Augustine speaks mainly of "figured locutions" (*figuratae locutiones*), which he associates both with likeness and with what is secret or hidden (*similitudo, secretum*; 2.16.23).[9] Somewhat later, he contrasts the "transferred words" of simple metaphor with allegory and enigma, which are figured locutions properly speaking (3.11.17). Strictly, then, figured locutions are the subset of transferred signs that include allegory, enigma, and other tropes of concealment or multiplication. Loosely, "transferred" and "figured" are interchanged (e.g., 3.10.14). Whatever their importance in the Christian scriptures, figured locutions might seem to be defective words. After all, they are opposed to fitting or immediate "given signs" as the most obscure and resistant examples of transferred meaning. In fact, as we also noted in the last chapter, figured locutions especially disclose for Augustine the seduction of signification, the signifying solicitation latent in any word. Figured locutions show this in at least two ways: they situate signification within persuasion, and they elicit an inexplicable pleasure.

The definition of sign in *On Christian Teaching* puts three terms in a relation of soliciting substitution. Augustine writes: "A sign is a thing (*res*) which, beyond the form (*species*) that strikes the senses, by itself brings something else into thought" (2.1.1). This definition, far from standing over everything that follows as a master category, is actually the first and dimmest step in a hierarchy. The sequence of attraction and redirection it describes is better seen in higher instances. The preliminary definition of sign is itself a sign or token for something better. In given signs, to move on and up a step, the seductive sequence is an effect intended by the sign maker and directed toward disclosing something in her soul. Some persuasion is assumed in every intended signification. Grammar serves rhetoric. The given sign incites motion toward the intention it signifies and so toward the one who employs it as sign. A given sign not only attempts persuasion, it issues a moral challenge: the hearer or reader must *complete* a motion through the sign. To stop short in a given sign is a moral failure. Indeed, to fixate on words as if they were things betrays vaunting weakness—a vanity familiar from professors of rhetoric (2.13.19–20).

Augustine has described this moral imperative in given signs even before attempting to define them. When outlining the *res* of scripture in *On Christian Teaching* I, he elaborately likens human activity to journeying: "suppose we were pilgrims, who could not live blessedly except in our homeland . . ." (1.4.4). Explicit metaphors of pilgrimage are supported by ancillary metaphors of ascent and exercise (compare 1.32.25 with 1.8.8, 2.38.57, 2.31.49). Human souls rest in God, ascend to God, reach the end of exercise in God, because God is properly conceived of as that "than which there is nothing greater or more sublime" (1.7.7). Human readers, human souls, would not be able to approach God except that "Wisdom itself deigned to match itself even with a weakness like ours. . . . [That Wisdom] is our homeland, but it also made itself the way to the homeland" (1.11.11). God's having made Godself the way is the source of signification—the power that drives the persuasive relation in every given sign. God's condescension enables linguistic signs to function as signs. For human beings, privileged wayfarers within the cosmic hierarchy, given signs explain and are explained by the in-fleshing of God's Word.

Augustine enunciates the analogy explicitly:

> Just as when we speak, so that what we carry in our soul might enter the listener's soul through fleshly ears, the word that we bear in our heart is made into sound, and is called locution; yet our thinking is not converted into that sound, but remaining whole in itself, it assumes the form of voice by which it insinuates itself into the ears, without itself falling into change; just so the Word of God was not altered, when he was made flesh, that he might dwell among us. (1.13.12)

In-fleshing—into sounds, scriptures, human skin—is justified and explained by a hierarchical principle of ascent. The justification lasts so long as ascent requires it. The divine Word takes flesh because that is the only way to talk to us (1.12.12). Such pedagogical love implies a hierarchical subordination, even of divine incarnation. "No thing (*nulla res*) should hold us on the way, when not even the Lord himself, so far as he has condescended to be our way, wants to hold us, but [for us] to move on, that we might not cling to temporal things weakly, however much they have been assumed and done by him for our salvation, but rather that we might run quickly past them" (1.34.38). The incarnation, which is the principle of both scriptural meanings and human persuasion, is only an instrument—and so a danger for those who hold on to it too tightly. In the same way, someone who dwells already in a house of faith, hope, and love may no longer need the building machinery of scripture (1.39.43, *quasi machinis*). It is safer to take down the scaffolding. It is wiser to keep running past the tempting instruments of exhortation.

Is it so easy to relinquish God's body or its divine words? What ever could take their place? And what exactly is Augustine running from?

Tempting Figures

Already in Book I of *On Christian Teaching*, even before the moral function of signs and things is diagramed so meticulously, figured locutions reveal something disconcerting about signs. They provoke a confession of rhetorical pleasure around bodies. Figures are tied to incarnation in many ways. Before Augustine speaks of figured locutions, he speaks of the figure of the human body (*humani corporis figura*) that some pagans assigned to god as the highest form (1.7.7). Others figured gods to themselves in whatever bodily excellence they found. Figuration is our customary relation to divinity. Jesus too signifies his own body under the parabolic bodies of others (1.30.33, the Good Samaritan). More generally, a figured locution makes a body out of scattered particulars or elusive abstractions. It gathers them into an imagined "body," as when one says that "all Christian action" is "marked out" or "transcribed" in the sign of the cross (2.41.62).

What Augustine can speak—what he must confess—is enigmatic delight in the incarnational trope of figuration and its graphic likenesses (*similitudines*). "And yet, I don't know why, I regard the saints more sweetly [*suavius*] when I see them as teeth of the church, tearing men from their errors, and bringing them into its body, with all their harshness softened down, just as if they had been torn off and chewed" (2.6.7, with reference to a verse repeated in Song of Songs 4.2 and 6.5).[10] The crucial adverb is *suavius*, a word of rhetorical praise, but also of erotic touch.[11] In the same scriptural figure, Augustine can consider the effects of baptism "most delightfully" when the church is praised "as a beautiful woman" (*pulchra quaedam femina*): the whiteness of her teeth is like that of newly washed, twin-bearing sheep—that is, new souls reborn under the twin command to love God and neighbor. Knowing the pleasure of figures for human understanding, the Holy Spirit disposes Christian scriptures so that the plainer passages satisfy hunger, while the obscure figures prevent boredom by stimulating appetite again (2.6.8). Even scripture must allow for satiety.

The enigma of pleasure in rhetorical figures becomes the engine of our persuasion through the scriptures. Augustine confesses his share in the pleasure before an image from the Song of Songs, an image repeated in the (presumptively male) lover's depiction of the (female) beloved's bodily beauties. Augustine receives that scriptural book as a tale of Christ and the church or the individual soul, but no allegory can remove the erotic charge of this image—or the intimate violence of churchly teeth chewing erring souls before swallowing. Beauty of a body ripe for bearing twins; beauty of sharp teeth for swallowing those newly reborn. In confessing the mysterious pleasures of figure, the official account of bodies seems to tremble—and then to bite.

Augustine's text has represented some scriptural bodies vividly, especially the body of Jesus. But it has done so while calibrating the effect. Augustine had already praised words for their capacity to mimic the effects of bodily signs (2.3.4). The gospels signify by recounting the odor of ointment poured on Jesus' feet and then wiped off with a woman's hair; by suggesting the taste of Jesus' body and blood as meal; by remembering the touch of the hem of his robe—a touch sufficient to heal another woman. Augustine mentions these examples to draw the conclusion that his reader has just performed: We can use words to speak of these things, but we could not use these things to accomplish all that we can with words. He implies that words must control meanings around the bodies that they represent— especially if the body is named "Jesus."

Still, our enigmatic delight in figures threatens to undo verbal control, to multiply bodily significations. Augustine has admitted in relation to the verse from the Song of Songs that the bodily image is more smoothly persuasive than the plain teaching of unfigured words. Even in words about Jesus, the perfume, the meal, the healing garment can be more attractive, more deliciously persuasive, than sober instruction. So, too, Augustine's retellings of Jesus' body threaten to overcome the controls placed around the incarnation. We first hear of figured locutions in relation to a miraculous cure: Jesus smears clay made with his spittle onto the eyes of a blind man (2.16.23, after John 9:6–7). The incarnation is explained by an extended analogy to medicine: just as a physician applies different treatments to injuries, and dresses wounds with bandages cut to size, so "the Wisdom of God [that is, Jesus], when caring for humanity, applied itself to healing, itself the physician, itself the medicine" (1.14.13). Personification as Wisdom—or the ensuing spiritual interpretation of the analogy—cannot quite conceal the figural implication: Jesus took flesh to press himself as healer against the believer's flesh.

Augustine knows the danger of figural language generally and of Jesus' body particularly. He first mentions Jesus' body when reproving those who want to dispense with human community in transmitting scriptures. If we are taken in by them, Augustine argues, we will stop going to church to hear the gospel preached, "waiting to be 'rapt up into the third heaven, whether in the body or out of it,' as [Paul] the Apostle says, and to hear there 'the ineffable words which a human may not speak,' or there to see the Lord Jesus Christ and to hear the gospel rather from him rather than from human beings" (pref.5.11). Jesus' body is in the third heaven, and the self-translating words heard there are ones we may not speak on earth. To pursue the body of Jesus directly would be to empty the churches and so undo, on Augustine's understanding, the divine generosity of both scriptures and incarnation. In this passage, direct access to Jesus' body is linked to the presumption of direct inspiration. Fantasizing the body as present means ignoring the pedagogy of scripture.

Picturing Jesus in heaven further risks reducing him to an Olympian deity—just another beautiful face in a temple frieze, a festival procession, a spectacle. Augustine inhabits a world—runs from a world—in which divine bodies are all too common in fact and in representation. Their statues are incensed, adorned, paraded. Their bodies are desirable, do desire. They can be surprised while bathing, as Diana by Actaeon, or uncovered while sleeping, as Cupid by Psyche. If Jesus is just another divine body, then he fits too easily into an economy of representations and desires, of seductive and dangerous epiphanies.

Augustine does what he must to prevent this pagan presumption, this deadly fetishization: he transfers the incarnate pleasure of scriptural figuration to a nearer "body," an inevitably abstract and doctrinally secured Church. The transfer takes place in various passages—though not most importantly when he explicitly reiterates the figure of the church as Christ's body (e.g., 1.16.15). Augustine controls access to Jesus' body by measuring scriptural figures or the memory of Jesus' rites according to church practice. Augustine regulates figurative speech when he provides the criterion for identifying it. The stated danger is that a reader will fail to recognize a figure when confronted with one. So Augustine curses the deadly carnality that construes figures literally (3.5.9). This "miserable slavery of the soul" takes a sign as a thing and so plunges the mind downward. Augustine sees the condition immediately in carnal Israel and gentile idolatry (3.6.10–8.12). Still the unstated danger is greater: a reader might read a literal passage under the lure of figural pleasure and so make allegorical or enigmatic what must remain plain if there are to be churches. So Augustine reiterates the familiar negative rule for identifying figural language: You presume that the scriptures are literal until you find a passage that seems to contradict "honesty [or decency] of morals" and "truth of faith" (3.10.14).[12] The passage must then be read figuratively. How do you measure decency and truth? By reference to the rule of faith carried in the church. The condition for interpreting scriptures is a certain communal foreknowledge of what they intend to teach. Lacking that foreknowledge, no reader can hope to identify figural locutions. Only by remaining a member of the community of believers does a reader have access to the rule or norm of faith that is the meaning of scriptures (3.10.15). We are denied the pleasure of recognizing figures if we refuse submission to the rule of faith. Our supply of figural pleasure is regulated—so the argument—by our nearness to the body of the church, a body with gleaming teeth, at once figurative and literal, ready to tear us from any mistaken exegesis.

If we attempt to identify figures without reference to the rule, we are likely to overinvest bodies with significance, to succumb to the irrational exegesis of superstition. We will stage mime shows on the pretense that the motion of bodies is self-interpreting, but then hire announcers to tell us what is going on (2.25.38). We will scan the flight of birds for portents in anxious minutes, but ignore what they do most of the time (2.20.30–31). We will try to predict biographies from the observed motion of stars or turn basic acoustic effects into objects of worship (2.21.32–22.34, on *genethliaci*; 2.17.27, on statues of the Muses). There is a whole ladder of idolatrous projection to be scaled. For Augustine, the projections tell nothing about divine meanings, but much about where we take our pleasures, whether in the splendor of light or in "fleshy shadows" (1.7.7; 1.9.9, *umbrarum carnalium*). No sophisticated, revisionist exegesis of pagan idolatry can save it (3.7.11). Pursued into superstition, fancying figurative meanings where there are none becomes "soul-copulation" with fallen angels (2.23.35, *hoc genus fornicationis animae*; compare 2.39.58, on covenanted *societas* with demons). We will gain in these imagined signs only a deadly *jouissance*, the endless scratching of desire deflected into swollen frustration (2.23.36, *imaginariis signis*; 2.7.10, *mortifera iucunditate*). The lure of intensifying readers' pleasures by multiplying what counts as text ends by cutting all pleasures short in living death.

To treat the luxurious fevers of this demonic theater, we must turn to the chaste rites of the church. Jesus' resurrection gives Christian believers "a perfectly manifest index" of their freedom (*manifestissimum indicium*, 3.9.13, as for what follows). The Lord himself and the tradition of the apostles deliver a new "*disciplina*," new rites, "some few in place of many, and these most easy to do, and most august in understanding and most chaste in their observance." When you perceive them, you know at once what they refer to, and you revere them not in fleshy subservience but in spiritual freedom. They are the opposite of the demonic spectacles, the mythical theophanies. Entry into the community that carries the rule of figurative interpretation is brought about by transparent, self-interpreting performances (cf. prol.6 on Paul's baptism). That community not only celebrates the meal of Jesus' body and blood, it distributes the body of Jesus onto the body of its members (2.3.4, 3.9.13, on meal). Members of the church are "spiritually born" of the same semen, the *semen verbi*, seed of the preached word and the incarnate Word (2.12.17). They drink their milk not from a mother's breasts, but from the same Word who tutors them through visible things (2.12.17). The semen and the milk, as images and as energies, are disbursed through the church. If Jesus likened the fate of the Temple in Jerusalem to the suffering of his own body, Augustine transfers Jesus' body into the new temple of the church (compare 2.16.26).

There is much to be meditated in the denunciation of lascivious idolatry and the chaste subordination of scriptural figures to the alleged literality of church. The rule of faith, to escape a regress, must be figureless, and the rites of Christianity, to avoid becoming demonic mimes, must require no interpretive caption. The "body" of the church must do better whatever fleshly bodies do without tempting them to fetishism. This is a conundrum rather than a conclusion. It also risks rhetorical failure. A figureless rule of life will not persuade, and a self-interpreting rite is no sacrament at all. Both undo the need for the rhetoric of incarnation, which supposes that the most important human teaching requires mediating flesh and its sounding words. Both commit interpretation to an institution—since, whatever the conceit of literalism or transparency, interpretation will be required, as

Augustine himself proves on nearly every page of this book. But what is most telling is that Augustine violates his own deepest pedagogy of hierarchical ascent when he privileges the plain letter or the candid rite. If grammar is a function of rhetoric, if the meaning of a sign is completed only in rhetorical turn, then any rule of treating or teaching can only ever be vindicated in arrival. What stands proxy for that vindication at any earlier point is the power of the figure to attract and sustain desire. But how can desire be attracted or sustained by the perfectly transparent "body" of the church—by the authority that has taken the place of the body of Jesus? And what are the risks for desire if it acquiesces in that substitution?

When figure cannot be trusted to sustain desire, when its sweetness, its smoothness, its skin, is judged inadequate to teach, the alternative is compulsion. The body of Jesus, mistrusted as figure, is supplanted by the "body" of the church, construed as better-than-figure, as continuously disciplined letter. The masturbatory pleasures of feigned figure, the demonic copulations of covenants for overinterpretation, are mortified by an authoritative community—which may have been figured in scripture, but which now acts in blunt letter. No need for a smooth tongue when you have sharp teeth. The body in which a kenotic God once came to teach has been replaced by a "body" that claims power over teaching in the name of his absence—or so *On Christian Teaching* sometimes suggests.

But Augustine does not stop running there. He stops writing one book only in order to start another—to take up the story of his own arrival in the authoritative community, his own persuasion to it. He begins to write *Confessions*, a text that imitates scriptural history by recounting stories about how God teaches bodies. This second book inscribes a particular life within the frame of scripture. Since so much of that life offended morals and repudiated true teaching, it must be read retrospectively as figure. Since the life turned decisively around reading about Jesus, its figurative renarration must incorporate or encounter a figure of Jesus' body. How can it stage that final body as the object of chaste desire? How can it portray Jesus without making him the subject—or star—of yet another demonic spectacle?

Prostituted Words

As Augustine tells it in *Confessions*, a decisive turn in his conversion of many acts came in reading a scriptural verse that quenched unholy desire and so made him a fit candidate for baptism. The verse, read under the dramatic solicitation of a disembodied and genderless child's voice, commands the reader, commanded Augustine, to "put on Lord Jesus Christ and make no provision for the flesh in desires" (Romans 13.13). Put on Jesus: like armor, like a baptismal gown, like a second body. *Confessions* tells how much it took for Augustine to be able to read those scriptural words as rhetorically effective—as something he could actually perform.

The moment of seduction by scriptural words has been prepared from the beginning of *Confessions*. The book is preoccupied by the application of words to bodies. Its narrative portion treats, from passage to passage, the endless intertwining of desires through bodies and the words they receive in order to be redirected, remade. The narrative might then seem eminently incarnate—and it is, but in no simple way. The Word became flesh to dwell among us, but in *Confessions* the flesh of that Word is figured mainly by anticipation or retrospect, as exhortation or repentance. At the moment the reader expects encounter, there is absence or evasion. Augustine tells how he untangled perverted relations of words and bodies, but he cannot bring on stage the body in which those relations are finally put right. Perhaps this taboo on representation respects the absence from churches of one form of Jesus' body—until he comes again. Perhaps Augustine is enjoined not to reveal the holy mysteries of Christ's body in the only way it is regularly present now, as eucharistic bread and wine. Or perhaps there are dangers in words about an incarnate God that cannot be untangled in any restaging—no matter how gifted the baptized rhetorician, how chastened his scripts.[13] Can Augustine ever figure the body of Christ safely within the recital of his protracted education away from demonic spectacle and toward scriptural reading?

Confessions famously begins by quoting scriptural praise of God to pose its own version of the question: How might a small portion of creation, the human being, fulfill its wish to praise God while corseted by mortality? God excites human desire to praise, gives human pleasure in praising. Augustine feels the desire and its pleasure. He traces it back to the faith he received from God through the Son's humanity and the ministry of human preachers. All the rhetorical elements of *On Christian Teaching* are already here: praise, desire, faith, preaching. So too are that interrupted book's tensions around flesh. If the humanity of Jesus inspired Augustine to faith, it was partly as an antidote to the frustrations of merely mortal desire and the fantasies of mythical metamorphosis. The example of Jesus came by preached words to a body bounded by death, sin, and divine displeasure (I.1.1).

The human body begins—in Augustine's text, in his mother's womb—as the dialectical opposite of uncontained, unrepresentable divinity. God cannot be circumscribed by bodies or by words (I.3.3). Human flesh is all too much contained—by the womb before birth, then by lack of speech. Skin confines mind. The mind's first signs are fumbled bodily expressions of desires or discomforts. Its original rhetoric must use tears, gestures, cries (I.6.8). "With groans and various sounds and various motions of members I willed to express my heart's sensations, that my will would be served" (I.8.13). The economy of signs is an economy of embodied desires.

Words, spoken and then written, are eagerly acquired as surer instruments for the accomplishment of desires. They do lessen the mind's bodily solitude, but only at a price. Augustine was taught to read Latin letters by beating. Looking back, he admits that he did not know how useful reading and writing would some day be to him—or to the conduct of human life, the spread of the gospel. He did know as a child how much he hated the beatings. Still he began to experience new pleasure—the pleasure of reading "false fables" that made him "itch more hotly" (I.10.16). The pleasure grew into curiosity about the "spectacles," the adult games of public shows.

In *Confessions,* Augustine rehearses a critique of performed poetry that would have been familiar to his first readers from many sources, but especially from Plato. Augustine indicts poetry on three counts: that it is irrationally powerful, that it is full of lies, and that it authorizes immorality. Poetry's power is irrational because it speaks beautifully to strong appetites—appetites for bodily pleasure, but more dangerously for praise and power. Beyond the seduction of poetry itself there lie the better managed seductions of commerce in poetry, the uses to which knowledge of poetry is put in the marketplace of prestige. Then poetry is acknowledged fiction. The educated admit that there was no Aeneas, that Juno never lamented his arrival in Africa or Dido his departure (I.13.22, I.17.27, I.13.21). The fictions about his wanderings are valued because they cover up darker facts—the petty sadism of schoolmasters, the onrushing violence of the river of human despair. Augustine accuses poetry in last place of authorizing immorality. It not only depicts Jupiter as an adulterer; it suggests arguments in which the god's acts excuse our own. Augustine quotes lines from Terence: a "worthless young man" points to a wall painting of Jupiter's seduction of Danaë in order to justify his own fornications (1.16.26).

The mythological poetry Augustine was forced to learn supposes that it can sing varied incarnations of multiple divinities. It does not suppose that those incarnations are safe or their representations stable. "Janus is not the only one that has a double face; many other divinities do too, including some goddesses," writes Pierre Klossowski. "If they offer one face in the temples, they have another in the solemn liturgies and stage scenes."[14] For each face, there is a different cultic response. On Klossowski's reading, this difference was for Augustine "but an incoherence that only served to perpetuate monstrous practices. We suspect currents and countercurrents." Klossowski ironizes in an academic voice. Currents, indeed: "the infinite amalgam of images" invited so many human performances—authorized so many expressions of the worshipers' "intimate plurality." The promiscuous pleasures of readers, spectators, worshippers are solicited and depicted in divine traffic with variable bodies.

Confessions tells us as little about Augustine's response to civic cult as it does about his sex life. But we do occasionally catch him performing a god—or, rather, a goddess: "It was assigned me . . . that I should speak the words of Juno enraged and grieving that she 'could not keep the Trojan king out of Italy'" (1.17.27). The task was not to recite Virgil, but to perform a prose paraphrase of the opening scene of the *Aeneid*: "And he was said to be more praiseworthy who in the dignity of the adumbrated character [*pro dignitate adumbratae personae*] excelled in likeness to the emotion of anger or grief, dressing thoughts in fitting words." *Adumbrata persona*: a role or character barely outlined, sketched by shadows, but also feigned or simulated.[15] For a young student of rhetoric, understanding a goddess's speech in poetry is being able to mime it. Reading well is performing convincingly.

With performance, Augustine's attack on poetry goes over into another and more sustained attack, also familiar from the Platonic dialogues and their echoes. From paraphrases of Virgil to more cunning persuasions: rhetoric means immediately for Augustine, as for Gorgias or Cicero, the art of moving public assemblies to some action or sentiment. Studying rhetoric is apprenticeship in the manipulation of public desires. On Augustine's diagnosis, the study is unfailingly motivated by the rhetor's clammiest desires. His teachers could speak according to the Ciceronian rules, "copiously and ornately," whenever they spoke about their lusts (1.18.28).[16]

A rhetor's words do not act in isolation. They function within an economy of images and performances that circulates desires through bodies. Here, as in *On Christian Teaching*, the economy is represented vividly—and almost too pleasurably. In *Confessions*, the depiction of the demonic traffic in tickling signs is countered by a sobering narrative of Augustine's own body and the bodies he (or it) loves. The bodies are subjects of disease and death, but also—of course—of desire as the engine and instrument of mortality. Augustine's father sees him at the bath and gladly tells Monica that they should soon expect grandchildren (2.3.6). The baths: the site of seduction and philosophy, of the superb seduction that is philosophy. But Augustine's puberty retold predicts no wisdom, no beauty, only an uncontrolled copulation that will yield children of sorrow, that will spin once more the funereal wheel.

Even so, philosophy appears in order to seduce. Augustine is in his eighteenth year, about to become a father himself. He hears about him the clanging of "the cauldron of shameful loves" (3.1.1). He progresses with rhetoric. Into his hands there comes a little book by Cicero, a text prescribed for the rhetorical curriculum. The *Hortensius* is an exhortation to philosophy, a redoing or reperforming of Aristotle's *Protreptic* (3.4.7). Reading the book changes Augustine's passions—and more deeply than poetic mime or rhetorical manipulation could. He begins unexpectedly to burn with love for wisdom. He wants to love wisdom, to seek it, to draw close to it, to hold it—to embrace it tightly (3.4.8). Wisdom still figures as a body—or Augustine already wants Wisdom to be a body.

Cicero inflames Augustine's desires by promising them complete satisfaction in the study of some more satisfying wisdom. The Christian scriptures couldn't yet persuade him, because he could not yet read them with the right eyes—or the right desires. So Augustine had to find another teaching. He thought that he found it in the "many and enormous books" of the Manichees (3.6.10). Augustine calls it *"religio"* only when he thinks of it as demonic ritual (as at 4.1.1). More frequently, when he thinks of it as doctrine, he likens it to the base counterfeit of philosophy, to sophistry.

Augustine's first description of the Manichees stresses that they were glib sensualists, quick-talking pimps of a gaudy lie (3.6.10). In their mouths, he found only "devil's snares and bird-lime": sticky mouths, like little nooses drawn, are sophists' traps. Augustine's description of the renowned Manichee bishop, Faustus, could be copied from Platonic scenarios for meetings between Socrates and his sophistic rivals. While Faustus is convincing so long as he can give his purring speeches, he cannot handle questions. Faustus lacks philosophy. He has mastered a rudimentary reading list—a few works by Cicero, fewer by Seneca, some poetry, some Manichean tracts, but nothing more. Faustus spends his days practicing speeches rather than pursuing wisdom. So of course he refuses to entertain Augustine's questions in public, to "converse informally" or to "give and take argument" in the Socratic style (5.6.11). When he is finally compelled to address questions in private conversation, Faustus shows himself ignorant.

The prolix volumes of "this unknown Mani" came in the end to seem so many "lengthy fables," less useful and less beautiful even than the most outlandish of poetic or rhetorical conceits (5.5.8, 5.3.3, 3.6.11). Better Medea flying through the air than the Manichean cosmology. Still, it took Augustine nine years to read beyond the false promise of reading pleasure in those sticky words. His progress was aided by other words, by attentive reading in philosophical accounts of nature, but also by encounters with other rhetorics. The chaste words of the Christian bishop, Ambrose, attracted his professional admiration, though he was still contemptuous of the things they signified (5.13.23). Augustine was still unable to read scripture or even to understand explications of it. He must learn to unriddle its figures—and especially the one figure, the one teaching body, that is its key.

The Word's Own Flesh

The long pedagogy of words and bodies reaches its conclusion in *Confessions* 7, 8, and 9. These central sections mean to make persuasive a dramatic peripety in Augustine's education for reading scripture: the episode in the garden. They frame this episode as an act of new reading, an unexpected persuasion, and a subversion of erotic desire. In it, scriptural figures take life by taking over Augustine's life. He learns to read them when he can perform them—not as caricatures of fictional gods, but as stable shapes of his own new virtue. The scriptures supply in the figure of Christ what no other poetry or rhetoric could give, but the moment of the gift also shows how little this one figure can be represented in Augustine's text. If Augustine's long pedagogy of reading is completed in the garden, if his desires for reading pleasure reach there a real end, the climax marks a final victory of words over bodies—especially the body of Christ. We can see this only if we find our way back to that garden again—and not for the last time.

Book 7 begins with the body as the bearer of death. It marks time by mortality. Augustine's adolescence is dead, his young manhood passing (7.1.1). Even before discovering the Platonic books that will be his tutors, Augustine understands that God cannot be imagined in the "figure" or "form" of a mortal human body. Still, he must go further in uprooting bodily imagination, because God is not some stuff diffused throughout the cosmos, like light in air or an ocean of water in a boundless sponge (7.1.2, 7.5.7). These gross images have physical effects on Augustine's thinking: they pull him down, sweep him back, irritate his eyes. Just as *On Christian Teaching* predicted, addiction to bodily signs also leads to false science, to finding secret meanings where there are none—say, in the "false divinations" and "impious deliriums" of astrology (7.6.8).

Augustine is helped out from under these ponderous images by "certain books of the Platonists translated from Greek into Latin" (7.9.13). While reading them, Augustine comes to see with the "eye of his soul" an "unchangeable light" above him (7.10.16). It is not the common light seen by "all flesh" or some mere intensification of it. This light is altogether different, above Augustine's mind not physically or spatially, but by causal eminence. Physical senses cannot disclose the fully intelligible; perishable body cannot encounter eternity. The prerequisite for wisdom seems to be ecstasy, exit from flesh. This is the culmination of the first motion in Book 7.

The second motion comes immediately: Augustine cannot describe his transient vision of the unchanging-unphysical without noting the lacks of the Platonists' books that led to it. He notes them repeatedly, in varying lists of supplements. Immediately before describing the vision of the other light, for example, he contrasts the partial truth of the Platonists' books with the fullness in the Christian scriptures (7.9.13–15). The contrast occurs entirely in scriptural language. Augustine does not juxtapose quotations from the Platonists' books with verses that correct or surpass them.[17] He uses quotations from the Christian scriptures to show both where the Platonists agree with church teaching and where they fall silent before its fuller account. One rhetorical effect is to overwrite the Platonic words, which are not permitted to speak for themselves in Confessions. A more striking effect is to emphasize the full range of the Christian voice, the resonance of the scriptures in all registers of truth. This is not a dialogue of two voices, not a Christian miming a Platonist. It is a single voice that sounds most strongly, most fully, because it so often sounds alone. Its fullness is meant to compensate for the mere ecstasy, the exit from body, that was the condition of the Plotinian vision.

In a first list of supplements, Augustine taxes the Platonists for failing to speak the full truth of the Word or Son of God: the Word came to make humans children of God, took flesh, took the form of a slave, and was obedient to death. So the Platonists also cannot see that God conceals high truths from the proud and despoils Egyptians, Athenians, or Jews of the truths they ignore or violate. Truth, too, comes in the form of a servant. The Christological emphases are repeated in a second indictment of the Platonists. Augustine accuses them of failing to teach charity because they do not know the humility of Christ (7.20.26). He then arranges a second string of scriptural passages, now entirely from the Pauline letters. Every truth from the Platonists is also in Paul, but the apostle knows as well that only the promise of Christ can effect moral regeneration, can bring about freedom from death. So it is not surprising that the Platonists ignore the means of moral conversion, that they lack the "face of piety, "tears of confession," and the "potion of our price" (poculum pretii nostri, 7.21.27).[18]

The charges against the Platonists are driven home by strikingly physical images for the believer's encounter with the God of Jesus Christ. Augustine could "enjoy" God only after he had "embraced" Christ as the mediator between God and humankind—the mediator who "mixed" the food of saving truth "with flesh": "'the word was made flesh' so that our infancy might be suckled by your wisdom, by which you created all things" (7.18.24). But the bodily images are immediately qualified into lessons for humility. The eternal Word "built a humble house for himself of our clay" so that his humility would teach us the humility by which alone we readers can approach God. Divine condescension can be displayed across the distance from bodiless divine to embodied human. The hierarchical distance matters more then the reality of created body. Incarnation means voluntary humiliation. The body is an occasion for moral instruction—a sign for a thing that is a lesson. The master analogy of *On Christian Teaching* begins to run in the opposite direction, from flesh to word.

The reversal becomes explicit in other passages, when Augustine qualifies vivid bodily images by folding them into the rhetoric of scripture. He thinks of the moment when he turns from the Platonists' books to the scriptures: "later when I was made gentle in your books and my wounds had been healed by your curing fingers" (7.20.26). "Curing fingers" recalls the fully embodied Jesus of the gospel narratives, but the citation is reduced to metaphor by the mention of books. The hesitation over bodies goes even farther just here. The crucial step in the itinerary of Augustine's reading, the transit from the Platonists' books to scripture, is left unexplained. Augustine testifies to his desire for the new reading: "I grasped most avidly the venerable stylus of your spirit, and the apostle Paul before the rest" (7.21.27). This is the crucial moment of the transfer of readerly desire, the step in reading so long prepared. But why did Augustine turn to Paul? The choice of text seems almost as haphazard as the finding of the right Pauline passage will be in the garden. What drew him to Paul—except perhaps some echoes from embodied childhood?

The rhetorical tension of Book 7 is not resolved in it. The passages that seem most to emphasize the importance of the incarnation perform curious evasions around the body of Jesus. When an unexplained desire finally leads Augustine to read scripture avidly, he reads Paul—and Paul as a teacher of morals. Paul mediates Christ: texts by the writer Paul stand proxy for gospel narratives about Jesus—and the gospel texts perform the miracles once attributed to Jesus' body. The dangers of corporeal imagination in regard to the divine are so pressing that a body can be associated with divinity only through layers of didactic mediation. In *Confessions*, desire for Christ can be expressed as anticipation, as promise, but not as encounter. For incarnation to supply the missing moral lesson, its brute fact must be adumbrated into figure.

Eden Without Bodies

Confessions 8, which ends with the scene in the garden, narrates conversions all along. It tells of resolutions to enter the Christian community by abandoning the world's network of bodies. The conversions are tied to texts, and their retelling in *Confessions* multiplies textual relations, nesting texts within texts. The progression through text—the narrative progression itself—approaches Christ only as direct representations of his body recede. What many readers regard as the central episode in Augustine's conversion is narrated in the absence of the one body that is supposed to make Christian conversion possible. It is a moment, indeed, when Augustine's own body is overwritten by a Pauline *verse* about Jesus' body.

Here is part of Augustine's dissolution into texts. Ponticianus, a mere acquaintance, comes to visit Augustine on some matter of business. He picks up a codex that lies out and is surprised that Augustine has been reading Paul (8.6.14). Ponticianus is surprised again when he learns that Augustine and his companion, Alypius, have never heard the story of the conversion of the great Egyptian monk Anthony. Ponticianus recounts the story in detail, though the details are not reported by *Confessions*. He must have told its most dramatic episode, its moment of decisive resolution. Attending liturgy, Anthony hears the gospel verse in which Jesus counsels the rich young man: "If you would be perfect, sell what you have, and give it to the poor, and you will have treasure in heaven; and come, follow me."[19] Anthony applies Jesus' words directly and immediately to his body: he resolves to abandon his possessions and his customary life in order to follow Jesus into the desert. Taking this resolution, Anthony places himself in direct rhetorical relation to Jesus. He inserts himself into the gospel in order to change its plot—to do what the rich young man refused.

Ponticianus talks on about Anthony's followers in the West. He appends a story of two imperial officials who chance upon a copy of the life of Anthony written by Athanasius. They find it in a garden. One of them reads the written life and applies it directly and immediately to their own situation (8.6.15). They decide to abandon their planned marriages in order to seek God in the desert of solitude. (Fortunately for the story, their fiancées agree.) Taking this resolution, they imitate Anthony's direct response to the words of Jesus.

Notice the multiplying textual mediations, the lengthening chains of rhetorical reception. Anthony acts immediately on the Lord's invitation, read out from a liturgical pericope. A text is written about his response to hearing. The text becomes an occasion for the unnamed officials to respond to the (same?) invitation. The bodily voice of Jesus is replaced by the gospel text, which is replaced in turn by a narrative that quotes it in illustration of its rhetorical effectiveness. (Since Jesus did not actually persuade the rich young man to join him, both the gospel and the written life of Anthony seem more rhetorically effective than his original speech.) The chain of texts is not finished. Ponticianus's telling of the double story to Augustine becomes the occasion for his finally fruitful reading of the Christian scriptures—for his being persuaded by a verse to put on Christ. But Christ stands far back in the rhetorical chains. Even his quoted words have been displaced. The verse to which Augustine answers is not an invitation from Jesus or a story about Jesus. It is an exhortation from Paul to put on Jesus. Put him on how? As words? And after how many textual substitutions?

Ponticianus leaves Augustine in turmoil, eager to respond to the echoing scriptural invitations, unable to do so. Augustine and Alypius go out into their garden. It is figured as many gardens at once. It is both Eden and Gethsemane. It is the garden in which Ponticianus's two officials converted to monasticism and the garden of the pears Augustine stole so long ago in the narrative of *Confessions*. Or it is a school garden in which a rhetorician practices for court. Augustine describes the scene as a "controversy" of contending voices, the "angry litigation" of Augustine against himself (8.11.27, 8.8.19). On one side are his "old mistresses," "vanities of vanities," and "violent habit" (8.11.26). On the other is "the chaste dignity of Continence, serene and cheerful without dissolution, coaxing decently" (8.11.27). Contending voices, but also contending figures or adumbrated persons. This Milanese garden is a stage for philosophy, a theater of moral personifications, filled with reproving gestures and exhorting voices.

We need to look again at that famous female figure, at "the chaste dignity of Continence." The personification of Continence has no face, only an expression of moral seriousness; no body, only hands with which to proffer "flocks of good examples." She is virginally fruitful with children of her immaterial husband, the Lord God. She smiles, but she does not speak. Her gestures are something like a silent "*figura* in which is traced" the last condition for entry into the Christian life (cf. *On Christian Teaching* 2.41.62). It is Augustine, the recovering rhetorician, who voices her gestures as challenging words: "Can't you do what these boys do, what these girls do?" Augustine is ashamed to be listening to his old pleasures rather than her smiled invitation. He imagines that she speaks again, this time to paraphrase Paul: "Deafen yourself to your impure members on earth that they may be mortified" (after Col. 3.5). Her paraphrase of scriptural words is an offer to hasten the body's inevitable death. Mortify earthly members: give them the death that they seek in their fevers, the death that is their destiny and due.

Continence mortifies members by having no body. Her husband is an uncontainable eternity; her children are moral lessons. Her "body" is a pure name defined by a series of oppositions to real and mythological bodies. She is the opposite of the unnamed and all too fleshly "mistress" we have seen torn from Augustine's side. Her *casta dignitas* must also oppose the staged *dignitas*, the feigned passion of that Juno Augustine once performed (1.17.27). Whatever Augustine sees in the garden, whatever he does, it must not be spectacle. Whatever words he supplies for Continence to speak, they cannot be a boy's mimed show. Continence is the least passionate of adumbrated persons. Augustine need not—must not—rage or weep on her behalf as he puts her speech into prose. If he weeps, it is not because he mimics her tears.

Christian writers before Augustine had figured Continence, among them the author of *Shepherd of Hermas* and Tertullian.[20] But their allegories need not be his—and his is no simple allegory. She is indeed a female figure, but at the very limit of figuration. In other narrations of this event, Augustine described her as Philosophy (*Contra Academicos* 2.25–26). In *Confessions*, "Philosophy" has become "Continence." She is more specifically attached to bodies, but as their mortification. If philosophical protreptic can intensify erotic desire into its sublimation, Continence denies it, contains it. She denies it in her very adumbration. Compare her with any of the Platonic figures of philosophic seduction, from Diotima (*Symposium*) to the personified Laws of Athens (*Crito*). Compare her mute gestures even with what remains of the persuasive voice in Aristotle's *Protreptic*, the model for Cicero's *Hortensius*. In the arc of his narrative, Augustine needs effective persuasion to kill off the mortal sinfulness of his endlessly desiring body.

Choosing the children of Continence, he refuses any (more) children by his own bodily exertions—much more, any copulations without issue. He fixes his erotic desire on a "woman" with whom he cannot procreate.

The emptiness of the figure of Continence testifies to the persisting danger in Augustine's account of rhetoric's bodily solicitations. It must be Continence rather than Christ because his appearance would risk too much attachment, too much spectacle. In comparison, Continence is a figure of adumbrated femininity who can answer those aging but still saucy prostitutes plucking at Augustine's sleeve.[21] But the more important point is that the mute, bodiless body of Continence can perform a last rhetorical substitution, a signifying seduction. Her appearance transfers Augustine's attention, his desire, his will from the whispering mistresses, *nugae nugarum et vanitates vanitantium*, to the figure of a "fertile" woman who poses absolutely no risk to his chastity. She has a husband, God, who cannot be cuckolded. She has her hands full with more than enough children, her moral examples. She smiles without a face, reaches hortatory hands without a body. She is peace and joy without profligacy. She is, we have seen, both Wisdom and Scripture, but she is also afterglow without risky frenzy. Continence invites the reattachment of desire, its transference, in a way Christ's body never could. She is the right sort of girl after a string of bad ones. To suggest that Christ might play this role in the rhetorical chain would be, for Augustine, much more than obscene.

Continence figures the end of any ordinary rhetoric—even the gnomic and apparently ineffective rhetoric of Christ's counsels to the rich young man. She is the space into which a finally orthodox reader's pleasure is directed without fear of its escape into bodily ecstasy. She is silent. She reaches forward only to offer *exempla*. She is a figure for the figures in didactic or hortatory texts, including the Christian scriptures. She cannot plainly speak what she means to teach, but she leaves no room for lascivious innuendo. Her voice has to be supplied for her by the expert reader. Augustine before Continence in the garden is like Augustine construing the figure of the *pulchra quaedam femina* in the Song of Songs (*On Christian Teaching* 2.6.7). In both cases, he has to supply the voice—or give voice to the exegetical promptings of the Holy Spirit.[22] In each case, the textual figure elicits and absorbs his desire. In *Confessions*, Continence mortifies Augustine's remaining rhetorical lusts by inviting their (re)attachment. She prepares him for the coming of a final text—in which an incarnate god can persuade without appearing on any stage. Augustine is ready to fix his reader's desire on a text with which he cannot procreate demonic theophanies.

Unable still to shake the old, wheedling voices, to mortify his earthly members, Augustine goes off from Alypius a second time, to weep alone—and for himself. It is now that he overhears the famous command chanted by a voice—whether a boy's or a girl's he cannot tell. For once a voice appears to him not as male or female, not as holding a fixed position in the economy of persuasive lust, but as doubly pure voice, voice without gendered body. Surely it is a *figura* speaking, one of the exemplary children of the silent Continence. But Augustine does not supply this voice—does not mimic it, improvise it, project it. The voice seems to come from one of the neighboring houses—or, just perhaps, from the "divine house."[23] "Pick it up and read it"—that is the chant. Bewildered at first, Augustine then receives the command. He rushes inside to retrieve his copy of the letters of Paul, the one that surprised Ponticianus. In it he reads, as if at random: "Not in riots and bouts of drunkenness, not in coupling-beds and impurities, not in strife and rivalry, but put on the Lord Jesus Christ and make no provision for the flesh in its desires."[24] The sentence has an effect on Augustine's will, and on his body: "I did not will to read further, nor was there need" (8.12.29).

Augustine has at last learned to construe scripture—by performing it, but also by stopping short of its troubling and pleasurable figures. He has quelled his reading pleasure in a single locus of scripture, without the need to unriddle the enigma of its figure. The figure here is Jesus' body in most intimate connection with the body of the believer. But the moral letter has persuaded Augustine, sating his desire in unpolluting action. Its letter has become the body that he can possess in chastity. Wanting to embrace Christ, Augustine had reported without explanation that he "avidly grasped the venerable stylus of your spirit, and the apostle Paul before the rest" (7.21.27). Augustine is the opposite of those who would dispense with the letter in pursuit of immediate illumination. He hardly wants to fly up to heaven to hear Jesus teach in the flesh—to become audience for another theater of theophanies. His encounter with Christ is mediated through the familiar genre of moral exhortation, but also through the text of Paul, the Spirit's best stylus. The voiceless appearance of Continence and the bodiless sounding of the ungendered voice yield to a spiritual stylus that moves without any scratching across the leaves of a codex. Persuasive voices yield to writing instruments that can record words capable of mortifying mortal bodies with too insistent desires. "I did not will to read further, nor was there any need."

The stylus called Paul exhorts Augustine to "put on Jesus and to make no provision for the flesh." This means, most immediately, that Augustine resolves to choose celibacy as a precondition for receiving baptism. His victory over old lusts is his escape from the world's theater of bodies—bodies in obscene myths and murals, in spectacles; bodies subject to the embarrassing signs of puberty or their procreative consequences; bodies of concubines or carefully vetted fiancées. But where in this moment of victory is the body Augustine could not find among the Platonists? Where is the "form of humanity" into which the eternal Word descended to suckle, to cure, to embrace him? However many gardens it might be, Augustine's garden is not the one outside the new tomb lent for Jesus' hasty burial. In that other garden, Mary Magdalene cries out for the body of her Lord and rushes to embrace it when she recognizes it at last (John 20:10–17). Augustine weeps for his sins, his frustrated misery, but not for the missing body of Jesus.

Put on Jesus, but do not fall back into the habits of bodily imagination. Put on Jesus, but do not perform a spectacle or treat him as an actor's mask. Put on Jesus, but not as a second and more sensitive skin. What remains of Jesus' body in the Pauline verse works to mortify what remains earthly in your body. It quells the demands of any flesh beneath. This new body comes to Augustine's flesh not as a miraculous touch or even a gospel episode heard at liturgy. It arrives in hortatory words read at random from a didactic passage in scripture. Augustine succumbs at last to divinely seductive words. He puts on the body of Jesus, but that body consists only of examples and counsels. It is a "body" of ethical words delivered without any risk of making a spectacle of divine incarnation. *Confessions* refuses to figure Christ in this decisive act of reading. It refuses even to savor the pleasure of the figure, since savoring it would mean touching the skin of a god with your own.

You put on Jesus when you read Paul rightly. Right reading is your incarnation. Augustine's reading of the Pauline verse at the end of *Confessions*

8 can appear to violate the exegetical precepts of *On Christian Teaching*. In its solitude and suddenness, in its random finding of the verse, it can even seem one of those cases of inspired interpretation that the earlier work wants to reprove. There is no church in this garden, only the figureless figure of Continence. There is no dilating exegesis under the rule of faith, only an instantaneous apprehension of a chaste meaning. This severe discipline of reading pleasure might be the one required by Augustine's stubborn case. It might be the only therapy possible in a world of myths, where beautiful gods seduce maidens and schoolboys play goddesses in drag. If so, then the story of how Augustine changed his reader's pleasure must also be a story that changes his readers.

"I did not will to read further, nor was there any need." Roland Barthes begins *The Pleasure of the Text* by likening a reader's pleasure to Francis Bacon's picture of the "simulator" or deceiver who neither excuses nor explains.[25] The reader's only negation is turning away from the page. In the garden, Augustine turns from the page, he assures us, because he becomes it, passes through its signs to the thing it teaches. He is able to do this only after an arduous education affixes his reader's desire to the bodiless figure of Continence. Having chosen her, he can at last put on a verse about the body of Jesus. Writing *Confessions*, Augustine tries both to recapitulate and to enact that education for his readers. You came expecting to hear the scandalous past of this unlikely bishop? You'll get no pornography here. You want a miraculous appearance by Jesus at the moment of his conversion? No theophany either. *Confessions* elicits readers' desires, attracts them to itself, only to step out of the way in favor of the scriptures—but the scriptures as plain letter. You will see only examples. You will touch only the stylus.

Poor reader, you have been duped in order to be saved. Is *Confessions* then an imitation of a gospel or its pedagogical parody? Is this what became of Augustine's talent for comic improvisation?[26]

"The Potion of Our Price"

One other possibility remains for divine bodies. In his most emphatic contrast between Platonism and Christianity, Augustine ends the list of Christianity's superior moral pedagogy by naming "the potion of our price"

(7.21.27). This may remind some readers that *On Christian Teaching* suspended the dangerous cycles of figural interpretation by invoking the church's transparent rites, with their antitheatrical theology of divine body, their riskless spectacle. In *Confessions*, too, the events of the garden are only prelude to Augustine's baptism. Perhaps Christ appears in the *Confessions* not in his own body, but in the distributed, the displaced eucharistic body that constitutes churches.[27] Perhaps a reader of *Confessions* can still carry desire out of the garden to the evocative descriptions of Augustine's baptism or his first participation in the Eucharist.

There are none. *Confessions* is more resolutely silent about Christ's body in the Eucharist than about the body that must be put on through baptism before approaching it.[28] One reader finds at the end of the narrative of *Confessions* a passage so full of eucharistic imagery that it is "perhaps the only place in our literature where a Christian receives the Eucharist in the literary text itself" (O'Donnell on 10.43.70).[29] In fact, the elliptical passage, like the mention of the potion or cup, hints only to those who know already what it says. For those who do not, it remains a stubbornly silent figure. The churches' rites remain transparent only for their initiates, only when unrepresented in the general economy of signs.

Is liturgical silence the subtlest seduction—because the highest pitch of deferred desire? Augustine's reader expects to meet Jesus in the garden, but finds only speechless figures, bodiless voices, and a stylus producing another text. She follows Augustine toward the church that claims to receive and distribute the divine body, only to find that its mysteries cannot be narrated. *Confessions* can only outline a divine body, can perform the *dignitas* of the *adumbrata persona* of Jesus only as retreat before risk, as indefinite withdrawal.[30] The body of this divinity will never be seen—cannot be surprised at a forest stream or uncovered in blissful sleep. It can be displayed only as what it is not—as bread and wine under the taboo of public silence. Is the absolute refusal of the risk of being seen in public seduction at its most sublime or the entire abandonment of seduction? If there are risks in supposing that divine bodies can be seen and desired, what risks are there in asserting that a divine body must refuse to make a seductive spectacle of itself? (Does the Christian God want incarnation less than Klossowski's Roman gods do?) What kind of seduction can relate to bodies only by mortification and to words only by authoritative exegesis? Jesus the Christ may be eaten by initiates he has rebodied, but he may not be figured for them. They may use their teeth, but not their eyes or ears.

Unless the muteness, the secrecy of their bodily communion restores their bodily life after words. Unless every mortification of desire does become, among the saints, its more intense redirection. Unless Augustine attempts the one seduction that can excite desire for the body of an incarnate god without delivering it up to demonic spectacle. Barthes writes, paraphrasing "psychoanalysis," that the erotic is the intermittent, is skin glimpsed between two pieces of clothing, bounded by concealing borders.[31] Silence in the *Confessions*—about scandalous copulations or liturgical mysteries—is skin between the borders of words. Some of the skin is Augustine's. Some belongs to Jesus. After the garden and its lessons in reading, we readers are invited to be uncertain about where one skin stops and the other begins. Our uncertainty is the condition for representing incarnation. We are supposed to be more confident when we eat it.

3

Freedom in Submission

All lovers love freely, and freely take upon themselves the command of the beloved. They treat his wishes as commands, and subject themselves to him as servants; to those standing outside this relationship it is all incomprehensible, they cannot grasp its laws.

Hans Urs von Balthasar, "St. Therese's Little Way"

In his soul there is one element which deliberates and aspires to domination, and another element which is submissive and obedient. . . .

Augustine, *Confessions* 13.32.47

I was in torment, reproaching myself more bitterly than ever as I twisted and turned in my chains. And you, O Lord, never ceased to watch over my secret heart. In your stern mercy you lashed me with the twin scourge of fear and shame. . . . In my heart I kept saying "Let it be now, let it be now!", and merely by saying this I was on the point of making the resolution. I was on the point of making it, but I did not succeed. . . . I stood on the brink of resolution, waiting to take fresh breath. I tried again and came a little nearer to my goal, and then a little nearer still, so that I could almost reach out and grasp it. But I did not reach it. I could not reach out to it or grasp it. . . . But this did not drive me back or turn me from my purpose: it merely left me hanging in suspense.

Augustine, *Confessions* 8.11.25

as he waits for the moment of his "conversion," Augustine's description of himself—bound, beaten, suspended—is that of a tortured slave. Unusually, though, no one else has enslaved him: he is enchained entirely by the stubbornness of his own will, suspended by desires that pull him in opposed directions and so elude release and resolution. The old girlfriends tug him one way, cool Continence another—toward God, he hopes, which is also to say toward a steadfast and faithful desire. He finds that he is not quite strong enough—not wholehearted enough, he says (*Confessions* 7.8.20)[1]—to shake off those old urges by himself, however. It seems as though he seeks self-mastery, the capacity to make his own choices and to choose Continence over indulgence; yet it turns out that what he so desperately seeks is *not* to master himself, but rather to be mastered. For all his talk of resolution, the most transformative moment in his conversion comes not in his will's command to itself, but in an act of strange obedience: "Take and read," calls that childlike voice from an invisible source, and Augustine obeys (8.22.29). *Whom* he obeys, in the absence of the speaker's identity, remains a little less clear to the reader than it seems to be to Augustine (or maybe we as readers are once again simply more curious about what seems to him an insignificant matter). It might be a child who speaks, it might be Paul who writes, but Augustine hopes that it is God he is obeying.

In his wish to be mastered by God, Augustine himself is implicated: he stages his own domination, even by the voice of a child; but perhaps he also shows God how well he submits. Well enough, finally, to seduce that divine domination, to transfigure his slavery and humiliation from signs of half-hearted, not-quite-continent desire into an imitation of Christ. The moment of his reading is both peaceable and dramatic: "At once, with the last words of this sentence, it was as if a light of relief from all anxiety flooded into my heart. All the shadows of doubt were dispelled" (8.22.29). The doubts do not pertain to doctrine, Augustine having been intellectually converted to Christianity well before this scene; they have to do with Augustine's ability to respond to the call, to sustain the intensity and the direction of his desire—precisely by submitting it to another. This is the moment at which he gives over his will, and with it his flesh, but it is a moment that cannot remain and will have to be repeated.

We take up in this chapter the pleasures of that submission, pleasures that by their very nature require resistance. Without the guilty delights of disobedience, the perverse pleasure of obeying—indeed, the very realization that obedience *is* pleasurable—risks going unnoticed. In fact, without the pull of disobedience, with its urge to play God, the pleasure of obedience might do worse than go unnoticed—it might become easy, and boring.

Luckily, the very nature of submission guarantees the necessary tensions. The peace of the conversionary moment passes, not altogether unlike the quick evaporation of the exuberant disobedient delight of stealing unripe pears. But both leave traces: the new obedience, conspicuous though it is, is not only imperfect and inconstant, but it always carries within it the lingering trace of resistance too. As James Wetzel notes, "No new will, regardless of its source or manner of arrival, could ever constitute a new self without first becoming part of the story of a single, temporally extended person. The past, in one way or another, will find its entry into the converted will."[2] Augustine carries within himself, as himself, the ambivalences of his narrative, and of his desires.

The complications of obedience run deeply, and we must be careful not to take his submissive urges lightly. The puzzling eroticism of obedience, in which we do not merely take upon ourselves the commands of the beloved, but greedily insist upon more commands, is often explained as the pleasure of irresponsibility. First, it frees me from having to figure out what to do; I am no longer responsible for finding, weighing, and determining among my options. More, if you tell me what to do, then it is your fault, not mine, if I do it. This explanation is often advanced, for instance, to explain the popularity of dominatrices with corporate executives, and no doubt it is sometimes true. We find, however, that Augustinian obedience is decidedly not seeking a way out of responsibility, but is if anything exacerbating it. The eroticism of submission is for him—as for many of those who seek it—not at all a matter of ease in the abandonment of responsibility but precisely a pleasure of and in intense difficulty and ultimate, frustrating-yet-desired impossibility; it is a twofold intensity of the shattering and sustaining of the will, both in and under the will of God.

That shattering and sustaining, both more corporeal than we sometimes realize, mark the dual pleasures of obedience. One pleasure is that of the sudden drop, in which the will breaks and the body bends, suddenly re-leased from its suspension. The other is the sustained restraint entailed by remaining in a state of renewed resistance. Both place the body in time: in the impossible brevity of the breaking moment, in the long stretch of en-durance. In the tension of these temporalities, flesh reaches, too, toward eternity—toward the atemporality of the *now*—let it be *now*—that always eludes the subject. The body is held willfully in as the will restrains itself: to keep supplication from too obviously becoming demand; to display its humility intentionally, shamelessly, yet without becoming proud of that display; to seduce God, and also the reader, into looking. In the shatter, there is an immeasurable instant of relief from resistance (and all anxiety), of seemingly perfect accord in the loss of self-willing; in the sustaining, the pull toward selfish desire is felt and fought again, a pull that is necessary if the shattering in all its intensity is to be possible. Hence, perhaps, the frequent "submissive" demand for ever-more-difficult commands, the sort we resist even in following; hence, for Augustine, the intellectual twists that sustain obedience in its impossibility, keep the fulfillment of divine com-mand ultimately out of reach and so guarantee that we are always drawn on, and in. With obedience, as with God, there is always more.

More is sustained in some measure by paradox, as paradox, defying resolution, defies being-over as well. There are at least three notable para-doxes in the play of Augustine's obedience: one dealing with the active and passive wills, one with humility, and one with resistance. We may consider them in that order.

Active and Passive Will

To the modern, and largely to the contemporary, mind, will is necessarily active, both in choosing among options and in causing action intended to bring about the chosen results.[3] Augustine's view is more complex; he attri-butes to will both activity and passivity.

The concept of active will makes sense only if will is linked to freedom. While Augustine's valuation of freedom—his sense both of its goodness and of its effectiveness—varies considerably and sometimes problematically over the course of his career, that he believes that the will is free seems unarguable.[4] Even when he turns away from the more celebratory version of freedom found in *On Free Choice of the Will* (388–95) to a greater mistrust of its uses in his late writings, Augustine holds on to his insistence on choice and responsibility, from which even the doctrines of grace and original sin do not absolve us.[5] Obedience is actually integral to freedom, and for that matter to responsibility, running contrary only when it is wrongly turned—that is, when it is turned away from divine gifts, rather than toward them.

Obedience cannot be the abandonment of freedom. If the pleasure of obedience, the pleasure of one will in submission to another, were only the pleasure of irresponsibility, then its danger would be obvious, often political, and, to put the matter crudely, bad. James Bernauer, in his analysis of theology in the work of Michel Foucault, frames the problem succinctly: "Common to all forms of fascism is the *obedient subject* and Foucault's philosophy of religion is in resistance to that figure."[6] It seems reasonable to ask whether Augustine's is too, or whether he, in his ascetic and ecstatic struggles to submit his will to God's, seeks out the fascistic figure with troubling eagerness; that is, whether his is a passive and irresponsible obedience that colludes with a repressively destructive dominance. Can Augustine's submission do anything other than lead us to just the wrong love, to just the wrong way of loving a worrisomely domineering God?

Clearly Augustine seeks out that domination. He famously (and quite actively) asks, or possibly orders, "Grant what you command, and command what you will. . . . Oh love, you ever burn and are never extinguished. O charity, my god, set me on fire. You command continence; grant what you command, and command what you will" (10.29.40). Here Augustine's is a supplication, adoration, and submission strangely caught up in a multiplicity of wills, seemingly several of his own and at least one of God's. He demands the inflammation of desire as much as the capacity to repress or restrain it, and he asks, further, to be ordered to that restraint, to be commanded to (struggle with) continence and against temptation. In his short work *The Excellence of Widowhood* (ca. 413), he is even more explicit in connecting divine commandment to supplication: "let us beg Him to give us what He commands us to have. He commands us to have what we do not yet possess, in order to remind us of what we should ask" (17).[7] God, that is, demands our supplication, makes us ask, by making impossible demands of us, commanding us to have what we do not. Thus is fed not only humility, but desire, reaching, or burning, for the perpetually tantalizing not-quite-there. Thus, too, is desire sustained.

Nor, lest this impossibility be still too simple, are God's the only demands Augustine seeks. He wants to draw other desires in order to meet them—and he wants to draw and meet them in order to be desirable to God. "May your mercy attend to my longing which burns not for my personal advantage but desires to be of use in love to the brethren. . . . Let me offer you in sacrifice the service of my thinking and my tongue, and grant that which I am to offer" (*Confessions* 11.2.3). The request here is not to be granted some object of desire, but to be allowed to give, to be of use, to meet desire; to be of value enough to be desired, to be worth sacrificing. Things get stranger still, still more overtly obedience-seeking, as "Grant what you command" becomes "Grant me now and in the future to follow gladly as you do with me what you will" (10.35.56). After that initial violent yet peace-inducing break of Augustine's will in conversion, God, we cannot help suspecting, has not been quite demanding enough for the demands of Augustine's will to obey. Augustine, accordingly, must intensify his faith, must love God more, to seduce the divine demand. And he must love God more because the God he loves demands so much; because in that demand, in the intensity of his desire, is the evidence of divine desire in return.[8]

As these curiously submissive demands and clearly demanding submission suggest, getting a sense of obedience and its play between activity and passivity requires that we further complicate our understanding of will. First, being free, the will must be under its own influence: "For what is so much in the power of the will," Augustine asks, "as the will itself?" (*On Free Choice of the Will*, 19–20). But he also notes, in a move with some Aristotelian resonance,[9] that one's will may become habituated to vice and thus under the control of forces not entirely one's own—not, at any rate, one's own any longer, as the seductive power of vice comes to be stronger than the resistant power of the will. Though it may thus be split against itself, the will is not excused by this sense of external control, because the enchainment is the outcome of an earlier choice that *was* free (no one made Augustine attach himself to those now-undesired old loves). As Book 8 of *Confessions* leads up toward its famous climax, Augustine declares to God,

The enemy had a grip on my will and so made a chain for me to hold me a prisoner. . . . By servitude to passion, habit is formed, and habit to which there is no resistance becomes necessity. By these links, as it were, connected one to another . . . a harsh bondage held me under restraint. The new will, which was beginning to be within me a will to serve you freely . . . was not yet strong enough to conquer my older will, which had the strength of old habit (8.5.10).[10]

In this instance, only one of these conflicting wills properly counts for him as willful. In the will of which he himself disapproves, he is, Augustine says, "passive and unwilling rather than active and willing," even though he admits, "I was responsible for the fact that habit had become so embattled against me" (8.5.11).[11] Through actively having chosen wrongly, over and over, the will is eventually habituated into a passive near inability to choose rightly. Here Augustine attributes will, or willful activity, only to the desire and choice for good, toward God, denoting other directions[12] of the will as passive.[13]

The direction of the passive will is finally nowhere. To be passive is not, as we might suspect, simply not to will, but to will nothing. And nothing, for Augustine, is evil. In the *Confessions*, evil is presented as the negative of creation—not as uncreated entity (this would put evil on the level of divinity), but precisely as what *is not*: an absence or privation of the full goodness of being. Thus is explained the apparent presence of evil in a world created solely by an all-good God. To will destructively is to will negation, the ultimate outcome of which is nothing(ness). In this, as much as in his own sense of undesired enslavement to worldly pleasures, is the passivity of Augustine's struggling will: that will is passive which wills (toward) nothing. So in seeking submission, Augustine, far from seeking to be absolved from responsibility, seeks a way out of passive enchainment to habits he no longer actively wills, to the habits of willing nothing, which yet exert on his will a powerful force.

As the demand for demand—*command what you will*—already tells us, the will freed from passivity, led from passivity into freedom, does not display the self-mastery we might expect. While willing and working against one's own better will is passivity or enslavement to "the enemy," freedom—the opposite of passivity—is not self-will, but perfect subjection to God's will.

"This is our freedom, when we are subject to the truth; and the truth is God himself, who frees us from death, that is, from the state of sin. For that truth, speaking as a human being to those who believe in him, says, 'If you abide in my word, you are truly my disciples. And you shall know the truth, and the truth shall make you free' (John 8:31–32)" (*On Free Choice of the Will*, 57).

Freedom—subjection to truth—demands not merely fulfilling God's desires rather than one's own, but also actively willing to do so—making that fulfillment into one's desire. To seek an active submission, one must lack neither seducibility nor resistance; one must be susceptible of being drawn into God's desire while retaining some desire against submission. Without it there is, at most, only a sort of coordination of desires, rather than an active obedience. The redeemed will is the will turned anew or converted to God, but not without resistance to the turning. What we must resist is, improbably enough, our own passivity.

The active will is the obedient will, the will in the fullness of freedom and joy and delight. Why, then, would we ever will otherwise, as if aiming at our own unhappiness? Moving beyond the classical responses, which understand weak or destructive wills as the consequence of either short-sightedness or ignorance, Augustine provides a more complex theory, taking up Paul's suggestion of a hereditary tendency to sin (Romans 5:12) into his own famous, and famously difficult, understanding of original sin. Original sin, keeping us from any possibility of being perfect in virtue, is another factor in sustaining the tensions of submission.

This original falling-away, the result of an original disobedience, is passed on to all human beings through the "seminal nature" of Adam.[14] In consequence, disobedience multiplies.[15] Disobedience to God gives rise to the will's disobedience to itself, in which we see the conflict between active and passive wills, and to the resistance of flesh to the will's command; even having wholeheartedly committed to some act, we may find ourselves physically incapable. Noting some willful abilities that we do have, and then some that we do not—such as the ability to shiver the skin in order to twitch off flies—Augustine comments, "man himself . . . may have once received from his lower members an obedience which he lost by his own disobedience." Man's own flesh rises against him (and woman's too, if not quite so conspicuously). So disobedience is its own punishment; it simply extends itself—"In short, to say all in a word, what but disobedience was the punishment of disobedience in that sin? For what else is man's misery but his own disobedience to himself. . .?" (*City of God* 14.24). And yet, in a strange and lovely redemptive move, the resistant value of disobedience becomes a part of the pleasure of obeying—obedience becomes the will's triumph over that resistance.

In other ways, too, the punishment for our turning-away, our distractibility from divine desire, is inherent, not external. Augustine complains of God's threat of "vast miseries," "If I do not love you, is that but a little misery?" (*Confessions* 1.5.5).[16] Wrong desire keeps us from being happy because it does not desire what will most delight the soul, what most purely enables our enjoyment. *That* desire, however, that best and highest and most delightful desire, demands that the soul turn away from concern with its own delights. The original sin is separation of the will, the turning away and splitting off of one's will from God, the disunification of these perfectly harmonious wills into a conflicting multiplicity. The passive following of the serpent's suggestion is transfigured into a more active disobedience, though habituation will render this disobedience passive once more, as false freedom invariably returns to enchainment. True freedom is the reunification and reharmonizing of will—not to do as one pleases, perhaps passively giving in to destructive desires, but actively to do in order to please, to find one's joy in the desires of the demanding divine.

Humility and Pride

For Augustine, as for many Christians of his and subsequent eras, the active obedience of the rightly directed will is caught up in the paradoxes of pride and humility: humility is required for active submission. Dogmatically, obedience is not mere incidental accord of will, happening as if in parallel to desire the same thing,[17] but an active submission of one will to another. "It is then said to be the moral habit by which one carries out the order of his superior with the precise intent of fulfilling the injunction. . . . Stress is put upon the fact that one not only does what is actually enjoined, but does it with a mind to formally fall in with the will of the commander."[18]

The last sentence, though it is not Augustine's, conveys a concept crucial to making sense of his valuation of obedience. Both obedience and disobedience entail a certain parallel between human and divine wills, but the nature of that parallel makes all the difference. The disobedient will strives to create divinely because it wants to be as like God's will as possible, imitating divine freedom by rebellion. The obedient will, ideally, subordinates itself to the will of God *because* that will is God's. Disobedience inadvertently honors by imitation,[19] while obedience struggles to avoid identifying with the will with which it nonetheless strives to accord.

Obedience to God is the active subordination of one's will by one's will to God's will with God's help. (The last manifests the need for grace in our fallen, distractible state.) Obedience, based in freedom, is what saves humanity once it has fallen from harmony, through passivity, into division; the very scene of the Christian salvation story is one of obeying. Christ on his knees[20] famously renounces autonomy: "not my will," he says, "but yours be done."[21] The question for human followers of Christ becomes, then, how to honor this subordination of will. In strongly Augustinian terms, Cardinal Ratzinger, later Pope Benedict the XVIth, elaborates:

> Jesus assumes, as it were, the fall of man, lets himself fall into man's fallenness, prays to the Father out of the lowest depths of human dereliction and anguish. He lays His will in the will of the Father's: "Not my will but yours be done" . . . . It is this very conforming of the human will to the divine that is the heart of redemption. For the fall of man depends on the contradiction of wills, on the opposition of the human will to the divine, which the tempter leads man to think is the condition of his freedom . . . . "Not my will, but yours . . ."—those are the words of truth, for God's will is not in opposition to our own, but the ground and condition of its possibility. Only when our will rests in the will of God does it become truly will and truly free.[22]

Ratzinger cites Augustine as having claimed that "the humility of Christ and His love, which went as far as the Cross, have freed us from the powers [of false Gods]."[23] At one point in the *Confessions*, Augustine even indicates humility as a, if not the, reason for the Incarnation: "You sent him so that from his example they should learn humility," he writes (10.43.68).[24] Ratzinger adds, "We now kneel before that humility."[25]

There is something deeply fascinating in the almost certainly unconscious arrogance of Ratzinger's Augustinian statement: *we now kneel before that humility*. In part, it emphasizes the embodied character of obedience: Augustine (urgently, willfully) seeks the voice that can command him to kneel as to take and to read—to make his flesh over in the performance of divine word, in always-risky imitation of divine Word. In the flesh we disobey and are redeemed; in the flesh Christ is crucified, and we drop to our knees before (the image of) this obedience.

Our humility before this figure suggests, of course, an asceticism of the will, a restraint and refusal of its stubborn pride, a willingness of the will to work against its own desires. Yet we might recall here Geoffrey Galt Harpham's point that asceticism "is always defined as a quest for a goal that cannot and must not be reached, a quest with a sharp caveat: 'seek but do not find.' "[26] The already risky quest for identification with the incarnate God seems to go further here, into a kind of outdoing. Presented with an example of ultimate humility (a complete, obliterating subordination of personal will: let not my will to live, but yours to have me die, be done) we humble ourselves before it, as if to suggest that we can go lower than that, deeper into this life-giving subordination of embodied will.

If one subordinates one's will to that of another, one at least implicitly declares that other's will to be superior. For instance, submission in the monastic tradition may be intended not so much to impart the wisdom of the elder as to enforce the humility of the novice.[27] Augustine connects the two in seeing submission of pride and of will as linked parts of his conversion: "By fear of you, you repressed my pride and by your yoke you made my neck submissive; now I carry that yoke, and it is gentle" (*Confessions* 10.36.58). But divine discipline, though always portrayed as desirable, is not always depicted as gentle or easy: "By your laws we are disciplined, from the canes of schoolmasters to the ordeals of martyrs. Your laws have the power to temper bitter experiences in a constructive way, recalling us to yourself from the pestilential life of easy comforts which have taken us away from you. 'Lord hear my prayer' (Ps. 60:2) that my soul may not collapse (Ps. 83:3) under your discipline" (1.14.23–15.24).

There is an evident, if not quite open, strain of pleasure in this bitter divine discipline, in the bending of the neck and the breaking of the will thereby demanded. By contrast, Augustine's sense of the obedience that adults might owe to other human beings is almost startlingly mild. Some measure of this mildness surely comes out of his sympathy for the superior, the one who would be obeyed. We read in his Rule for monastic houses, "By your ready and loving obedience, therefore, you not only *show compassion to yourselves* (Sirach 30:24), but also to your superior. For . . . the higher the position a person holds, the greater the danger he is in" (*The Rule* 7.4). Human power, with its weight of responsibility and its constant struggle against the temptations of pride, is conceived here as a burden rather than a pleasure.[28] *Pride*, love of one's own power,[29] is opposed by humility's willingly powerful abandonment thereof. The power of humility is that of the will that can restrain its own desires—in itself a sign of strength—in subordination to another will. The temptations of power and pride are fairly evident, but humility comes with its own kind of power and so with its own contrary temptations. Displaying oneself as the lowest of all, one risks coming out on top.

We are not fully bound by obligations of obedience to any human beings; most obviously, as Augustine notes, "There is never an obligation to be obedient to orders which it would be pernicious to obey" (*Confessions* I.7.11). Obedience to God is a different matter. Even the order to kill one's own offspring is not pernicious if divine—which is not to suggest that it is justified by anything except its source. Despite such ethically problematic[30] counterexamples, such obedience is dogmatically held to rank high among the virtues, because it entails putting aside one of our most cherished "possessions," the will, in favor of the effort to please God.[31]

But for Augustine especially, *only* obedience to God is to be unlimited— for the sake, as we have seen, of the one obeyed as much as out of concern for the negative possibilities inherent in obedience to a fallible will.[32] It seems fairly obvious that if one regards God and only God as infallible, then God and only God may be obeyed without constant checking-up, or careful limitation. But God is also alone in being free of the first deadly sin: "Lord you alone exercise rule without pride, since . . . you have no master" (10.36.59). Even self-mastery, so often our own ideal and so seemingly the ideal of asceticism's violent discipline, is linked for Augustine to pride and in fact to the original, disobedient preference for having one's own way: for being like God, but going about it wrongly. Pride becomes a form of passivity.

This paradox is intensified by another, one that results more directly from the claim that obedience is owed (only) to God, while at the same time God is identified not only as the authoritative Father, but as the obedient son. In this pairing, the poles of obedience and command are each at their ultimate. We might not dare to attempt to experience absolute command, knowing our own fallibility and resisting our own temptation to pride, but we might perhaps dare to endeavor to emulate the son's inhuman obedience. Of course, the paradoxical arrogance inherent in this humble act is already evident, already seen in the notion of kneeling before humility in a subtly surpassing imitation of divine submission. And we are thus drawn to kneel because humility carries its own kind of pleasure—and its own seductive desire to be seen, to be beautiful in the graceful bowing-down of will, to draw God's attention with that beauty, as the created world draws ours.

Yet despite his own desire to resist pride, Augustine's is not a will that readily bends. It is too much and too strong for him to turn over to another on whom he would always be checking, another whose pride in the submission of Augustine's will would have to be limited, unless that other were to make him or herself not worth obeying, precisely by that pride. And beyond the dangers of submission to a will itself wrongly directed, it is always a bit of a disappointment to turn one's will over to another who does not, or cannot, regard this granted dominance as a considerable accomplishment on both sides. Disappointment, unlike the combination of fulfillment and exacerbation, is no incentive to desire. Too willful to wish, perhaps even to be able, to obey with reservations, Augustine must seek (thus, in the intensity of his seeking faith, bring out) a will that can be unreservedly obeyed, a will that can delight in his obedience without danger to itself. Thus he can only imperfectly seduce the power of human domination: his faith turns the full force of its seductive desire only to God.

Surpassing divine humility, even by humbling oneself before it (how else, except with pride, could one respond?), is itself forbidden, and this tells us of the impossibility of perfect obedience—of the necessity, and not merely the happenstance fact, of an inherent streak of resistance. We are to model ourselves, impossibly, on God's ultimate humility in Christ, giving our own wills over; and we give ourselves over to God's ultimate mastery in the Father. In an added difficulty, however, this is obedience to a master who tends not to issue orders very directly.

Augustine finds indications of God's will in scripture (12.30.41), but he is also well aware of, and indeed insistent upon, the rich multiplicity of interpretation onto which biblical texts open.[33] Thus, textual indications of divine will are ambiguous. Adding another layer of difficulty is the fact that we do not completely know *ourselves*. "I myself," Augustine declares, "cannot grasp the totality of what I am" (10.13.15).[34] We cannot, then, be quite certain that our will is ever quite wholeheartedly submissive, let alone that we have interpreted correctly those commandments to which we submit; the breakthrough moments of perfect peace flow back into the struggle of uncertainty, and the will to break (through) again. The constant risk that our attempted humility will become a source of pride becomes in turn a ground for further humility: even if we are obeying almost perfectly, we cannot be *certain* that we are obeying the right commands.

Nor do we always know *where* God works. Augustine, though somewhat disapproving of his parents who laughed at his punishments and the often hypocritical teachers who administered them (1.9.14), nonetheless hints that God is at work in such chastisement, even professing extravagantly: "Lord my God, I sinned by acting contrary to the commandments of my parents and of those teachers" (1.10.16). As Leo Ferrari remarks, "The irate schoolmaster of Augustine's infancy therefore becomes the scourging God who purifies his soul through the many punishments of life."[35] Sometimes heavenly mercy, sustaining us in humility, is indistinguishable from the humiliation of worldly mockery; while we must be cautious in obeying human orders, we must also be alert to the divine possibilities in them.

So we can and must give our wills wholly only to the authority whose commands retain an anxiety-provoking edge of interpretive uncertainty, uncertain too of the source and completeness of our own obedience. Even an appeal to divine mercy is of no help here; for Augustine, true obedience must not come from fear of punishment, but from love and its concomitant desire to please, its will to have the beloved's will fulfilled. Knowing that one might not be punished for failure is thus beside the point.[36]

Untrusting of most other sources, Augustine seeks dominance by inwardly demonstrating it over and upon himself. But inward domination is not enough: he must still be mastered by another. Which is to say, he must be able to sustain his faith that he is in perfectly expert hands, no matter what happens—a perfectly masterful expertise his faith can attribute only to God. Divine dominance is seduced by the urgent need of the faith that holds it to be perfect.

Without ever being certain, we must with a wholehearted will give our will over, yet retain that wholeheartedness, which is to say: that will. This too is the paradox of kneeling before the cross, which we now see as a double paradox of active and voluntary obedience to another will, and of outdoing an ultimate humility, undercutting an ultimate submission, as the only way to honor it.

Submission and Resistance

This ultimate humility risks falling into banality if it comes too easily. Here the character of Alypius, with whom Augustine undergoes his conversion, provides an illustrative contrast. Alypius is in that polysemic garden with Augustine, and he is the first person Augustine informs of his transformative experience in taking and reading. Alypius picks up the same text, which Augustine has helpfully marked, and takes the next verse for himself: "Find room among you for a man of over-delicate conscience." Augustine notes that "it very well suited his moral character, which had long been far, far better than my own" (8.12.30).

It is true that Alypius seems less subject to temptation than Augustine, to the point of being easily and "naturally" chaste. He likewise urges Augustine to celibacy: "It was Alypius who prevented me from marrying," claims Augustine, "because he insisted that if I did so, we could not possibly live together in uninterrupted leisure, devoted to the pursuit of wisdom, as we had long desired to do" (6.12.21). (It is somewhat startling for a thinker so devoted to Paul to attribute his celibacy to a friend's desire for company and not to his own desire for single-minded devotion to religious matters.) Yet there are other sides to Alypius's "moral character" as Augustine has chosen to present it. He is dangerously impressionable, for starters. He is also persistently lured by spectacles of violence—lured too, it would seem, by the desire to have his own resistance to desire violently overcome. Carried off to the gladiatorial shows by a group of friends, he indulges in his own bit of melodrama: "You may drag me there bodily, but do you imagine that you can make me watch the show and give my mind to it?" This is a taunt that has the desired effect of encouraging his friends to test his resolve. He shuts his eyes on the alluring scene but at a roar from the crowd he cannot resist peeking. From that point on, he is lost. "His soul was stabbed with a wound more deadly than any which the gladiator, whom he was so anxious to see, had received in his body," laments Augustine. Alypius grows "hot with excitement"; his eyes cannot get enough; his curiosity is insatiable (6.8.13). Later, even the sight of Augustine's submission to his desire for women tempts Alypius to entertain thoughts of marriage: "He was amazed at my state of bondage, and amazement led to the desire to test it for himself" (6.12.22). Alypius likes to look. He submits himself to visual impressions—especially to visual impressions of domination and submission. He leads himself into temptation, at least the temptation to watch, and commands himself to continence.

Indeed, it begins to seem that it is more his capacity for submission than his lack of heterosexual drive that makes Alypius superior to his former teacher. He is far, far better at submitting than Augustine. Or is he? At times, Alypius seems to give way too easily; his submission is too passive; there is no resistance to be overcome, thus no suspense: no break, no drop, no struggle to stay. To the extent that Augustine's resistance is higher, he may be far, far better at submitting after all. In fact, obedient submission without resistance is not merely uninteresting but in fact impossible, not merely as a pragmatic matter, but by definition.

As we have repeatedly noted, the desire to submit moves against itself, making Augustine's craving for wholeheartedness more paradoxical still. The inherence of resistance keeps the will actively engaged, and it keeps humility challenging. Harpham writes, "Desire is, of course, asceticism's abiding problem. But it is simply wrong to say, as so many have, that Christian asceticism excludes desire, for it manifestly exploits the desires to achieve spiritual perfection. . . . Be like Daniel, Bonaventure counsels, 'a man of desires.' 'Ask grace not instruction,' he insists, 'desire not understanding.'"[37]

It is perhaps fortunate, then, that the reining-in of willful desire so often intensifies it. Joyce Schuld writes that for Foucault, "'repression' is the weakest rather than the strongest use of force in power relations. Indeed, he would agree with Augustine that it often paradoxically stimulates and spreads the very desires and pleasures it sets out to control."[38] Psychoanalysis, of course, makes a similar point, noting that repression can both conceal gratification and intensify desire.[39] To obey continually does not only strengthen the habit of obedience—it also strengthens the disobedient urge and hence the gratification and triumph inherent in successfully obeying. But to be as nearly certain as possible that one is being obedient and not self-serving, one must fight the very gratification one seeks.[40] Chaste and dignified though she may be, Continence must be resisted a little bit, too.

We must resist even the temptation to be untempted. "The greatest temptation is not to feel temptation," as Harpham notes.[41] The ease of non-desire is not an option; not to want is death, not the eternal (over)fullness of life. There is no merit in not resisting, no submission without a trace of the desire to dominate.

Obedience may, impossibly, be an attempt to get out of the cycle of pleasure by renouncing even the choice of one's renunciations—except, of course, that one must choose to do so. Obedience sustains the necessary imperfection of the willing self—that is, of the subject who seeks the satisfaction of attainment or accomplishment—essential to keeping the ascetic goal from being reached. The more I fulfill my intention to perfect my submission, the less my will is my own, so the less *I* fulfill *my* intention, but of course that was my intention, all along.

Here, too, Foucault echoes Augustine; as Jeremy Carrette notes, "The key insight for Foucault was that Christianity held a paradoxical self . . . found in a self-sacrifice."[42] The self is something not simplistically to be destroyed but in a complicated mode to be gotten over. As Bernauer puts it, "Th[e] capacity for self-renunciation was built from the ascetic power with regard to oneself that was generated by a practice of obedience, and from the skepticism with respect to one's knowledge of oneself that was created by hermeneutical self-analysis. As we will see, Foucault later came to warn Christianity of the dangers of that obedience."[43]

But dangerous is not exactly the same thing as bad.[44] Nothing is more boringly antithetical to the intense ascetic will than having nothing to surpass.[45] One value of obedience, in fact, is the way in which it sustains this twist in desire. If my will is *only* what another wills, even if that other is God, then I am without will and cannot obey voluntarily (that is, at all); if I will to obey, if I obey freely, then my will is done even as I humbly say, let yours be done, instead. If I happen already to want what it is that you want, my "obedience" is accidental. The impossibility of perfection in submission sustains the ascetic pull, keeps drawing us in; like faith, it sustains the challenge.[46] I can obey perfectly only in a move to which ascetic submissiveness could never admit: by breaking the limits of the willing self, by making my will one with God's will, which is of God's very substance[47]—and then *I* am not obedient, after all, because there is no more *I* who might obey. Perfect obedience would mean a perfect unity of my will and God's will into one will. "God and I, we are one in this work,"[48] said the Augustinian-influenced Meister Eckhart, and he got himself in trouble, too. But this is the only abolition of will: into the perfection of divine fulfillment where the subject, obedient or otherwise, would make no sense. And even from this "mystical" fusion—or this impossible break—the subject returns, and the paradoxes of sustaining obedience return with it.

The puzzles of Augustinian obedience do not pertain solely to the human will; an absolute submission would also undermine the notion of divine omnipotence upon which its perfect possibility depends. We should take seriously here the notion of power best developed by Foucault, indebted to Nietzsche, which pairs it necessarily with resistance.[49] Power pushes only where some force pushes back (even this makes power, force and resistance too nearly thinglike, but of course language deprived of nouns becomes awkward). To offer an obvious and probably unnecessary reminder, this renders neither power nor resistance necessarily good or evil. Harpham lays the relation out clearly in his discussion of asceticism:

> Resisted power is doubled, mirrored, self-contradicted, self-confirmed—as multiple, relational, and unstable. . . . And yet only resistance can make power coherent. . . . Without resistance, in short, power is inconceivable. Resistance is neither an addition to nor an aspect of power; it is the site and condition of power. . . . Even to speak of "power" and "resistance" as thought they were independent terms may be a case of what Nietzsche calls language "doubling the deed," but we cannot correct language's error by resolving the two terms into one.[50]

In understanding this, we need to keep another, related point in mind: power and resistance need not function only as forces directed from one subject to another. Not only might they work in social, cultural, or political structures in which it makes little sense to try to identify agency, but they also, and often, function within a subject, as Augustine's sense of resistant will within himself already suggests ("The mind commands itself and meets resistance" [*Confessions* 8.9.21]). Harpham points out that the inherence of resistance is essential to asceticism: "Ascesis is the strong form of the universal condition, the cultivation of repression's tempting failures. Through such cultivation, the self is simultaneously opened up (or 'transcended') and closed off. Ascetic discipline does not seek an impossible perfect repression; indeed, it requires resistance."[51]

It is this necessary coexistence of resistance and power that requires us either to abandon or to modify dramatically the doctrine of divine omnipotence. Resistance must be as real as the power against which it pushes, and not merely pro forma. But this makes an absolute, irresistible power, an all-powerful power, impossible; not merely something we have never encountered, but a nonsense formulation. And that means that even in submitting to God, the one who wills submission retains responsibility.

Obedience throws this dogmatic tension into relief. The maximum of obedience should be the minimum of resistance—immediate, complete, and effortless acquiescence to the will of the one obeyed, simply because it *is* that will. That is, the perfection of obedience seems to be the absence of resistance to the master's power—but in such absence, there remains no power either, and no possibility of pleasure—think of Alypius, who seems so oddly disappointing in his virtue, who submits too easily. If resistance is not a mere token—if God is not guaranteed in advance to "win"—then obedience must always be just a little bit in doubt. Always a little bit in doubt, and always sustained by the faith through which, into which, we draw and are drawn into God. God's power *is* insofar as Augustine's faith draws it, his submission kneels to it, and his obedience to it neverthetheless resists.

God is omnipotent and omniscient—also beneficent—to the extent that Augustine seduces God into so being by faith. And it is crucial that other responses are imaginable, that faith and not merely reason or observation is at work. Indeed, a nearly silent undercurrent of reproach runs through *Confessions*; God is always with him, but often silent or out of evidence. God is everywhere and nowhere in this text that is constantly addressing and being addressed by God, seducing and being seduced by God. God is the effect of Augustine's seduction of the world, of his submission to the need to resist its temptations, if joy and excitement are to be sustained.[52] Sometimes the tables may even be turned: as we have seen, Augustine in the intensity of his demands may very nearly play at dominating God.

In fact, it is not so clear who dominates here, as we find ourselves back at an earlier point: if my will is God's altogether, and if God's will is of God's essence, then the I-God distinction fails to hold well either, or, to quote Eckhart, "God's existence must be my existence and God's is-ness is my is-ness, neither less nor more."[53] Augustine wants to retain the human/divine distinction, but he must, to do so, also retain the paradoxical imperfection of his submission. Insofar as obedience *is*, it is necessarily imperfect; were it to be complete, it would no longer be obedience. It is its very imperfection that makes it possible, and that makes it a suitable object for the intensity of the ascetic will.

The Eroticism of Obedience

The asceticism of the will that intensifies into obedience is also eros, another way of seeking to disrupt the boundaries of the self and to be drawn forth in an infinite seduction. For Augustine, to obey is an act of love, and, as we have seen, his love for God is a quest for the only kind of obedience in which he can indulge without restraint. His God seems to seek just that. "What am I to you," Augustine asks, "that you *command* me to love you, and that, if I fail to love you, you are angry with me and threaten me with vast miseries?" (I.5.5)

To love God is not simply, of course, to have some sort of theological emotion. Augustine's love is both an asceticism of the will and a surplus of adoration and desire. In this it blends two currents in Christianity more often sharply distinguished. Bernauer makes the distinction clearly, between asceticism, grounded in "the fearful obedience to God and the suspicious examination of oneself through temptations and tests," on one hand, and a confidence in divine love, on the other.[54] He remarks, "If one stream of Western culture's Christianization-in-depth is its dangerous esteem for obedience, a more fundamental and promising current is its confidence that love is the center of the mystery, in exposure to which we live our lives."[55]

In general, this seems an accurate assessment. For Augustine, however, these currents necessarily flow together; the mystery is that obedience can (without losing its tensions, its difficulty, its dangers and even its pain) be so joyful; that adoration can so simply, so seeming-necessarily, drive one to one's knees.

This pleasure demands, as we earlier suggested, an intense responsibility: despite his occasionally disquieting respect for authority, Augustine has a sense of obedience that runs contrary to the demands of the fascist "obedient subject." The temptation to obey in a totalitarian context is the temptation to evade thought and responsibility by externalizing and centralizing both. However, at least two elements in Augustine's understanding of right obedience forbid such evasion. First, I must know if orders issued are pernicious or not, and I must be careful and compassionate with the one I obey. Nothing here is, or can be, unthinking. Second, and perhaps more importantly, we cannot evade responsibility to the elusive, illuminating internal Teacher—that is, our responsibility for responsiveness to the Word, which speaks *because* we are listening.[56] We must always suspect that the voice commands because we have demanded it, that we bear this responsibility too. "A just human society is one which submits to you," Augustine declares in the *Confessions*, "But happy are those who know that you are the source of moral precepts" (3.9.17). Not all submission to worldly authority will be in accordance with these precepts, and we are not absolved from responsibility for what we obey, not even when we obey the voice of God—a voice we only hear within, or seducing us further without giving definitive answers.

All of this keeps obedience in a troubling and open space—in tension, as eros is, with the ethical as well as the political. To quote Harpham again, "Ethics implies closure and decision, an end to temptation; asceticism repudiates such a possibility. Ethics honors the distinction between 'being tempted' and 'resisting'; asceticism acknowledges no such distinction. Ethics worries the differences between *what* you might resist; asceticism demands only *that* you resist. Asceticism, then, is the resistance to ethics as well as the basis for ethics."[57] Obedience, so central to many ascetic modes, is doubly resistant: it is the resistance to one's own resistance and refusal, at the heart of asceticism yet in tension with it, its ultimate impossibility guaranteeing that to learn how to kneel is something that no subject will ever quite master, the elusiveness of mastery (and, always, of the Master) sustaining the pleasure of the search, the intensity of the break within the sustained restraint, the challenge of divine commandment.

If obedience could disappear into its own perfection, becoming at once unnecessary and impossible, then we would need, and we would desire, neither breaking nor restraint: we would have no desire at all. But in the disappearance of (dis)obedience there would be as well the double disappearance of the flesh in which obedience is possible and the word by which it is commanded. The God who obeys, on whom we model our obedience, is the carnal, incarnate God, who is, as incarnate, curiously near absence in the *Confessions*, as if dissolved into the text, or perhaps safely hidden away by it. The God to be obeyed is the one who speaks, however elusively. Seeking to overcome the stubborn disobedience of his own flesh, while yet sustaining the intensity of his pleasure in its seducibility, Augustine sustains as well the delightful and agonizing tensions of the fleshly will and creates them again in the tease of the text, leading us to take and read of pleasures that were not at all those we were seeking.

We read of the errors and trials of the body. Obedience belongs to the flesh: Christ *can* obey only by virtue of incarnation. And he does obey, clearly stating that the crucifixion is not what he would will, and going through with it anyway. For Augustine, this is the Christian insight that Platonism in its other modes has missed—the physicality and the suffering: "that 'he took on himself the form of a servant and emptied himself, and was made in the likeness of men and found to behave as a man, and humbled himself being obedient to death'" (7.9.14).[58] This contrast, as Louis Mackey notes, "leads Augustine to conclude that although they understood the spirituality of the divine and condemned idolatry, the Platonists were too proud to acknowledge the Word in its humiliation."[59] Though they must have tried to avoid hubris, the Platonists would never have imagined obedience to a God who could kneel.

We do not always, of course, experience carnality as humility, or as submission; in fact, it is precisely where the temptations of pride are posed.[60] The tensions of submission are also those of flesh in the image of divinity. What Augustine seeks is the flesh made perfectly Word, made perfectly accordant with—perfectly obedient to—the word of God. In modeling his obedience on Christ's, he attempts as well thus to model his flesh, to make it mutually transparent to the commanding word, knowing even so that there remains a distinction between "my" will and "thine." Without it, he could never obey.

Augustine falls back, as do we (though striving to be enfleshed word) into body-and-text.[61] He cannot identify either his text or his flesh with God's, but he cannot, as either a Christian or a Platonist, altogether disidentify them either. Our words, like our bodies, obey our wills only imperfectly, echoing their imperfect accordance with their divine versions in their inability wholly to capture that of which they speak, especially when they speak of God. Yet our bodies, like our words, take perverse pleasure in continuing to try, in pushing against their own necessary restraint, trying to reach divinity beyond their own limitations. And perhaps at their very limits, as the flesh reaches word, as word is made carnal, as obedience pushes itself through to its own absence in fullness, just glancingly—in a moment that will mark our memories and complicate us—we touch on divinity after all, a touch that, though it can neither grasp nor stay, can still suffice to bring us to our knees.

4

No Time for Sex

> The disavowal of time does not imply an abrogation or even a dialectical surpassing of temporality, but rather its radical deepening, an eradication of time by rooting oneself more deeply in the ground of time.
>
> Elliot R. Wolfson, *Alef, Mem, Tau: Kabbalistic Musings on Time, Truth, and Death*

> We cannot really say that time is, except in so far as it tends not to be.
>
> —Augustine, *Confessions* 11.14.17

The one who cleaves faithfully to the beloved brings time to a standstill, as absolute attentiveness accomplishes a miracle of full presence. Or so we can hope; so we seem to recall. Such a perfectly unchanging state of erotic absorption has never been attained, yet it was already there in the beginning. Indeed, Augustine knows just where to find it—in heaven. That is, in the heaven (*caelum*) of Genesis 1.1: "*In the beginning God created heaven and earth.*" For Augustine, this transcendental figure, which he renders "heaven of heaven" to distinguish it from the physical sky, partakes in the eternity of God's love, though a creature. It—or, perhaps better, *she*—is doubled by the formless *terra*, which likewise evades temporality—not, however, by participation in divine immutability but rather by dissolution into sheer mutability (*Confessions* 12.9.9–12.15.22). Opposites here very nearly meet at their limits: "heaven and earth," perfect focus (*intentio*) and utter dissipation (*distentio*), both represent erotic, as well as cosmic, modalities that seem to liquefy temporal distinctions. "May I flow into you, purified and melted by the fire of your love," prays Augustine (11.29.39).

The erotic undoes temporality, but it does so by deepening or intensifying it. If there is no time for sex, so to speak, this is not only because we are, for better or worse, most often occupied with other kinds of acts. There is no time for sex because there is no time like the present—no time *but* the present—and the present is always giving us the slip. What is longingly anticipated immediately converts to memory, and memory's ever expanding storehouse of images swiftly gives rise to further fantasies: we seem incapable of resting *in* the moment. Yet, paradoxically, sexual pleasure arrives only in abandonment *to* the moment, a moment of no duration (as Augustine insists [11.15.20]) that nonetheless enfolds the endlessness of bliss.[1] What is overtly the case with the sexual is, moreover, characteristic of all human experience, to some extent: we are always stretched across memory and hope (or dread), fractured by temporality, out of step with our selves. In this extension is the taut reach of our desire—the desire of desire, perhaps—as well as the dissolving depths of our convertibility. By our very distension across time, not despite it, we may be brought to the edge of eternity.

To get there, we must turn back to memory, as Augustine repeatedly does. Emerging in the space—"a place, no place" (10.9.16)—opened in the ongoing withdrawal of presence,[2] memory's capaciousness is the measure of time's unfurling; it is also where temporal distinctions seem to collapse. Memory harbors habit, overlapping with animal instinct ("both beasts and birds have memory" [10.17.26]) and colluding, potentially, not only with the disciplined life of ascesis that intensifies eros but also with the monotonous tug of lustful addiction that dulls it ("the images of things imprinted by my former habits still linger on" [10.30.41]). It is also the seat of imagination and thus a source of novelty: limned by the shadows of a fertile forgetfulness (10.16.24–25), it withdraws from itself so as to draw itself back in a repetition that is also a re-creation.[3] The archives of memory enable both the time-resisting momentum of iteration and the time-disrupting in-breaking of newness, in other words.[4] As displaced presence, memory pulls us back to the future, in a profound disarticulation of temporality.

As we have seen, Augustine remembers that he loved. He also loves to remember. And remembering—confessing—is itself an inaugural act of love. Beginning in Book 10, we are caught up in the moment of that love. No longer looking back, even if steeped in recollection, Augustine confesses "not what I have been but what I am" (10.4.6). We no longer look back, either. Rather, we listen in eagerly, as he declares his love for God tirelessly, counting its countless ways and gateways and thereby rhetorically prolonging the moment of amorous address (e.g., 10.6.8)—so many bites of sound piling up in the halls of memory, ours as well as his. In Book 11, he moves deeper into his meditation on time and also seems to lean more heavily forward, as the urgency of his desire intensifies: desire for the absent but anticipated presence of the other is also desire for the otherness of the future, desire for the otherness of one's ever-becoming self.[5] On fire for God, catching us with his heat, Augustine is also on fire for truth—the truth about time, as it happens. "My mind blazes to solve this most intricate puzzle. Do not close it off, my lord God, good father, by Christ I beg you, do not close off from my desire these things both familiar and secret, lest I be kept from penetrating them!" Indeed, for God to deny his ardent desire to penetrate would be unjust, since it is God who has aroused this desire, by displaying the seductive mysteries of creation so openly. "Give me what I love," pants Augustine, "for I love, and you gave me this" (11.22.28). Yet even as he seems to strain toward the future with new impatience, he also slows down dramatically, as if with a lover's restraint, folding back on a past far more distant than his own life history.[6] Indeed, he turns back to the very beginning of time, as we have seen. The beginning of time is also the beginning of the book. Beginning at the beginning, Augustine will not make much forward progress, after all: doled out syllable by syllable, the secrets of scripture draw him not ahead but ever deeper. Yet in the fathomless depths of Genesis 1, in the deepening of time itself, he discovers the eternity he seeks. Gazing into the abyss of his own soul (13.14.15), he also hears angels reading the very face of God, uttering words without syllables in the melting of tenses (13.15.18). In the beginning he discovers his end, in the labor of interpretation his sabbath rest (13.35.50–13.38.53).

The later books of the *Confessions* thus effectively perform what they preach about time and eternity, continuously looping the remembered past toward the anticipated future in the reach for unending bliss. Converting the future into memory and the past into hope, these writings thereby continue to seduce presence, extending desire toward the other, extending desire toward *becoming-other*, extending desire, yearningly, across time, in the effort to exceed time—suspending desire, tremblingly, at the very brink of time. This is a performance repeated in Augustine's other great narrative work, the *City of God*, and this chapter will also consider his account of beginnings and endings—of creation and resurrection—in that text. There we are reminded that there was no time for sex in Paradise. There will be no time for sex in heaven, either. There will be an eternity, as there was in the beginning. In the meantime, there is the pleasure of suspense. . . .

Seducing Memory

Book 10 of the *Confessions* opens, in perhaps untimely fashion, with a meditation on the "fruit" of confession. Having already been engaged in confessing for nine rather long books, Augustine now pauses to look back and wonder what use there might be, if any, in so much self-revelation. He hopes to be read by others, and to be read generously, yet seems doubtful of this outcome (10.3.3–10.4.6). God is his ideal reader, his most desired reader, but this too presents a problem. For God is his ideal and most desired reader precisely because God already knows him more intimately and fully than he knows himself (10.5.7). God can interpret correctly both what he writes and what he leaves out, what he gets right and what he gets wrong, because God has seen it all. Why, then, does God *need* to read him? Why does *he* need to write?

Perhaps Augustine needs to write his *Confessions* so as to become himself a text transformed by a divine reading—which may or may not be redundant for God but is definitely not so for Augustine. Perhaps Augustine writes not only to know himself known but also to know his knower—or, rather, to remember the one who never forgets him (13.1.1). Searching for his God, he enters "the fields and spacious palaces" of his own memory, finding in them a treasure-trove of images stored up from data received by his senses. Everything is there—except what he has forgotten. It can be summoned at will—except when it eludes his will. Though some images surface easily on demand, others show themselves more reluctantly, if at all, he confesses, and still others force themselves on him when he wishes they would not, a particularly bothersome instance of this being the sexually arousing figures that still come to him in dreams (10.30.41–42). The memory is full of mysteries, then; it is full of secrets. In addition to open fields and spacious palaces, it enfolds countless nooks and crannies. It plays with him, seductively, sometimes hiding what he wishes to expose, sometimes exposing what he would rather not see. It draws him in further in this teasing game. He is amazed by what he finds in its "huge court," capacious enough to encompass heaven and earth and sea and all that his senses have drawn from them—except what he has forgotten, he repeats. Strangely, his memory encompasses even his own self. "There I meet myself," he observes. He meets himself in multiple guises (as we know from the prior books) but most strikingly, perhaps, as the very one who presently wanders through memory's vast caverns and deeps that cannot be plumbed. The image he offers lodges itself in our own memories, in part because it is so difficult to conceive. Augustine's memory is part of him yet it also exceeds and includes him: "the mind is too narrow to contain itself" (10.8.15).

He has shown us much already, possibly even more than we wanted to see, but there are further treasures to uncover in the "immense capacity" of memory (10.9.16). Besides the veritable cosmos that has entered through the gateways of his senses (10.10.17), there are also abstract concepts (10.9.16, 10.11.18–10.12.19) and imprints of emotions (10.14.21–22). There are memories of remembering (10.13.20) and of forgetting (10.16.24–25). If the former might seem to open onto an infinite regress, the latter appears to Augustine to cancel itself out—which perplexes him even more than the notion that his own memory contains him. He has been able to accept, fairly easily, the fact that he can recall grief without necessarily being overcome with sadness (10.14.21–22), but he marvels that he can remember forgetfulness at all, as if the very presence of forgetfulness in his memory should erase itself. "Who can comprehend how this can be?" he queries rhetorically, regarding his own ability to remember oblivion (10.16.24). Surely he has already provided adequate grounds for explaining either the memory of the concept of forgetfulness or the memory of an occasion of forgetting. Nonetheless, he chooses to be seduced by the pleasures of astonishment, and in so doing he shifts the framing of the thought. Forgetfulness in the memory is not like recalled grief; rather, it is like the trace of darkness in light, of silence in sound—or of eternity in time.

For there is no memory without oblivion. We cannot recall what we have not forgotten, cannot retrieve what has not slipped our minds (10.14.21–22). It is the haunting awareness that something (*but what?*) has been lost that draws memory beyond its borders, teases it with secrets, opens its depths. Augustine suggests that some memories are irretrievable: "What we have lost, what we have utterly forgotten, we shall not be able to seek" (10.19.28). Yet how can we be sure that any forgetting is final? We may yet remember that we have forgotten, and to remember forgetfulness is to begin to search—to begin not to forget.

There is also no temporality without forgetfulness, it would seem. Oblivion is the disappearing of a past defined as such by its very disappearance. Conversely, to remember what has been forgotten is to evoke presence, albeit a presence that seems to be gone as soon as it arrives: to be fully attentive is impossible, or very nearly so, for the mind is always giving itself the slip.[7] Forgetfulness does not only safeguard the past-to-be-remembered, however; it also enables the selectivity of memory, as well as its mutability—thus its futurity. Augustine prays that he may forget his own evils by being filled with the goodness of God (1.5.5), that he may forget Aeneas and other such "poetic fictions" while remembering how to read and write (1.13.22), that he may forget the past so as to be open to the eternal delight that awaits him (11.29.39; cf. 9.10.23). To forget oneself is, in other words, to become susceptible to transformation, whether for good or for ill (1.13.20–22). All may be forgotten, so long as God is not; whoever forgets God, becomes an abyss (13.21.30).

Yet how can we remember God? How rescue ourselves from the abyss of our forgetfulness or, for that matter, of our memories? It was, after all, the search for God that sent Augustine on this seemingly endless journey through memory's seemingly boundless vaults. And in its seductive vastness he may finally have discovered what he sought. "See how I have travelled in my memory seeking you, lord, and I have not found you outside it. Nor have I found anything about you that I have not remembered from when I learned of you" (10.24.35). Augustine has not found God *outside* his memory, but has he found God *inside* it? Yes, but only what he recalls being taught. "You were not in my memory before I learned of you," he asserts with surprising confidence (10.26.37). This is a distinctly disappointing outcome—anticlimactic, at the very least. But perhaps Augustine has forgotten his own forgetting of God. After all, it frustrates him to be reminded of what he cannot remember: "In regard to the darkness of my own forgetfulness, it is like the time that I spent in my mother's womb. . . . I pass over that time, for what does it have to do with me, since I cannot recall anything of it?" (1.7.12). To be sure, no one can remember her own beginning. But we can remember forgetting, perhaps.[8] Has Augustine forgotten *that*?

Indeed, Augustine continues to seek the one in whom he has his beginning. He shifts his tactics, however. Having very nearly cornered himself within the imaginary walls of his own palace of expansive yet still limited remembrance, he now allows his spatial constructions to collapse. "There is no place," he remarks briskly. Truth is "everywhere" (10.26.37). He continues to search his memories—what else?—but no longer contains them as such. Or, perhaps better, he no longer splits himself from them but allows himself to be drawn to their presence. Now he loops back to his beginning point—the search for God, yes, but more precisely the search for the God who pulls him in and leads him on with the beauty of creation, beauty that he remembers vividly, across the full register of his senses.

Beauty itself remembers, and it also reminds him of something. "Heaven and earth and all that is in them everywhere tell me that I should love you," Augustine has written earlier. And love God he does. But what does that mean? What do I love when I love God? he has asked repeatedly. He imagines himself, somewhat absurdly, taking a poll of creation, asking earth, sea, and heaven whether any of them is what he loves when he loves God. Each confesses in turn: "I am not God." "We are not God; search beyond us." When he begs for more, he is given one further hint: "God made us." The cosmos remembers its creator, then. It reminds Augustine of his own creator—though not, of course, in so many words. Rather, as he puts it, "My question was my attentiveness (*intentio*), and their answer was their beauty (*species*)" (10.6.9). Augustine attends to the world, and it answers with beauty, which is why he was attending in the first place. Beauty holds him suspended in the moment, and it does so by refusing to satisfy him. It seduces him into wanting more, and this wanting is what lures him to explore the phenomenon of memory, in search of the faculty that will grant him access to sublime realms. Yet memory too refuses to satisfy, failing to divulge even an image of God. Memory, too, seduces, then, not least with its own teasing forgetfulness. Augustine cannot recall existence in his mother's womb; he cannot recall his divine creator. But he remembers his forgetfulness, astonishingly. And he remembers beauty, which reminds him of something—something he has been seeking for a very long time.[9]

"Late have I loved you, beauty (*pulchritudo*) so ancient and so new, late have I loved you!" he now declares. Augustine has been diverted by the beauty of creation, which has rendered him forgetful and caused him to procrastinate. Yet that same divine beauty has also been calling him to his senses—calling to him precisely through his senses. "You called and shouted and broke through my deafness; you flashed and shone and banished my blindness; you shed your fragrance and I drew breath and now I pant for you; I tasted and now I hunger and thirst; you touched me, and I have blazed up in your peace" (10.27.38). He is paying attention, belatedly—but then time is always out of step with itself. Beauty's memory pulls him toward the future, feeding his desire. He wants more! He is afraid he will settle for less.

Book 10 is the book of memory, but it is also the book of temptations. In the later chapters, Augustine catalogues with unsettling precision all the ways that the world seduces him, beginning with the power that sexual desire still exerts on him, despite his success in maintaining physical continence. "There still live in my memory, of which I have spoken much, images of such things, which were fixed there by my former habits; and they pop into my head, lacking strength when I am awake but when I sleep leading not only to delight but even to consent and something very like the deed" (10.30.41). Having evoked such a powerful memory of remembering, Augustine proceeds to itemize the seduction of physical pleasure (*voluptas*) as it affects each of the senses: "for pleasure pursues what is beautiful, sweet-sounding, fragrant, tasty, soft" (10.35.55); he discusses the seduction of curiosity and the seduction of admiration as well. *Any* of these might merely distract and divert him; indeed, his text here performs such a distraction by memory. Yet it is also the case that *any* of these might render him still more attentive to his own delight, and thereby draw him still further in his longing for God. As Michael Mendelson puts it, "*memoria* for Augustine does not have its primary value as a means of preserving the connection between a past and present self; its most valued function is that of transforming one into a self for whom there is *no* past."[10] With a little luck, memory may continue to seduce his love unto eternity.

Extending Desire

"It seems to me that time is nothing other than a stretching out (*distentio*)," observes Augustine in Book 11, "but of what thing, I do not know, and I wonder if it is not of the mind itself" (11.26.33). As we have already begun to see, time's distension within memory—"the belly of the mind" (10.14.21), as Augustine calls it—makes space for the stretch of desire, even as desire paradoxically seems to seek time's undoing. "See, my life is a stretching out (*distentio*)," exclaims Augustine, in a tone that is now distinctly plaintive, as he contrasts the oneness of the eternal God with the dispersion of humanity—"we who are many, pulled in many directions by many things (*nos multos, in multis per multa*)." He prays that he may be "gathered up," that he may "forget the past, not being distended but rather extended (*non distentus, sed extentus*), not toward the transitory things that will come but toward the things that lie before"—eternal things, that is. Weary of his own scattered distraction (*distentio*), he prays for presence of mind (*intentio*) (11.29.39). At the same time, he hints that to gather himself is also to extend himself. But what *is* the difference between distension and extension, between distraction and attraction, between the stretch across time and the stretch toward eternity—between desire and . . . *desire*? The difference is almost nothing. Then again, almost everything depends on it.

Admittedly, the distinction may at first seem easy to spot and thus to require little discussion. Augustine clearly privileges what is eternal and unified over what is transitory and multiple. *Distentio* corresponds to the latter, suggesting a state of fragmented desire that results from the frantic pursuit of elusively transient beauties remembered, and thus also anticipated, but never quite grasped. *Intentio*, in contrast, suggests a focused attentiveness, a collected presence, that draws close to eternity: for in eternity, as he has told us, "all is present" (11.11.13); the "years are one day, and that day is not every day but *this* day" (11.13.16). Yet, as we have also seen, *distentio* is at the same time opposed by *extentio*, which is thus aligned with *intentio*—and this complicates matters. The gathering or punctual contraction that occurs in the middle of the text of *Confessions* (in Book 10, on most reckonings), and in the midst of time's flow as well, is not the end, except in so far as it is also the beginning.[11] To be attentive is not simply to turn inward but also to be pulled out of or beyond oneself, transformed by the irresistible momentum of love. To be attentive is to *draw out* the moment.[12] It might thus seem tempting to emplot *distentio-intentio-extentio* as a temporal sequence or even a narrative supersession; this would not, however, suit either Augustine's distinctly nonlinear understanding of time or his equally complex textual practice. Temporality is not, for him, *simply* a state of mind; it *is*, however, complexly linked to mental states of distraction, focus, and ecstasy, and one does not merely follow on the heels of the other. As M. B. Pranger puts it, "If Augustine does have his mystical moments in the *Confessions*, they do not cease to be part of this very process of procrastinating the present through memory, oblivion, and hope."[13] (We will have a bit more to say about Augustine's mystical moments later.) Indeed, the present of Augustine's *Confessions*—the sustained intensity and cumulative density of his prayerful address to God—is always looping itself through memory and fantasy, as we have seen. Such arts of distraction may, paradoxically, seduce attentiveness, both deepening and expanding alertness in the reader who abandons herself to the pleasures of this text.[14]

The stretch of desire that is no longer merely a dissipating distension is a suspension, perhaps. In the earlier books of the *Confessions*, as we have seen, Augustine is caught up in waves of swelling and spilling—repeatedly wasted and spent by so much love.[15] His story goes nowhere because it goes everywhere: even his conversions multiply, and nothing—including continence—really halts the dissipating effect of lust. This itself is a kind of suspension, but it is one that can and will be transformed, not least so as to be made more sustainable. By Book 11, the tension of longing seems to be at once held in (*intentio*) and drawn out (*extentio*). Desire must be caught, and also thought, at the border of time and eternity, the reader now apprehends—at the border that both separates and joins the creature and the creator, then.

Such an ambiguously in-between place opens up excitingly for Augustine within scripture itself. Indeed, the Bible's seductive secrets will draw and hold him for two more books. Beginning to romance the text, he declares confidently: "Ask, and you will receive; seek, and you will find; knock, and it will be opened to you. For everyone who asks receives and who seeks finds and who knocks is opened to. These are your promises" (12.1.1). At the close of the work, he is still approaching the anticipated threshold of bliss: "Let it be asked of you, let it be sought in you, let it be knocked on your door: thus, thus let it be received, let it be found, let it be opened" (13.38.53). Such a prolonged suspension is almost a stasis—the rest of a sabbath day that has no evening (13.36.51). "Augustine ends his book with a beginning," notes Charles Mathewes, with regard to a writer who ultimately prefers to let his questions as well as his texts remain open.[16]

It is in the very first verse of the Bible that Augustine discovers the figure who perfectly models such a desired state of suspense. He discovers this figure through a process of verbal extension that is also an intensification: "In the beginning God created heaven and earth," he reads, and immediately transposes "heaven (*caelum*)" into "heaven of heaven (*caelum caeli*)," with a little intertextual help from Psalm 113:16. The reach of transcendence is thereby registered—this is no merely cosmic firmament—but so, too, is the depth of its mystery. This depth nearly bottoms out in the next biblical line, as attention shifts from the sublime heaven of heaven to the unsettlingly subterrestrial *terra*: "The earth was formless and invisible, and darkness was on the face of the deep, and the spirit of God was moving over the face of the waters." As it happens, these two verses, together with the two figures they contain, will keep Augustine busy for much of the remainder of his *Confessions*. Not until he is halfway through the last book, the thirteenth, will he move on. The heaven and earth of Genesis 1:1–2 fascinate him not least because they sit at the boundary where temporality opens onto eternity, as previously noted. They do so, moreover, through a curious doubling that itself doubles the split already opened between the extension and the distension of desire.

The word *terra* seems as unstable as the shifty ground that, according to Augustine, it signifies. "What should it be called?" he queries, as if he has been asked to name the creature himself (12.4.4). The "earth" inscribed in verse 1 is subsequently not only displaced by a mobile set of terms drawn from verse 2—the darkness, the deep, the waters—but also neutralized, if not quite annihilated, by the nothingness (*nihil*) that Augustine understands it nearly (but not quite) to be. A "nothing something" (12.6.6), "near nothing" (12.7.7), "almost nothing" (12.8.8), it evades gender along with all other marks of differentiation. And yet, like the Platonic *khora* that it so closely resembles (if resemblance is not too contradictory a notion in this case),[17] the Augustinian *terra*, perceptible by neither the intellect nor the senses (12.5.5), evokes the maternalized feminine, in the guise of a radical receptivity that is also a radical fecundity. When Augustine tries to imagine what "she" might look like, he succeeds only in picturing a monstrous shuffle of "countless and varied shapes (*species*)": "My mind turned up forms (*formae*) that were hideous and horrifying, appearing in confused order, but forms nonetheless; and I called it formless not because it lacked form but because it had one so bizarre and incongruous that, if it had appeared before me, my senses would have recoiled and I would have been deeply disturbed." Such a terrifying terrestrial potency is practically nothing precisely because it can be changed into absolutely anything. Indeed, Augustine soon realizes that changeability itself must be the invisible formlessness that he has been trying vainly to visualize. If only he could capture the moment of transition from one form to the next—if only he could perceive that which is "capable of receiving all the forms into which changeable things are changed" (12.6.6). If only he could remember the time in his mother's womb (1.7.12)! Then he would be able to see through time to eternity, in the fertile betweenness that is the womb of all things.[18] Taken to its limit, in a distension of time's very distension, the flow of sheer mutability approaches the stasis of perfect immutability: for without form, there is no longer, or not yet, any division of times (12.9.9, 12.11.14).

In its very disturbing monstrosity, Augustine's *terra infirma*—his *terra informis*—exposes the ambivalence of desire. Unmasked, its very invisibility may force us to avert our gaze. We desire what seduces us by hiding from us, but in the *nihil aliquid* we apprehend that there is no stable "whatness" at all, no *thing* to elude us, only an unending flux of becoming. There is too much (to) desire—and also not enough—as transience melts into eternity. This abysmal fecundity within creation is, intriguingly, mirrored not only in the disturbing play of images surfacing from the depths of Augustine's memory[19] but also in the overwhelming multitude of interpretations welling from the font of scripture, as he perceives it (12.27.37). Like the sound that precedes and gives rise to all forms of song (12.29.40), scripture's sonority may engender a diversity of resonant truths, asserts Augustine (12.31.42). Its bottomless deep evokes both wonder—"*mira profunditas!*"—and awe-full desire: "It is a horror to attend (*intendere*) to it, a horror of honor and a trembling of love" (12.14.17).

The timeless depths of sheer transience both draw and overwhelm desire, then. But what of the sublime heights of perfect faithfulness? Unlike her more dubious double, the scriptural figure of heavenly devotion, as Augustine imagines her, does not seem designed to inspire horror. "The heaven of heaven is some intellectual creature, which, although by no means coeternal with you, trinity, participates nonetheless in your eternity by powerfully restraining her own mutability through the sweetness of your most happy contemplation; cleaving to you without any lapse since her making, she exceeds every whirling vicissitude of time" (12.9.9). We do not have to gaze upon this paragon of creation, because we can see through her eyes, and those eyes are directed, dutifully and unfalteringly, at God—her "only delight (*voluptas*)," whom she "draws by her most persevering chastity." In all of this she is, Augustine notes explicitly, a model for every soul. We do not have to gaze upon her, then, because we must instead *become* her, by matching the intensity and constancy of her desire for God. Reveling in the divine presence, she neither anticipates nor remembers anything else (12.11.12). If we *did* look at her, however—if we allowed ourselves to be thus distracted—surely she would impress us with her well-shaped and well-preserved beauty. While *terra's* generativity evades time by taking distension to the limit where mutability eclipses form, the heavenly *creatura* extends toward eternity by allowing form to eclipse mutability.

Does this sublimely chaste lover simply mark the distance, at once moral and ontological, between what cleaves to divinity and what is next to nothing? Augustine may seem to have thrust a heaven-over-earth verticality so strongly into the first verse of scripture as to subject all subsequent reading to its priority.[20] To read him thus, however, is to forget the queered gravity of his erotic cosmology, which tugs in many directions at once. "*Pondus meum amor meus.* My weight is my love: by it am I carried wherever I am carried" (13.9.10). It is to forget that *distentio* may so easily become *extentio*—that his *heaven* sits so close, in his reading of verse I, to his *earth*.[21] It is thus also to forget the bent logic of his theory of time.[22] The farther we turn back, the more we are drawn forth; the deeper we are pulled into the flux, the closer we draw to the stillness. Desire unravels temporality by extending time's stretch, refusing any final goal or object—refusing to come to an end. Thus distension becomes suspension, the blossoming of a mindful expectancy, where restfulness emerges within movement, presence within absence, that which is almost divine within that which is almost nothing.

There is not a time, but there *is* an abysmally heavenly moment when joy arrives, when we see "face to face" and know "all at once"—even if we only recognize it in memory's hindsight (12.13.16). There is not a space, but there *is* an abysmally heavenly point where transcendence and transience touch—even if we only glimpse it as we pass it by. Despite her personification as creature and lover, heaven is of course not a person any more than earth is. Augustine may call her—it—a city or a house, wisdom or mother (12.15.20).[23] He may imagine a chamber to harbor the soaring songs and wordless groans of his love, a maternal embrace to gather him close in his dispersion (12.16.23). But it—she—is not exactly a place, nor a before nor an after, either. She—it—is the face of the ever-convertible deep, his and also our own.[24] "*Mira profunditas!* It is a horror to attend to it, *horror honoris et tremor amoris*" (12.14.17). Thus Augustine reads scripture, and now we read him. *Sound* tosses so much meaning to the surface of this confessional text, as we are confronted with an "inexplicable combination of momentary presence and an underlying unfathomability," as Pranger puts it, hauntingly—unfathomable moments "at once eternal and intermittent and as such both sweeter and grimmer than can ever be grasped."[25] Indeed, it is almost more than we can bear to face: and so it is with horror and trembling that we gather and extend ourselves to honor what we cannot grasp, to love without end.

Sex in the City of God

Love without end is heavenly love: that much we know by now. Having represented the heaven of heaven as a figure of everlasting desire in his *Confessions*, in the *City of God* Augustine pauses to wonder, at quite some length, what it might mean to *inhabit* such a state—or city. Here, as in his *Confessions* though on a grander scale, temporality is stretched to the limit.

Past fictions, future hopes, present possibilities—all point to the event of incarnation. In that event, temporality is intensified and thereby eternalized—"so fully in the moment that it can have no past or future and, consequently, no re/presentable present."[26] But how can one *imagine* such a fecundity of eternity harbored within time's measured steps? This is the question that Augustine sets for himself once again. Seeking to extend his mind toward the end of all ends, Augustine ultimately directs his gaze to the resurrected bodies unveiled in the heavenly city. Breathtakingly beautiful, infinitely desirable, these are bodies to die for, for they are bodies that will not die. Adorned by the scars of their difference, they nonetheless share the same eternity of bliss, freed from all necessity—even from the need for sex and procreation, it would seem. But what about sex *without* procreation? What about unnecessary, purely doxological sex? What about sex for the eternal joy of it?

En route to such an unimaginable future, Augustine detours through beginnings only dimly recalled. He detours once again through the book of Genesis, then. "The world was not created in time but with time," he observes, adding with regard to the temporality of the act of creation itself: "What kind of days these are is difficult or even impossible for us to imagine, to say nothing of describing them" (11.7).[27] He is certain, however, that the cosmos is in no sense co-eternal with God. Rather, it is infused with the dynamism of radical mutability that adds the sparkle of unpredictability to its unfolding history, even if God foreknows all. Zooming in on the creation and subsequent development of humanity, he is struck by the essential sociability of an extremely diversified species, all descended from a single ancestor (12.22, 12.28). God is pleased by such "unity in plurality," and so too is Augustine (12.23). Sociable by nature, the race is, however, fractious through sin: a shadow lies over it from the start. Already "there arises in the human race something like two societies or cities, not manifestly but in the foreknowledge of God" (12.28). When sin emerges into clear view, it is as a perversion of a nature inclined to love: Adam allowed himself to be led astray by Eve because "they were so closely bound in partnership," while Eve for her part seems to have been lured by a charitable desire to accept the serpent's words as truth (14.11).

This "original" sin of willfully misplaced desire lodges in the soul but is manifest in the body as well. Thus, as soon as they turn from God toward other loves, Adam and Eve feel ashamed of flesh that now seems to have a will of its own: "immediately they were embarrassed by the nakedness of their bodies." Augustine continues: "They even used fig leaves . . . to cover their *pudenda*, the 'organs of shame' [Gen. 3:7ff]. These organs were the same as they were before, but previously there was no shame attaching to them." The organs are the same, and also not the same, for now Adam and Eve feel "a new movement in their disobedient flesh, as a punishment corresponding to their own disobedience" (13.13). The physical stirring of desire is, then, the punishment that fits the original crime of rebellion. The shame that arises concurrently with this disturbing movement is the trace of a memory of lost innocence.[28]

It is through the veil of shame that Augustine must peer to perceive the state of humanity before the fall, but he does so in order to follow the trajectory of a salvation that is more than a restoration. To wonder about prelapsarian bodies is already to begin to imagine resurrected ones, it would seem, and it is to do so from the perspective of what is lacking in fallen ones. The resurrected body, he asserts, will submit with "an obedience so wonderfully complete that the body will fulfill the will of the spirit in such a way as to bring perfect assurance of indissoluble immortality, free from any feeling of distress, and relieved of any possibility of corruption, any trace of reluctance." This body, melting into perfect obedience, "will not even be such as it was in the first human beings before their sin" (13.20). It will be even better! To fall into perdition, it would seem, is to take the first step on the path to greater perfection. But what are the implications of such bodily obedience for heavenly love?

Augustine prefers to pursue this question through a meditation on the effects of sin and sinlessness not on the body but on the soul, for love is at base a matter of the soul, or better yet of the will. He follows the psychological theory of his day in holding that the will expresses itself in four basic emotions: desire (*cupiditas* or *concupiscentia*) for what one wants, joy (*laetitia*) in the having of it, fear (*timor*) of what one does not want, and grief (*tristitia*) in the having of *that* (14.6). All of these emotions are both natural and necessary, he insists, and the only thing that distinguishes a heavenly love from a sinful one is its object. He dismisses attempts to split terminological hairs. The real split that fractures human hearts and history opens not between the longing of *amor*, the attachment of *dilectio*, or the generosity of *caritas*, he insists, but between a desiring will rightly directed and one that is wrongly directed; it is desire wrongly directed that is conventionally referred to as lust—*cupiditas* or *concupiscentia*—but even that is no more than linguistic habit (14.7). Not to desire, rejoice, fear, or grieve would be not only strange but wrong, in this life; even Jesus had emotions! Such movements of the soul will, however, be stilled when time is no more (14.9).

The range of emotion was constrained in Paradise as it will be in heaven, though less absolutely. The first couple knew only one emotion, joy, for "their love for God and one another was undisturbed, and from this love arose great gladness, since what they loved was not withdrawn from their enjoyment." Augustine explicitly rejects the possibility that Adam and Eve already felt desire or fear before the fall. What, then, would the relations of this glad pair have been like, if only they had had time for sex before their flesh rebelled? In the presence of so much joy and so little desire, perpetual chastity might seem to have been the most likely prospect. Not so, insists Augustine firmly. But how could he know? "Be fruitful and multiply" (Gen. 1:28) says it all, as far as he is concerned. Their happiness would have been sustained while human society propagated itself; upon its reaching plenitude, all would have been granted an even greater happiness, the security of eternal bliss (14.10).

Having come so close, Augustine once again defers direct discussion of paradisal sex. Instead, he attends to the observable phenomenon of the postlapsarian *libido*. Here the emotional and the physical meet, and the effect is disturbingly powerful: "there is none greater among the physical pleasures." Such an exceeding *voluptas* registers temporally as a presence that is intensified to the point of its own undoing: "in the very moment of time when its limit is reached, almost all sharpness and (so to speak) vigilance of thought is obliterated." One might wonder where the lapse is in such an ecstatic eclipsing of time. Isn't this what we have been seeking all along? Almost—but not quite. For the meeting of minds and bodies is no real meeting but arises out of and subsides back into a morass of dividedness: in this temporal world, sexual desire is always out of step with itself, Augustine insists. Never mind the gap that can open between desire and the will to procreate, or between desire and the love for a chosen partner; desire is even "sometimes divided against itself," as physical arousal may come and go when one least wants it to. "In this astonishing way, lust does not even serve wanton lust," he marvels (14.16). Such profound disunity within the self is shameful; and shame is what leads humans to cover their unruly genitals, Augustine observes once again. That shame attends fallen desire is to him not merely scripturally attested but self-evident: intercourse between marital couples—far more illicit sex—seeks privacy; "it blushes to be seen" (14.18). "A man would be less put out by a crowd of spectators watching him visiting his anger unjustly upon another than by one person observing him when he is having lawful intercourse with his wife" (14.19).

We might begin to suspect that Augustine is getting something very wrong here. Has he forgotten what he taught us in his *Confessions*? Desire profits from the slippages of time as well as the seductions of secrecy, and it is desire that draws us to God. As so often, however, he seems to lapse so as to extend himself further. Pushing through the veils of falsehood and forgetfulness, he continues to pursue, in an ambitious reach of imagination, a sexuality without shame—the kind that Adam and Eve *might* have had, but did not. "If there had been no sin, marriage would have been worthy of the happiness of Paradise, and would have given birth to children to be loved, and yet would not have given rise to any lust to be ashamed of" (14.23). Here, making heavy use of the subjunctive mood, he writes of a past that would have been, had sin not intervened. He writes of a past that never was, then—a willed past that embodies fantasies of the will's absolute mastery. Augustine is topping God's act of creation in order to anticipate God's act of redemption. With every member rendered fully obedient—even that one unruly "part"—there would have been no cause for shame in Eden, as *he* imagines it. Sexual intercourse would have been conducted under conditions of strictest self-control. "Then the instrument created for the task would have sown the seed on 'the field of generation' as the hand now sows seed on the earth," he suggests (14.23). He repeats the point, now including reference to the female partner: "The man would have sowed the seed and the woman would have conceived the child when their sexual organs had been aroused by the will, at the appropriate time and in the necessary degree, and had not been excited by lust" (14.24).

This may seem like sex so plainly vanilla that one would wonder why Adam and Eve would have bothered. But look again. The Augustine of the *City of God* does finally seduce us, and he does so, we would suggest, in large part by offering us fantasies of a control that is so over the top—so unnatural, so perverse—that it finally undoes itself, as mastery and submission meet (and dissolve) at their limits. However, he ultimately detects such heavenly possibilities less in the fictive past of a Paradise lost than in present realities more bizarre than any fiction. Previously he has insisted on the plausibility of his willful reconstructions of what might have been, forcefully denying our right to incredulity while admitting that "we have no example to show how this could come about" (14.23). Now he confesses that what he is going to describe—what *is*—will seem unbelievable. Yet unbelievable things happen all the time—even sex as we know it would seem incredible to someone to whom it was unfamiliar, he observes (12.24). And oddly, the more incredible his reports become, the more we may want to submit to the seduction of his control—which is also to say, to submit to the seduction of his tales of hyperbolic control. Why shouldn't the penis be subject to the will, "seeing that so many other parts are now in subjection to it" (14.23)? There are some people, he relates, who "can do things with their body which are for others utterly impossible and well nigh incredible when they are reported." Like what? Well, for instance, they can wiggle their ears or move their scalps; swallow improbable items and regurgitate them on command; make uncannily inhuman sounds such as bird calls; create music by passing odorless gas through the anus; sweat or cry at will (14.24). In the absence of concrete examples of paradisal sex, the argument continues to proceed by analogy. Perceiving possible problems with his prior comparison of the penis to the hand that sows seed, Augustine cites the mouth, face, and lungs as examples of bodily organs that lack skeletal structure yet can still be controlled by voluntary muscles. So why not the penis? Or for that matter the vagina? "The male seed could have been dispatched into the womb, with no loss of the wife's integrity, just as the menstrual flux can now be produced from the womb of a virgin without loss of maidenhead," he argues. "For the seed could be injected through the same passage by which the flux is ejected" (14.26). Such descriptions may not seem erotically compelling, not least because the relation between will and pleasure, *voluntas* and *voluptas*, is left troublingly unclear.[29] But we must remember: these are inferences and projections, the best Augustine can do as he tries to imagine what never was—sex in Paradise. Had there only been time for it!

But what about sex in *heaven*? For it is to a heaven that has not yet arrived that Augustine is really trying to take us, and himself, via this narrative detour into a past that never was. And heavenly bodies, as he has told us earlier, will be even better than prelapsarian bodies; so too, presumably, will heavenly sex top sex as it would have been before the fall. By the time Augustine reaches the final book, much of which is devoted to the discussion of resurrected bodies, he is pulling out all the stops in his attempt to stretch the boundaries of what might be believed. Miracles multiply at such a rate in his text that any sense of the natural or normal is strained to the breaking point. If the particular miracles recorded in scripture necessarily loom large in popular awareness, Augustine wants also to call our attention to the ongoing, paradoxically quotidian, irruption of marvelous events that typically remain overlooked even by the people in the very communities where they occur. Relatively well known, he avers, is the case of the blind man of Milan whose sight was restored when Bishop Ambrose discovered the bodies of the martyrs Protasius and Gervasius. Less well known, however, is the astonishing cure of a deeply buried rectal fistula that Augustine himself has witnessed—and now narrates at what might be deemed excessive length. This strange story swiftly gives rise to other tales of healing: breast cancer, gout, hernias, demonic infestations, paralysis, coma, and a dislodged eyeball are all among the ills miraculously cured yet too little talked about, Augustine feels. An underdressed man is unexpectedly granted money for a coat. Children's corpses are revived, and this happens more than once. In the face of such excess, Augustine is beside himself: "Now what am I to do? . . . I cannot relate all the stories of miracles that I know." Yet he also cannot resist sharing a few more. Indeed, he seems quite overwhelmed by the impossibility of his self-appointed task of making *all* miracles known to *all*: God knows he has tried, but it is simply not feasible for any bishop, however diligent, to impress these tales on the memories of the entirety of God's people. Even those who have heard the stories "do not keep in their minds what they have heard" (22.8).

If the miracles of this world exceed the capacity of the mind, so too do the miracles of the world to come. Or rather, the miraculous is what *spans* the two worlds or "cities." But how is one to imagine bodies in the other world—resurrected bodies? Can Augustine's excitedly cited instances of miracles already witnessed provide enough of a clue as to what lies ahead?

Aided now not so much by the credulity of the faithful as by the incredulity of questioning skeptics, he reaches for the limit cases that will expand his imagination further. Does resurrected life begin before birth, and if so when? Will a miscarried infant be resurrected? (22.13) These are fruitful queries in their very strangeness. Consideration of tiny humans, whether prenatal or postnatal, gives rise to the further question of the size of resurrected bodies—no small matter, as it happens. What *does* flesh unfolded in time look like, from the perspective of eternity? What if there was no time for its unfolding, in the case of babies—much as there turned out to be no time for sex in Paradise? Augustine answers confidently with regard to those who die as infants: "By a marvelous and instantaneous act of God they will gain that maturity they would have attained by the slow lapse of time." There will be no loss of flesh—no loss even of flesh's potential—in the resurrection, he assures his readers. If anything, there will be gain in excess of expectation. At this point, Augustine toys with the idea of a sort of heavenly egalitarianism that would eliminate all differences of stature, in which case—he is sure—God would add extra matter "so that all would attain the stature of giants" rather than unfairly diminish the gigantic proportions achieved by some (22.14). He rejects this possibility, however, in favor of the notion that each individual will embody the height that he or she had, or would have had, at the age Christ achieved—roughly thirty years (22.15). Just as differences in height will be preserved, so too will sexual difference, he further elaborates (22.17).

Nonetheless, the possibility of gigantic stature reemerges, and it does so precisely in the context of Augustine's affirmation of the preservation of the particularities of difference, when he turns to address another of the questions raised by skeptics, regarding lost body parts. "Now what reply am I to make about the hair and the nails?" he asks. It would seem that the bits cut off from each body must be restored in the body's eternity (he has already promised that nothing will be lost), yet the insult to beauty that would be presented by the resulting excesses of hair or toenails presents a problem for Augustine. Thus, he suggests the analogy of a potter reshaping a pot: "All that is required is that the whole pot should be remade out of the whole lump, that is, that all the clay should go back into the whole pot, with nothing left over." This has implications for more than the reincorporation of parts that have been cut off (or are otherwise lost, discarded, or even excreted), as it also allows for a reshaping of form more generally, arranging differently what is too fat or too thin, for example, while each body still retains its distinctiveness somehow, as tellingly preserved in the transcendent beauty of scars (22.19). Surely, however, such a conservationist stance implies that resurrected bodies will be either significantly bigger or much, much denser, if all that ever belonged to them, across time, is reintegrated. Would they not extend almost infinitely? Augustine admits as much, after taking what is a rather bizarre (even for him) detour through the perplexing digestive issues raised by cannibalism (what flesh belongs to whom?). He does so despite his continued attraction to the notion that resurrected bodies will preserve their original or potential mature height: "there may be some addition to the stature as a result of this," he confesses (22.20). Even when a limit has been set at a Christlike thirty-something, the body still exceeds.

Augustine's attempts to imagine resurrected bodies are not altogether different from his attempts to imagine the "nothing something" of matter's mutability. In both cases, eternity presents a challenge that registers visually and spatially: when temporal distensions are contracted, form implodes; when form is stabilized, space distends. Augustine is sure that eternal bodies are perfectly beautiful, but when he tries to imagine them, they seem monstrous in either shape or expanse. His best solution, as we have seen, is that of the potter: reshaping matter enables bodies to be kept in proportion, and in heaven, he insists, everyone is perfectly proportioned—and also endowed with a glowing complexion, he adds, for resurrection bodies, gorgeously colored, shine like the sun (22.19). Augustine's commitment to the preservation of difference disrupts his attempt to adhere to classical definitions of beauty, however. One might expect that perfectly proportioned bodies would all look the same, but if continuity of physical matter is retained, as he insists it must be, at the very least size will vary—which immediately reintroduces the problem of proportionality, albeit on a different scale. He is inclined to enjoy variety of shape and hue, anyway: "Eyes love beautiful and varied forms, bright and pleasant colors" (*Confessions* 10.34.51). Now the example of martyrs convinces him that other visible differences will also be preserved: the body would not be the body if it did not sport its history of scars. The beauty of the resurrection thus draws curiously close to the grotesque, but it seems thereby intensified, not diminished: the scars of the martyrs' wounds are what we *want* to see (*City of God* 22.19). And, as we have learned in Book 10 of *Confessions*, beauty would not be beauty if it did not cause pleasure and draw desire.[30]

But what happens to desire in the resurrection? In Paradise, desire was both unified and satisfied in advance, as it were—and therefore was not really desire at all, being always already cancelled by joy. Sex in Paradise, had there been time for it, would have drawn very near to eternal bliss, then, while participating nonetheless in the temporality of a divine creativity through which "the seeds display themselves and evolve as it were from secret and invisible folds into the visible forms of this beauty which appear to our eyes" (22.24). Less even than there was desire in Paradise will there be desire in heaven, one might think, and indeed Augustine has asserted that heavenly existence will be passionless. After all, the will's satisfaction—human happiness—is secured for eternity, nor is there need for sexual reproduction when the human race has achieved preordained plenitude, as well as immortality. "Both sexes will be resurrected," Augustine has assured us, but the sexual organs themselves will no longer have any use. "The woman's sex . . . will be exempt from intercourse and childbirth. The female members will not be adapted to their former use but to a new beauty (*decor*), which will not excite the desire (*concupiscentia*) of the beholder—for there will be no desire—but will arouse the praises of God" (22.17). The garments of shame have indeed been shed, it would seem. The genitals are not to be used, but are simply to be looked at and admired for their beauty, beauty that will cause the beholder to praise God. The instruments of desire's satisfaction are thus aestheticized, rendered purely decorative. "For practical needs are, of course, transitory," Augustine reminds us, "and a time will come when we shall enjoy one another's beauty for itself alone, without any desire. And this above all is a motive for the praise of the Creator, to whom the psalm says, 'You have clothed yourself in praise and beauty' [Ps. 104:1]" (22.24). Resurrected bodies, which may also be clothed in no more than their beauty, arouse no more than admiration and praise in one another,[31] and not for themselves but for their creator.[32]

Indeed, in heaven, all that any part of the body will be used for—though *used* is not really the right word—is to praise or to incite praise, and these are utterly unnecessary functions, he emphasizes. "All the members and internal parts of the incorruptible body, which we now see distributed through various necessary uses, will assist in the praises of God, because now there will be no necessity but a happiness that is full, certain, safe, and lasting." The hidden harmonies of the body will be exposed, he adds, and although it is by no means clear what this will look like, Augustine assures us that minds will thereby be set aflame with "delight in rational beauty" and moved to praise the creator. Such praise is its own ever-increasing reward, it would seem. Within it, the blessed saints encounter, "face to face," the God who is "the end of our longings"—who will be "seen without end, loved without stinting, praised without weariness." In heaven there will be "unfailing enjoyment in the delight of eternal gladness, forgetful of sins, forgetful of punishments." There will be no memory or expectation then, for all will be present. "There we shall be still and see; we shall see and we shall love; we shall love and we shall praise. Behold what will be, in the end without end!" (22.30).

But isn't this all that desire ever desired? Intriguingly, Augustine's attempt to banish longing from his heaven seems only to have intensified it. In the absence of any necessity, to will is pure lust. For temporal desire is entwined with need: we need to eat, and thus we desire food. However, the satisfaction of hunger induces pleasure that draws desire beyond need. "When I am passing from the discomfort of lack to the peace of satiety," observes Augustine, "the snare of desire lies in wait for me in the very transition; for the transition itself is a pleasure" (*Confessions* 10.31.44). In short, need leads to desire, which leads to pleasure, which leads us to desire more than we need. So it is in this fallen world. In heaven, however, desire begins with pleasure and never departs from it. It is as if all food were dessert, all sex unlinked from procreation or other uses and ends.

The "as if" may be important, for in heaven as Augustine imagines it in the final chapters of the *City of God*, sensual delight seems to have contracted into the visual. As Margaret Miles puts it, "The primary 'organ' of resurrected sexuality is the eyes. . . . Scopophilia, the 'perversion' that *replaces*, rather than acts as preliminary to, genital sex plays a major role in Augustine's account of the resurrection."[33] Indeed, the saints like to look, Augustine is convinced, and they are all beautiful—exceedingly, needlessly so. Saved from the distractions of time, they gaze at one another and their gazing overflows ceaselessly with love and praise of God. But how are we to understand all this heavenly *looking*? We have already seen that Augustine unsettles conventional concepts of beauty, drawing it close to the borders of the grotesque. Has he not also complicated traditionally Platonic understandings of contemplative vision by rendering it so strangely *literal*? He insists that the saints will see God *"in the body itself (in ipso corpore)"* while acknowledging that he is not sure what that means. Will they also see God *"by means of the body (per corpus)"*? he wonders. If so, will their eternal eyelids never close? Alternately, if they look with spiritual sight, what is this, and how does it relate to bodily seeing? Is it a kind of X-ray vision, working even when the physical eyes are closed, capable of perceiving directly what is immaterial and thus invisible? Or is it more like the ability to sense the life force (*vita*) invisibly animating visible bodies? Considering both possibilities, Augustine inclines toward the latter option: "Perhaps God will be known and visible to us in such a way as to be spiritually seen by each one of us in each one of us, seen by the one in the other, seen in him or herself, seen in the new heaven and the new earth, seen in the whole creation as it will be, seen also through bodies in every body, wherever the eyes of the spiritual body are directed with their penetrating gaze" (*City of God* 22.29). This is a striking, even a startling, theological assertion, in its thoroughgoing incarnationalism, or perhaps better, panentheism: to meet the divine "face to face," to see spiritually, is to perceive God *embodied in creation*—fully, and all at once. Conversely, to perceive the beauty of bodies in their plentiful excess, in the fullness of their resurrected glory, is to see God.

John Peter Kenney has argued persuasively that Augustine disavows the soteriological efficacy of contemplative vision in *Confessions*, based on its disappointing transience, while affirming its cognitive or intellectual usefulness. (It is not inconsequential that the disappointment of dissipating transience—a joy that is "momentary and fleeting, crashing to an end in an instant," as Kenney puts it[34]—also applies to Augustine's description of sexual pleasure in *City of God*.) Contrary to the assertions of the Platonists, contemplation is not an end in itself but must, according to Augustine, give way to confessional self-reflection and eschatological hope, in which the soul comes to grasp simultaneously its own abject weakness and its creator's potent grace. Even Kenney may, however, underestimate the distance that Augustine places between himself and a strictly noetic understanding of contemplation—a distance measured not only by his particular understandings of (active) divinity and (passive) soul, but also by his affirmation of the abidingness of materiality. Reading Augustine's understanding of contemplative vision in *Confessions* against the horizon of Book 12 of his *Literal Commentary on Genesis*, Kenney posits that "intellectual vision," however limited in its power to save souls, remains for Augustine the highest form of contemplative perception and is, moreover, "clearly delineated from either sensory vision or the attenuated version of it that he calls spiritual vision."[35] Our reading of the final chapters of *City of God* suggests, however, that Augustine there understands spiritual vision less as an attenuation than as an intensification of physical sight, a kind of seeing that apparently also encompasses the merely intellectual, its objects correspondingly spiritual precisely insofar as they are also vividly physical. In other words, the Augustine of the *City of God* seems to depart decisively from a conventionally noetic understanding of contemplation, in which vision is privileged in its capacity to be rendered a merely metaphorical sense. As Miles describes his view: "Spiritual vision relies on physical vision. . . . Moreover . . . the accurate 'seeing' of physical objects irreducibly involves the exercise of spiritual vision; to see accurately is to see lovingly, to participate in the very substance of the God-who-is-love."[36] This is a position that Augustine takes explicitly in resistance to the Neoplatonist Porphyry (*City of God* 22.26), yet he may not be so much departing from Platonic tradition as exploiting—even exploding—an alternate strand of that tradition, as Miles also suggests.[37] The startling fusion of bodily, spiritual, and intellectual vision depicted in *City of God* is lightly anticipated in the *Literal Commentary* itself, when Augustine suggests that all three kinds of seeing will persist in the resurrection "but there will be no false impressions with one thing being taken for another" and all visions will be enjoyed with "vivid and immediate clarity"(12.36.69). Vividness and fallibility are, in this text, characteristic of bodily sight in this life, immediacy and infallibility characteristic of intellectual sight, which (unlike bodily sight) requires no mediation of mentally formed images. In the resurrection, however, it would seem that imaginal or spiritual sight ceases to mediate, conceal, or dissimulate with regard to bodily sight but rather enables the transformation of physical vision into divine insight.[38] If such an understanding of spiritual vision approaches the perspective of Book 22 of *City of God*, it is arguably also consistent with

Augustine's strong attunement in Book 10 of *Confessions* to the power of creation to seduce through *all* the senses and thereby (potentially) to draw us toward God.[39]

Indeed, it becomes difficult to understand, finally, why Augustine should not attribute to resurrected bodies the pleasures of mutual touching, tasting, smelling, and hearing, as well as gazing. Admittedly, the visual is a form of sensory perception that uniquely, in his opinion, never quits and thus seems particularly well suited to eternity (*Confessions* 10.34.51), but one might question this attribution of uniqueness: after all, the problem with contemplative vision, according to *Confessions*, is that it is here and gone again "in the flash of a trembling glance (*in ictu trepidantis aspectus*)" (7.17.23). Moreover, when Augustine describes his sharpest and most satisfying experience of eternity's in-breaking, shared famously with his mother, he moves easily between language of vision and that of hearing and touch: "and while we spoke of it and gazed longingly toward it [i.e., eternal Wisdom], we touched it lightly for a full heart's beat (*toto ictu cordis*)" (9.10.24).[40] In fact, Augustine is able on occasion to imagine that the saints in heaven will still be able to enjoy tasty dishes, noting that resurrected bodies, not needing "any material nourishment to prevent any kind of distress from hunger or thirst . . . will eat only if they wish to eat" (*City of God* 13.22).[41] He is able to imagine the harmonious sound of eternal praise.[42] As Miles puts it, "characteristic of Augustine's description of resurrection experience is synesthesia, a flooding of the senses in which 'perceptual modes come together in unexpected combinations' to create vivid pleasure."[43] Is the beauty that lures him not something that traverses the entire sensory range, even as it also exceeds it, bursting into the beyond of the "spiritual" through the conversions of an imagination that is always more than strictly visual? "You called and shouted and broke through my deafness; you flashed and shone and banished my blindness; you shed your fragrance and I drew breath and now I pant for you; I tasted and now I hunger and thirst; you touched me, and I have blazed up in your peace" (*Confessions* 10.27.38).[44]

In the life of eternal bliss, as it unfurls in Augustine's imagination, desire and pleasure are ever exceeding one another, thus ever increasing, in a spiral of beauty and praise. Paradise as it might have been thus turns out to be a pale image of heaven as it surely must be. Satisfaction cannot kill a desire that is unnecessary to start with, any more than vision can attenuate a beauty that exceeds both sensation and imagination. Praise is given not as to an admired or beloved object, but within a loop of divine self-delight. More, desire thus drawn together, thus concentrated, is explosive, a single spark bursting the boundaries of the self. The praise of God drawn forth from all these gorgeous bodies is also God's own joyful desire, concentrated into the flesh. Augustine struggles to glorify desire right out of existence, even as he attempts to transform what is in excess of both nature and will into the beautiful, the fitting, the proportionate, the proper. But the too-much of corporality keeps on overflowing. We face the question not only of where the body ends, but when, as eternity folds the past of Paradise into an infinite future. The beauty discovered in such fleshly plenitude persists in linking itself to desire, which bursts out into praise for the creator yet is somehow not supposed to touch the bodies themselves, for they can never be possessed. Still, it remains the beauty of bodies that draws us in, and the excess of desire, divinely overwhelming the autonomous will, that breaks us apart.

Time and Desire

That there is a fundamental relation between desire and time is a distinctly (if not a uniquely) Augustinian insight. Temporal articulation—or disten-sion, as he dubs it—reflects the displacement of presence inherent to con-sciousness. "O Lord, you were turning me around to look at myself," writes Augustine. "for I had placed myself behind my own back, refusing to see myself" (*Confessions* 8.7.16). This displacement, this *slippage*, of the self within time conditions and is conditioned by desire. The present flees: we see it only as it slides into memory, only as it begins to be forgotten. We anticipate its return, but that too must become available to us as a matter of recollection: we remember anticipating. Desire, in its most misleadingly simple guise, is the wanting of what one does not have. Presence is what we desire, then—the coincidence of self with self but also of self with the other(s), indeed with all else. And presence is what must be lost if we are to gain it, through the stretch of desire across time. But how does this happen?

That temporality cannot be understood without eternity is another dis-tinctly (if not uniquely) Augustinian insight.[45] In Augustine's favored terms, time is *distension*, but eternity is *extension*. And the present, in contrast to both, is *attention*, *intention*—*intensification*. A point of no duration, poised between time and eternity, it is also the matrix of both, it seems. Time emerges as a distension of the present through an imaginative production of memory that performs and displays (but does not reproduce or even represent) the infinitely complex processes of differentiation borne on creation's mutable flux. Eternity, in turn, emerges as an extension of the present through a contracting and deepening of focus that draws us to attend to the unities of identity and connectivity harbored within creation's restful plenitude. Time that loses its purchase on eternity threatens to become a wasting dissipation—or so Augustine fears when he confronts his mental distraction in confessing his own history. Eternity that loses its purchase on time threatens to become a sterile stasis—or so some of *us* might fear when we confront Augustine's own tendency toward transcendentalization.

But let us continue to think time together with eternity, and desire with both, as Augustine does. If desire stretches itself across time in the longing for an elusive presence, what happens to desire when it reaches the point of dissolution, thereby entering into the presence of presence? Is there desire outside of time—does it survive eternity? Often we are tempted to conceive of eternity as the future: it has not yet arrived, or we haven't yet reached it; alternately, it seems to consist in time's infinite extension. Augustine approaches such an understanding of eternity by imagining it as the temporal prolongation of Paradise—an anticipated future that never was. His experimental fantasy leads him to conclude (provisionally, as it now seems to us) that there is no desire in the eternal bliss of the resurrection. In the resurrection, or in Paradise as it *might* have been, we will not desire, he proposes, because we will have all that we need or want. Small wonder, perhaps, that there is no time for sex in *this* fantasy—or only lost, anticipated, and wasted time.

However, eternity is, finally, revealed to be an extension not of the future but of the present. The closest temporal analogy is not an unending flow of fleeting moments but a suspension or a *drawing out* of a single moment. Eternity is what the focused attentiveness of the present *would* be if we were fully *in* it, rather than always already watching it slip by. Sexual pleasure—the thing most glaringly absent from Paradise as Augustine imagines it—may be as close as most of us come to eternity in time, as Augustine also almost (but not quite) suggests. The most intense of sensual delights, it focuses and defines "a moment in time" even as it causes us to forget ourselves and thus to withdraw from memory's distension, he avers. Sexual pleasure quickly burns itself out, however; moreover, when the vigilance of consciousness returns, we discover much in ourselves that is out of step with the desire that brought us to that moment of pleasure in the first place (*City of God* 14.16). Other experiences of focused joy or rapture leave us similarly bereft in their inevitable aftermath—a heart's beat of illumination lingering only in memory (*Confessions* 7.17.23, 9.10.24). For Augustine, *voluptas* remains balanced at the point between time and eternity, then; it does not quite get us to heaven, though it almost does. Indeed, its potent memory may keep us mired in time. Nonetheless, it *does* disclose something of eternal bliss. For eternity rests in pleasure, albeit a sublime pleasure—a felicity, a delight, a blessedness. And pleasure is not only what satisfies desire; it is also what makes it grow. If an imperfectly recollected Paradise kills desire by giving us exactly what we need before we have a chance to want it, an enticingly anticipated heaven makes us want ever more by always giving us more than we need so that we will continue to want more than we have—and all at once!

Time's stretch is ever in danger of becoming a grasping, a futile attempt to hold onto what was or will be. Eternity's reach is not a grasping but an opening, an opening to the depth of the moment. This is the difference, perhaps, between desire and . . . *desire.* Yet how is that difference fleshed out, so to speak? In his bold attempt to conceptualize eternal bodies—which does not, it is by now clear, simply mean bodies that last forever—Augustine finally engages in a radical deconstruction of the Platonic doctrine of transcendence as he takes desire around another turn. Eternity is disclosed not in the overcoming but in the intensification of corporality, he suggests—in the spiraling joy released as love and beauty exceed one another, "through bodies in every body" (*City of God* 22.29). Eternity is harbored within the flux of temporality, then, even as God is secreted within the abyssal capacity of bodies to smell, taste, feel, hear, see—finally, to *love*—the abyssal beauty of bodies.

There is no time for sex in heaven. There is an eternity.

In eternity, every day is *this* day.

What are we waiting for?

Conclusion
Seductive Praises

It is in His company that this need in us becomes opening, utterance, and call.
It is He who through our heart and our mouth invokes Himself.

Paul Claudel, *La rose et la rosaire*

God, although nothing worthy of His greatness can be said of Him, has
condescended to accept the worship of men's mouths, and has desired us
through the medium of our own words to rejoice in His praise.

Augustine, *On Christian Teaching* 1.6

The eroticism of Augustine, or at any rate of his texts, proves to be
every bit as complicated and frustrating as eros usually is, textually
or otherwise. Certainly, as generations of sometimes bored, sometimes bewildered students can attest, the seductive quality of the texts is not always
obvious. It is hard to say just what it is about Augustine's works that might
give rise to that quality. Other writers engage those elements of his subject
matter that strike us as seductive, especially corporeality and theology; other
texts are at least as abstract and elusive; but few seem to have the intensity

of eroticism that the *Confessions* has, either in their topics or in the experience of reading them. Augustine adds to corporeality, theology, and elusion a seductive reversibility; a play of substitutions that at once satisfies and arouses our eagerness to know; and, not least, sheer beauty, evident even in translation. In this conclusion, we take one last look at the reversals, substitutions, and beauties at play in the *Confessions,* to see what draws us both toward the text and toward one another's readings, even in our divergence.

The most evident substitution and elusion concern the interplay of word and flesh, a writer's variant on the mysterious Incarnation. Augustine draws us by what draws him, and yet part of his seductiveness, as we have seen, is the challenge of figuring out just what that draw is. In each of our chapters from the introduction on, we have not quite been able to tell if he is seducing us "just" with words, or with the promise of his flesh (or, at any rate, words about his flesh). That flesh, like Christ's, always seems to slip away just at the verge of its unveiling—to slip into abstractions, or other stories, revealing itself in unexpected and not quite gratifying ways. One might well suspect that this lends some weight, along with some subtlety, to the long-received version of Augustine as simply hostile to corporeality and especially to sex. That is, perhaps he does not declare outright that the pleasures of the flesh are evil, but he remains so very uncomfortable with them that he veers off at the possibility of discussing them, into more comfortable and disembodied abstractions that are seductive, at best, only to philosophers. Perhaps he wants to slip past fleshly disturbance into words alone, as if they could really be separated from flesh, or even all the way through words and into the word-exceeding abstractions of Neoplatonism. But Augustine is Christian, after all, and not only a Platonist, and Christianity starts with a Word made flesh.

It is true that the account by which the *Confessions* recasts Platonic cosmology in Christian language does not have a promising beginning for those of Augustine's readers resolute in their incarnationalism. Augustine writes of the Platonic books, "I read there that the Word, God, is 'born not of the flesh, nor of blood, nor of the will of man nor of the will of the flesh, but of God'" (John 1:13).[1] This certainly seems to declare, and implicitly to favor, the disembodied Word. In the next line, though, things change: "But that 'the Word was made flesh and dwelt among us' (John 1:

14), I did not read there" (7.9.14). Platonism can account for a great deal, and it lends its satisfying philosophical complexity to Augustine's readings of the scriptures he had previously rejected as childish (7.21.27). But it does not account for flesh—in all its humility, its weakness, its fleeting-ness—rendered divine. Augustine insists that divine embodiment is the key notion missing from the Platonic texts—a notion with implications for any number of other ideas, including the relative values of pride and humility. In embodiment is the "divine weakness" of a God who takes on human form, a kind of divinity that human beings might share (7.18.24). Refusing to disavow either the incorporeality of God's will or the corporeality of the Incarnation, Augustine maintains, and in some measure creates, tensions that persist throughout the history of Christian theology.

Though the conversionary passage in Paul, the one that Augustine takes and reads in the Milanese garden, tells us to put on Christ, as if covering our skin in a protective, not quite corporeal gown (8.12.29), Augustine also declares that God, as Christ, puts on a coat of human skin (7.18.24). This curious swapping is indicative: while he wants to hold to the distinc-tion between human and divine with a firmness uncharacteristic of Platonic or Neoplatonic thought, Augustine everywhere gives us reason to doubt that distinction.[2] We are to put on God in willful disregard of lustful flesh; God puts on us, accepting vulnerability and humiliation in the urgency of the divine desire for human redemption—a redemption entailing, in considerable measure, human desire. The humility for which we strive is the recognition of that divine weakness inherent in being human—which does not thereby cease to be divine. Paul enjoins us to make no provision for the flesh in its lustful desires, an injunction so potent that Augustine takes it on as his own[3] and finds it transformative of his own desires. Yet at the same time that very flesh is what God, desiring perhaps to be heard as well as read, to arouse those desires that only flesh can arouse,[4] provides for himself. It would be a bit much to claim that Augustine is comfortable with this extraordinary tension; he is not, in fact, very often comfortable at all—but he is (seductively) honest about it, refusing to do away with either side. Both the pull away from the distractingly desirous flesh (which is tugged at by old girlfriends who care nothing about scripture) and the pull toward the rich fullness of the senses (by which God displays, and is dis-played in, the beauty of the created world, showing that it is good) are important—and powerful—in Augustine's work.

This tension is maintained in both divine flesh and its human emulation. The transfiguration of the humble is not an obliteration of it; weakness does not become power, nor humility pride, and the eternal divine in the passing flesh does not arrest its transience. Rather, we are pulled toward oppositions we must both resist and embrace: toward matter and the flesh, but not to be stopped in the transient only. On Augustine's complex understanding, bodies are neither simply good nor unequivocally bad; they misbehave, disobey, and pass away in time—but they are, too, the only possible sites of virtue, of obedience, and even of eternal life.[5] And what we might conceive as "good" (power, virtue, eternity) is not what is possible *despite* the "bad" (weakness, concupiscence, transience); they are dizzyingly complicit. We "transcend" the flesh not by becoming fleshless but precisely by this complication: into every worldly, sensuous love God does not intrude but is enfolded, drawn in by the very love of beauty that communicates, and is communicated by, divine creation.

Augustine's insistence on the divine weakness consequent upon the Incarnation reminds us of the startling divine vulnerability characteristic not only of a God who can be crucified, but also of a God who seeks human love, which is also to say, who makes humanity for the sake of a delight that wants, or needs, to be shared.[6] Augustine even argues that human beings are created with the desire to praise their creator (I.I.I)—that is, to express that delight. The "weakness" of a God who needs is the "power" of a God whose joy can overflow into the beauty of a creation that cries out its creator's name, its very existence an act of praise. If beauty is an answer, it is an answer that goes on questioning us rather than a conclusion to be drawn from the evidence—it shows us a mystery, God present everywhere in what is not itself God. And mysteries are, persistently, seductive.

Like the beauties of the world, human believers sing God's praises. "'You are great, Lord, and highly to be praised' (Ps. 47:2)," says Augustine, opening the *Confessions:* "'great is your power and your wisdom is immeasurable' (Ps. 146:5). Humanity, a little piece of your creation, desires to praise you, 'bearing its own mortality' (2 Cor. 4:10), bearing the witness of its sin and the witness that you 'resist the proud' (I Pet. 5:5). Nevertheless, to praise you is the desire of humanity, a little piece of your creation. You stir humans to take pleasure in praising you" (I.I.I). In this outpouring, we begin to see a bit more of the reason for this work's ability to capture both attention and desire. Even in the opening paragraph, one of the text's distinctive features is already evident: a great deal of it is written in the second person,[7] unusual in most textual forms, and conspicuously so in a work that is autobiographical, philosophical, *or* theological, let alone all three. The direct address draws us in immediately, although, granted, we are not the addressee; the *you* so urgently sought, so desperately and sensuously (if sometimes belatedly) loved in these pages, is God. But no reader can read *you* and feel wholly unaddressed.[8] The effect of the second person is itself seductive: "Surely when I call on him," Augustine writes, "I am calling on him to come into me" (I.I.I). The second person invites God, but like the unresolved contradiction, it invites as well the reader who knows the text with eye and ear and moving lips,[9] "into the text as conversation partner, opponent, supporter, and co-author."[10]

Or as co-speaker, joining Augustine in that dramatic opening, declaring to God God's own greatness and worthiness of praise, a declaration that is an act of praise itself. Augustine's ideal reader will find herself speaking with, joining Augustine in this joyous address to the God they share, reciting in common the more or less familiar scriptural lines—or, if not sharing these particular words, nonetheless joining him in the act of praise (II.I.I), a bit of heaven (a place of continuous praising [*City of God*, esp. 22.24, 22.29]) on earth. The text is an extended prayer, in which petition (to know God) is fused with praise, or at the very least it is frequently disrupted by prayer—and the prayer is, along with the letter, one of the few linguistic genres consistently to make use of the second person. Prayer may also be, as Jean-Louis Chrétien argues, "the religious phenomenon par excellence,"[11] with "the God to whom it says 'you'"—the very fact of address— "constituting a moment in the meaning of its religiosity"[12]—even when it expresses (as Augustine so often does) bewilderment or (as others do) doubt.

Praise is not informational; indeed, its content may even in a way be tautological, as when Augustine in those opening lines praises God as being worthy of praise. Praise is language in excess of meaning, or at any rate of denotation,[13] and yet, for Augustine, it is the very deepest, and most important, meaning of language as well. Humans are made to praise God, Augustine says, but this is not because God somehow needs to be informed or reminded,[14] and neither is it because (as popular religious views so often seem to have it) God is so vain and yet so fragile that those who decline to praise will be smitten by dire punishments. It is rather because praise, as we see both in the intense and attentive response to worldly beauties and in the eternal commentary of the resurrected on the beauty of risen bodies, *is* the joy of speaking, and of writing; it is the joyful call in response to the call of joy.

And this call that praise is does invoke response, from the very beauty that called it. It hardly seems likely that God would respond to Augustine's self-revelations; again, Augustine can make no novel revelation to God, since God already "knows," already "sees" without the aid of Augustine's literate significations. Contemplating, then, the profitability of his confessions, Augustine concludes that to confess to God profits not God, but the one who confesses—not by unburdening the speaker, not even by forcing him to confront himself, but by, curiously enough, revealing God. "May I know you, who know me. May I 'know as I also am known' (I Cor. 13:12)" (*Confessions* 10.1.1). Knowing himself truly is knowing himself as a creature of God; knowing himself rightly is allowing God to "enter into [his soul] and fit it for yourself" (10.1.1). With his love "stirred up," he is able to find (and then to remember) God both inwardly (10.25.36) and through the beauties of the world (especially 10.6.9). Self-knowledge, intensified in revelation to God, and God-knowing, the revelation of God, are intertwined (also see 10.3.3).

It is to God Augustine wants most to reveal himself, God he wants to discover him in the seductively graceful text, reading Augustine in its beauty as Augustine reads God in the beauty that at once answers and attracts his intent attention. Failure to reveal himself to God has a curious effect: "I would be hiding you from myself, not myself from you" (10.2.2). However he may elude our prurient inquisitiveness, then, Augustine is not concealing himself from God, in part because, again, God has no need of reading. God already knows all about Augustine, anyway: "you hear nothing true from my lips which you have not first told me" (10.2.2). Augustine desires truth, he says, "in my heart before you in confession, but before many witnesses with my pen" (10.1.1)—writing becomes a curiously secondary confessional mode. The act of confessing is at once a calling-to in petition (Augustine everywhere calls on God, to hear him, to have mercy on him, to help him understand) and the call of praise: "He who is making confession to you is not instructing you of that which is happening within him. . . . Let my soul praise you that it may love you, and confess to you your mercies that it may praise you" (Ps. 118:175; 145:2) (5.1.1).

The seductive *you* appears in a context of both passionate desire for and self-revelation to this divine other—a combination hardly unfamiliar to us from our earthly loves. And its effect too mirrors what we hope for in those worldly loves: the beloved is revealed in turn; revealed, in fact, in the very call. Saying *you*, Augustine has drawn God into divine revelation[15]—not subsequent to, but implicit in, Augustine's prayerful confession of himself. As Pranger argues, Augustine gives us less a description of himself, or a narrative of his history, than a dazzling performance of turn and return, of conversion in prayer:

> [W]hat at first glance looks like an orderly narrative, is in fact a running text full of signposts that contain, in a preliminary and temporary fashion, the author's efforts to reflect the depths and heights of addressing himself to God. Small wonder that we have a prayer here rather than a firm narrative. For it is only through prayer as a performative that the mind attaches itself to its own source—doing things with words—thus bridging the gap not only between itself and its maker but also between the self and the self.[16]

Prayer seeking such revelation more commonly entails not the appropriation of scriptural voice, nor even this verbal performance of drawing the eternal into the temporal present, but silence. In the fourteenth century, the Dominican Johannes Tauler writes, "And therefore you should observe silence! In that manner the Word can be uttered and heard within. For surely, if you choose to speak, God must fall silent."[17] Augustine himself sometimes warns of praying that talks too much.[18] But in the *Confessions*, God does not speak conversationally back in the spaces left silent, but rather speaks *through* the language addressed to him. Thus prayer serves not to tell God how great God is—a function that has always seemed to us peculiar—but rather to reveal that greatness *to* the speaker, awakening further desire, praising in order to love. Thus, all of Augustine's language in the *Confessions* takes on the character of praise: its point is not to impart information, but to draw revelation, a revelation necessarily brief, incomplete and imperfect,[19] and at the same time astonishing and joyous, even blissful.

God is the *you* par excellence, the addressee who summons the address by which the one called is revealed. But, as the reversibility already alluded to might lead us to suspect, Augustine also addresses himself: "Do not be vain, my soul. . . . Even you have to listen. The Word himself cries to you to return" (4.11.16). Putting himself in the second person, he reminds himself that in calling he too is being called—and surely the effect of this calling is just as much to "come into me." He is called to come back to the God who has never left him—for example, "He is very close to the heart, but the heart has wandered from him" (4.12.18); "You were with me, and I was not with you" (10.27.38). More, to come into the summoning Word he must come into himself; at first, he cannot find God because "I was seeking for you outside myself" (6.1.1). Augustine reminds himself to turn his desire to, and take his pleasure in, God, by which he does not to cease to love the world, but begins instead to love it properly, and more fully than he has before. He calls to himself, in a sort of second-person reflexive, for the same reason he calls to God: in order to recall the two to each other. By telling or retelling, he returns love for love (2.1.1, 11.1.1) and at the same time word for word (10.6.1), his words of praise answering to the love that God's word evokes in him. "Prayer," writes Chrétien, "appears to be always surpassed and preceded by the one to whom it is addressed. It does not begin, it *responds*."[20] It responds by calling, by the event of address. Here is seductive reversibility at its most vivid: in this extended prayer, to speak is already to be spoken to, and vice versa.

Yet in all of this call and response, those we might most expect to be addressed in the second person are not.[21] We recall Roland Barthes's own use of the direct address: "The text you write must prove to me *that it desires me*."[22] When does the *Confessions* talk to *us*, its readers, to prove that it desires *us* and not just God? Certainly Augustine is aware that people will be reading him, as we revealingly say—though, again, the Augustine who gives himself to be read in the *Confessions* is much less revealed than we might expect, more caught in a play of elusive and inconclusive revelations. In this he mirrors the God he would seduce, a God constantly distant and veiled, however proximate and revealed (the mirror, at once echoing and inverting, is another seductive strategy or site). Augustine "reveals" himself with all the seductive elusiveness of divine revelation. And so his readers must mirror both Augustine and God. We, too, must be seductive, not least in our own desires. Augustine leads us in different directions, down different readings, precisely because we also lead him—in, of course, another play of reversibility.

What leads us to lead him? If people read him, Augustine says, and especially if they understand him, it will be because they love: "those whose ears are opened by love believe me" (10.3.3). Having heard rightly, those whose ears are opened can then speak rightly, joining Augustine in praise. Thus he comes to accept his readers, toward whom he initially seems surprisingly unwelcoming: "Why then should I be concerned for human readers to hear my confessions? It is not they who are going to 'heal my sicknesses' (Ps. 102:3). The human race is inquisitive about other people's lives, but negligent to correct their own. Why do they demand to hear from me what I am when they refuse to hear from you what they are?" (10.3.3) Yet these readers, who seem to exist here only in the third person, are his only readers, really, those of us other humans who will apply ourselves to the body of his text; those who, if they love, will believe—though "believing" ought not to be taken as holding the *Confessions* to be straightforwardly factual report, any more than such a description would apply to Augustine's belief in scripture. It might, rather, be taken as a willingness to pray along, to speak the praises of the *Confessions* as if they were also our own.

And, in fact, we who read the *Confessions* in the love of truth are also, Augustine seems sure, those who share scripture (12.25.34), who speak it with him. The present readers have tried to sustain openness to Augustine's texts, to sustain our complicated, exasperated love for them as a condition for understanding, which has likewise been the condition of our seducibility. In this we have read him rather as he reads, and appropriates, scripture—not only in our "strong readings," but also with the thought, "Why not rather say both, if both are true?" (12.31.42)

Augustine hopes to bring those who read his work to the same revelation of God that the *Confessions* have granted him: "But I am stirring up love for you in myself and in those who read this, so that we may all say 'Great is the Lord and highly worthy to be praised' (Ps. 47:1)" (11.1.1). That is, not only Augustine in writing of himself, but we in reading of him, are most importantly led not to the facts (if they are "facts") of his life thus recounted, not even to the theoretical analyses of time, memory, and materiality in the later books, but to the God revealed in them in passing glimpses, in elusive touches, in the flash of a trembling glance. While we were fixing our impatient gaze on Augustine, waiting for him to reveal just a little bit more of himself, he has slipped in his startling substitute, instead revealing God.

In this revelation, the text's element of prayer takes on an added importance, and this leads us back again to the play of word and flesh. The God who puts on human flesh is vulnerable—mortally so, as the crucifixion demonstrates. But he is vulnerable as well to desire, made so by desire for it—and for the words that express, create, and address that desire.[23] For Augustine, desire and prayer are inseparable.[24] In the same sermon in which he warns against being verbose in prayer, he declares, "Longing desire prays always, though the tongue be silent. If you are ever longing, you are ever praying. When sleeps prayer? When desire grows cold."[25] The desire in the *Confessions* is the desire to be known in order to know (10.1.1), to reveal in hope of revelation. It twists and turns, but it is never allowed to languish.

Prayer, especially if not uniquely, returns this vulnerability. Chrétien calls it "a wounded word": "[I]t is always a tearing that brings it about that the lips open," he writes, adding that the prayer is "wounded by this hearing and this call that have always already preceded it, and that unveil it to itself, in a truth always in suffering, always agonic, struggling like Jacob all night in the dust to wrest God's blessing from him."[26] The speech that is prayer is ordeal throughout, Chrétien argues, always called toward an impossible perfection in which God speaks to God in an embodied human voice.[27] A text that is always in some way prayer, then, is a particularly apt evocation of a Word made flesh, sharing both the urgency of address and a powerful vulnerability.

Still, this vulnerable and urgent desire seems to circulate between Augustine and God, perhaps through the world, but not so obviously through the reader. The *Confessions* wants us to desire God—but *does* the text desire us, or have we only fooled ourselves into believing it might, as an excuse to write about it? The answer is in its beauty. Sentences so artfully constructed desire readers, and though Augustine would surely praise God's lack of need for signifiers, there must still be some point to the beauty he cannot quite give up, however he might praise plain prose. Beauty is what calls us, what responds to our attention with the further provocation of desire.[28] The call of the text's beauty is ambiguously addressed. We have said that

God has no need to know what Augustine's words denote, what they signify in any ordinary sense, but God too may have need of their beauty, which is also their drawing power, their way of calling God by self-revelation. We are curious to hear about Augustine's life (he declines to satisfy us), perhaps even able to benefit from his example (he hopes to inspire us), but we are also alert to the seductions of his textual beauty (he succeeds in drawing us). The circle of intimacy extended by Augustine's confessions about his acts with friends is extended further, to include us in the intimate relation between Augustine and God. God already knows, and so does Augustine, but now we do too. In the very act of telling, Augustine invites us in, extending, however reluctantly, his address. Perversely, we respond to his reluctance with our desire to seduce the text in turn, to lead it where it might not quite have wanted to go.

And we follow it where it goes in multiple directions. Through the beauty of the text, we are always drawn both to the untouchable body of Continence and to the body of Christ made almost, only ever almost, sacramentally visible in these words.[29] The God to whom Augustine draws us is not quite so incorporeal as he sometimes, in his worries about sensuous temptation, wishes; the very words that strive to replace the flesh guarantee that they cannot succeed.

Augustine, we have said, slips between flesh and words, words not always even about the flesh, though always, in sublime disregard of his own anti-rhetorical stance, words with a potent sensory appeal. Though the *Confessions* seems—though, in real ways, it is—a text startlingly without a body, especially without a divine body, though it is a text in which language seems not only to have seduced, but to have absorbed or usurped, the flesh, it is also a text in which every word is drawn to the body. The mutual seduction of bodies and words entails, like any seduction, resistance: bodies and words are mutually seductive in that they are not only drawn to, but perpetually elusive of, one another.[30] Augustine's prose in the *Confessions* is so intensely aural and oral that it is constantly at the edge of poetry, not only in its rhetoric of praise but in its very sounds and textures—in its sensuousness, which is not lessened as its topics become more abstract.

In those densely philosophical late books, the sexy body of the young Augustine has not been emaciated and diluted,[31] nor has it simply been transcended into abstract speculation. The bodily nature of the text need not emerge in accounts of the body, any more than pleasure must be conveyed by recounting it; the very text that mediates, as if in an effort to distance us safely from the temptations of holy flesh, also draws us. Not that the body is lacking altogether. Book 10 gives us the stunning "late have I loved you" passage in which the desire for and pleasure in God run through all of the senses, but in which, too, the rhythms, repetitions, and assonances of the language caress and enfold.[32] It is in this same book that the beauties of the world tell the attentive Augustine of their creator. We can label the senses through which he loves his God "spiritual,"[33] but only if we refrain from modern distinctions and allow the spirit its full embodiment: these are not senses distinct from the flesh, but the senses of the body transfigured beyond ending. The abstractions of memory are contemplated as the inward presentation of the body's sensations (10.8.13), while those of time are analyzed in the sounds of a hymn (11.27.34–11.29.39); creation, too, is at one point compared to the formation of sound into song (12.29.40). The turn to philosophical considerations does not leave the body behind; that body is still taking a lot of joy in the sheer overflowing grace of creation (13.2.3). These descriptions are not simply analogies to the body—which, because they are clear and familiar, would hardly be unexpected—they are analogies to bodily *pleasure*, the sensuous and not merely the sensory.

The enjoyment of the body is not, of course, unproblematic in these late books, any more than it was prior to Augustine's conversion. There is a constant sense of struggle to find just the right mode of taking pleasure without being trapped in a reductively materialistic aestheticism. There is perhaps a greater sense of urgency about bodily discipline, especially in Book 10 (particularly 29–35), than in the earlier books. The turn to pleasures without end, even as it affirms the desirability of sight and scent and sense in general, also struggles to reject the temporality that conditions those senses. The real tensions, between the world as revelation and the world as temptation—between two modes of sensuous seduction—pull at one another throughout the text.[34] At times, the transfiguration of beauty looks quite like a transcendence of creation altogether; at others, nothing could be clearer than the sensual carnality of divine appreciation. But in every case, again, the language—even the language of rejection—is beautiful. It persuades, eliciting like figuration an inexplicable pleasure that transforms and intensifies the intellectual delight of the ideas. And yet the text avoids both the sensual transformations of time of which Augustine was surely experientially aware, and the bodily beauty of Christ that mystics a millennium later would describe in unreluctant and sometimes startling detail.[35]

The danger of approaching that body, even in words, lends to those words another function beyond their complex prayerful invocation and appropriation: it leads Augustine to veil and to substitute, as he does with bodies throughout. Those layers of intervening text perform a double function. They chastely stand between the reader, and the writer, too, and the terrifyingly persuasive body of Christ; they tantalizingly evoke, reveal, and reveil that same body. If Augustine can allow himself to be seduced by Continence, it is precisely because she stands as the resistance to seduction, and this almost keeps him safe—but only almost, because, in a paradox familiar to us from ascetic practice generally, he must be seduced by her even as she councils him in resistance.

Both Augustine's seduction and his seductiveness require these tensions, by which he leads some of us more to one side, some more to another, but all of us, he hopes, however deviant our paths, to God—that is, to a joy without end or reservation, traced and resisted in the ever-tempting flesh, drawing our voices into a multiple and sometimes dissonant chorus of praise.

Notes

Introduction: Pleasurable Temptations

1. Unless otherwise noted, citations of the *Confessions* in this work are translated from the Latin in James J. O'Donnell, *Augustine, Confessions: Text and Commentary* (Oxford: Clarendon Press, 1992), also available in an electronic edition at www9.georgetown.edu/faculty/jod/augustine.

2. For a complex account of conversion "as a performative concept," see M. B. Pranger, "The Unfathomability of Sincerity: On the Seriousness of Augustine's Confessions," *Actas do Congresso International As Confissoes de santo Agostinho 1600 Anos Depois: Presenca e Actualidade* (Lisbon: Universidade Catolica Editora, 2002), 210.

3. Ute Ranke-Heinemann, *Eunuchs for the Kingdom of God: Women, Sexuality, and the Catholic Church*, trans. Peter Heinegg (New York: Doubleday, 1990), 75, 76.

4. Geoffrey Galt Harpham, *The Ascetic Imperative in Culture and Criticism* (Chicago: University of Chicago Press, 1987), 61.

5. See Patricia Cox Miller, "Pleasure of the Text, Text of Pleasure: Eros and Language in Origen's Commentary on the Song of Songs," *Journal of the American Academy of Religion* 54 (1986): 241–53.

6. Margaret R. Miles, *Desire and Delight: A New Reading of Augustine's Confessions* (New York: Crossroad, 1992), 10, 12, 38, 53, 66, 131.

7. Ibid., 39, 122.

8. Ibid., 9–10.

9. Ibid., 52–53.

10. Ibid., 64, 67.

11. Roland Barthes, *The Pleasure of the Text*, trans. Richard Miller (New York: Hill and Wang, 1975), 6, 38.

12. Miles, *Desire and Delight*, 11–12.

13. Ibid., 80–81.

14. Ibid., 99.

15. See Miles's discussion (ibid., 98–99) of "the vexed question of whether, or how much, a historical author can be blamed for concepts that can be shown to have proven destructive in their institutional effects."

16. Ibid., 129.

17. Barthes, *The Pleasure of the Text*, 55.

18. Miles, *Desire and Delight*, 39.

19. Barthes, *The Pleasure of the Text*, 17.

20. Miles, *Desire and Delight*, 122.

21. Barthes, *The Pleasure of the Text*, 4.

22. Miles, *Desire and Delight*, 129–30.

23. Ibid., 125.

24. Barthes, *The Pleasure of the Text*, 31, 39.

25. Ibid., 4, 25.

26. Ibid., 26.

27. Ibid., 7.

28. Ibid., 32.

29. Jean Baudrillard, *Seduction*, trans. Brian Singer (New York: St. Martin's Press, 1990), 22.

30. Ibid., 81.

31. Ibid., 22.

32. Barthes, *The Pleasure of the Text*, 16.

33. Miles, *Desire and Delight*, 70, 128.

34. Ibid., 130.

35. Ibid., 11.

36. Ibid., 98.

37. See *Retractations* 2.1.1, with reference to *Ad Simplicianum* as a crucial turning point in his understanding of grace and sin.

38. Carol Harrison, *Rethinking Augustine's Early Theology: An Argument for Continuity* (Oxford: Oxford University Press, 2006), 7.

39. Hunter's essay on Augustine and the body is forthcoming in *The Blackwell Companion to Augustine*, edited by Mark Vessey. This argument is anticipated in Hunter's earlier work; see especially "Augustinian Pessimism? A New Look at

Augustine's Teaching on Sex, Celibacy, and Marriage," *Augustinian Studies* 25 (1994): 153–77.

40. M. B. Pranger, *The Artificiality of Christianity: Essays on the Poetics of Monasticism* (Stanford: Stanford University Press, 2003), 21–22. Pranger elsewhere directly addresses the nonlinear temporality of the *Confessions* itself: "Time and Narrative in Augustine's *Confessions*," *Journal of Religion* 81 (2001): 377–93; and "The Unfathomability of Sincerity."

41. Barthes, *The Pleasure of the Text*, 36.

1. Secrets and Lies

1. The very proliferation of metaphors at the beginning of Book 2—described by Robert O'Connell as "a barrage of near-Swiftian imagery"—has both an intensifying and a dissipating effect. At the same time, Augustine here artfully blurs or veils the distinction between the literal and the metaphoric, e.g., in the just-cited line, "I flowed and boiled over in the midst of my fornications" (2.2). In O'Connell's view, "the metaphor of fluidity takes a frankly biological turn at this point" yet one might debate how "frank" or explicit this turn is. O'Connell himself notes that even the term "fornication" for Augustine is not always or exclusively sexual and rightly suggests that it is an overly literal reading of Augustine's richly imagistic language that has led to "extravagant judgments" with regard to his supposed hypersexuality (*Images of Conversion in St. Augustine's Confessions* [New York: Fordham University Press, 1996], 25, 15–16).

2. Citations of *Against Lying* follow the translation of Rev. H. Browne, *Nicene and Post-Nicene Fathers* 1.3 (Grand Rapids, Mich.: Eerdmans, 1890). Latin edition: *Corpus Scriptorum Ecclesiasticorum Latinorum* 41 (Vienna: F. Tempsky, 1900).

3. Peter Brown, *The Body and Society: Men, Women, and Sexual Renunciation in Early Christianity* (New York: Columbia University Press, 1988), 389.

4. Margaret R. Miles, *Desire and Delight: A New Reading of Augustine's Confessions* (New York: Crossroad, 1992), 38.

5. O'Connell, *Images of Conversion*, 15, 31.

6. As recognized by Margaret Miles (among others): "In Augustine's colorful Latin, the *Confessions* is overwhelming; it is next to impossible to maintain a stance of critical detachment. . . . The reader is quickly seduced into passionate relationship" (*Desire and Delight*, 9).

7. Jean Baudrillard, *Seduction* (New York: St. Martin's Press, 1990), 81.

8. Jacques Derrida queries, "Is the whole literature on faked orgasm, which today would fill several libraries, a literature on the lie, even the serviceable, generous, officious lie (*mendacium officiosum*), if this feint of orgiastic ecstasy can remain

silent or at least not articulated in words?" Later in the same essay—after noting in passing that Kant would definitely have classified the faked orgasm as a lie—he inserts a rather convoluted parenthetical: "(And there is more than one lecture that could be devoted to what links the history of the lie to the history of sexual difference, to its erotics and its interpretations, without ever quite excluding, quite on the contrary, that the paradigm of the lie has an essential link to the paradigm of pleasure.)" Several libraries could be filled, more than one lecture could be devoted—and yet not a single book is noted by Derrida, not a single lecture written. The (implicitly feminine) faked orgasm is both an excluded excess and a parenthetically enfolded secret within the history of the lie—"at once at the heart of and exterior to any concept of the lie" ("History of the Lie: Prolegomena," in *Without Alibi*, ed. and trans. Peggy Kamuf [Stanford: Stanford University Press, 2002], 36–37, 44).

9. Jacques Derrida, "Typewriter Ribbon: Limited Ink (2)," in *Without Alibi*, 109.

10. Augustine's reference to "making truth" (*facere veritatem*) in confession fascinates Derrida, who returns to it repeatedly, e.g., "Circumfession," in Jacques Derrida and Geoffrey Bennington, *Jacques Derrida* (Chicago: University of Chicago Press, 1993), 47–48, 56, 137, 233, 300; *On the Name*, trans. David Wood, John P. Leavey, and Ian McLeod (Stanford: Stanford University Press, 1995), 39; "Typewriter Ribbon," in *Without Alibi*, 109; "Composing 'Circumfession,'" in *Augustine and Postmodernism: Confessions and Circumfession*, ed. John D. Caputo and Michael J. Scanlon (Bloomington: Indiana University Press, 2005), 23. See also Michel Foucault, "About the Beginning of the Hermeneutics of the Self," in *Religion and Culture: Michel Foucault*, ed. Jeremy R. Carrette (New York: Routledge, 1999; original, 1980), 170. M. B. Pranger explores the performativity of Augustine's confessional discourse more broadly, with reference to its relationship to truth, memory, and time, in "The Unfathomability of Sincerity: On the Seriousness of Augustine's Confessions," *Actas do Congresso International As Confissoes de santo Agostinho 1600 Anos Depois: Presenca e Actualidade* (Lisbon: Universidade Catolica Editora, 2002), 193–241.

11. As Derrida describes "literature" in *Geneses, Genealogies, Genres, and Genius: The Secrets of the Archive*, trans. Beverley Bie Brahic (New York: Columbia University Press, 2006), 17. The link between the confessional or testimonial and the literary is made explicit in his *Demeure: Fiction and Testimony*, trans. Elizabeth Rottenberg (Stanford: Stanford University Press, 2000).

12. Derrida, "Typewriter Ribbon," in *Without Alibi*, 111.

13. As Paul Griffiths argues, Augustine, who endorses a fairly strict definition of the lie—namely, "insincere speech that directly contradicts what its speaker

takes to be true"—considers the lie to be "among the clearest examples of sin." To confess is to attempt to speak without sin, in an act of self-disowning by which speech acknowledges "precisely its own inadequacy for anything except confession of its own inadequacy" (*Lying: An Augustinian Theology of Duplicity* [Grand Rapids, Mich.: Brazos Press, 2004], 31, 54, 92).

14. Baudrillard, *Seduction*, 79.

15. J. M. Coetzee, "Confession and Double Thoughts: Tolstoy, Rousseau, Dostoevsky," in *Doubling the Point: Essays and Interviews*, ed. David Atwell (Cambridge, Mass.: Harvard University Press, 1992), 292.

16. Foucault, "Hermeneutics of the Self," 179.

17. Elliot R. Wolfson, *Language, Eros, Being: Kabbalistic Hermeneutics and Poetic Imagination* (New York: Fordham University Press, 2005), 232.

18. Baudrillard, *Seduction*, 33.

19. Cf. Derrida, *On the Name*, 37: "But isn't it proper to desire to carry with it its own proper suspension, the death or the phantom of desire? To go toward the absolute other, isn't that the extreme tension of a desire that tries thereby to renounce its own proper momentum, its own movement of appropriation?"

20. Miles, *Desire and Delight*, 25–28.

21. Baudrillard, *Seduction*, 22.

22. On shame in the *Confessions*, see also Virginia Burrus, *Saving Shame: Martyrs, Saints, and Other Abject Subjects* (Philadelphia: University of Pennsylvania Press, 2008), 110–25.

23. Lyell Asher, "The Dangerous Fruit of Augustine's *Confessions*," *Journal of the American Academy of Religion* 66, no. 2 (1998): 227–55, at 240.

24. On the scriptural resonances of this narrative—above all the allusion to Genesis 3—see Leo C. Ferrari, "The Pear-theft in Augustine's 'Confessions,'" *Revue des études augustiniennes* 16 (1970): 233–42; Ferrari also notes that the tale may betray a Manichaean hangover. That the literary allusions at work are still more complex is argued by Danuta Shanzer, who calls attention to a significant parallel in Horace, Epistle 1.7 ("Pears Before Swine: Augustine, *Confessions* 2.4.9," *Revue des études augustiniennes* 42 [1996]: 45–55).

25. Baudrillard, *Seduction*, 31.

26. Miles, *Desire and Delight*, 92.

27. Ibid.

28. See, e.g., Luce Irigaray, *This Sex Which Is Not One*, trans. Catherine Porter and Carolyn Burke (Ithaca, N.Y.: Cornell University Press, 1985; French, 1977), 28–29. On Baudrillard's own resistant seduction by Irigaray, see Sadie Plant, "Baudrillard's Woman: The Eve of Seduction," in *Forget Baudrillard?*, ed. Chris Rojek

and Bryan S. Turner (London: Routledge, 1993), 88–106, and Virginia Burrus, *The Sex Lives of Saints: An Erotics of Ancient Hagiography* (Philadelphia: University of Pennsylvania Press, 2004), 156–58.

29. More on this in Chapter 2.

30. Danuta Shanzer, *"Avulsa a latere meo*: Augustine's Spare Rib: *Confessions* 6.15.25," *Journal of Roman Studies* 92 (2002): 157–76, argues persuasively that Augustine's linguistic reticence—in particular, his avoidance in this text of the generally neutral term *concubina*—reflects an attempt to blur the distinction (already ambiguous "on the ground") between concubine and wife, so as to present their relationship as a virtual marriage.

31. Shanzer (ibid., 175) reads it as a "bitter expression" that "problematized marriage."

32. The depiction of marriage as a legal contract pertaining primarily to the production of heirs arises from a quite concrete social context. As David Hunter notes, Augustine refers on "more than a dozen occasions" to the signing of *tabulae matrimoniales*, or marriage contracts, which identified "the intent to marry and the contents of the dowry" as well as "the purpose of the marriage," namely, "for the sake producing children" ("Augustine and the Making of Marriage in Roman North Africa," *Journal of Early Christian Studies* 11, no. 1 [2003]: 74–75).

33. Margaret R. Miles, "Not Nameless but Unnamed: The Woman Torn from Augustine's Side," in *Feminist Interpretations of Augustine*, ed. Judith Chelius Stark (University Park: Pennsylvania State University Press, 2007), 168–69.

34. For Miles, she is even less than a trace: "her 'namelessness' signals the absence of her subjectivity from the text"; "she disappears from our view . . . without a trace" ("Not Nameless but Unnamed," 169, 183).

35. Shanzer, *"Avulsa a latere meo,"* 157–62.

36. As Shanzer points out, though Augustine's citation of Genesis 2.24 in the *Literal Commentary* 9.1 reads *"et conglutinabitur ad uxorem suam et erunt duo in carne una,"* this citation is exceptional. "Almost everywhere that Augustine discusses the passage, he cites the text as in the Vulgate of Genesis"—e.g., *"et adhaerebit uxori suae et erunt duo in carne una." "Avulsa a latere meo,"* 160.

37. Citations of *On the Good of Marriage* are translated from the Latin in Corpus Scriptorum Ecclesiasticorum Latinorum 41 (Vienna: F. Tempsky, 1900).

38. Shanzer, *"Avulsa a latere meo,"* 176.

39. Danuta Shanzer, "Latent Narrative Patterns, Allegorical Choices, and Literary Unity in Augustine's Confessions," *Vigiliae Christianae* 46, no. 1 (1992): 43–50, demonstrates the links between the allegorical choice motif in Book 8 and the figures of Wisdom and Folly introduced in Book 3.

40. See Shanzer, "Latent Narrative Patterns," 47: "For the figure of Scripture (C. 3.5.9) is in fact Sapientia herself." Shanzer traces the figure of Scripture in

Augustine's *Confessions* from her first "unrecognized epiphany" in Book 3 to her angelic reading in Book 13.

41. Baudrillard, *Seduction*, 10.

42. Ibid., 54.

43. As Gerald Schlabach puts it, "The fable was not the Manichaeism that his friends may have shared, but the pretense of human society itself" ("Friendship as Adultery: Social Reality and Sexual Metaphor in Augustine's Doctrine of Original Sin," *Augustinian Studies* 23 [1992]: 125–47).

44. Schlabach suggests, in a similar vein, that Augustine here (and elsewhere) calls for a love that clings but does not grasp—that, indeed, this is for Augustine the crucial distinction between a "continent" and a "lustful" love ("'Love is the Hand of the Soul': The Grammar of Continence in Augustine's Doctrine of Christian Love," *Journal of Early Christian Studies* 6, no. 1 [1998]: 72).

45. Kim Power, *Veiled Desire: Augustine on Women* (New York: Continuum, 1996), 101–3.

46. Alan G. Soble, "Correcting Some Misconceptions About St. Augustine's Sex Life," *Journal of the History of Sexuality* 11, no. 4 (2002): 568.

47. Citations of the *Literal Commentary on Genesis* are translated from the Latin in Corpus Scriptorum Ecclesiasticorum Latinorum 28.1 (Vienna: F. Tempsky, 1894).

48. Yet the specter of the homoerotic haunts marriage from the margins, threatening to expose the queerness of even its hetero-erotic center: if the goal of procreation is all that distinguishes it from other faithfully maintained bonds of "libidinous love," that goal is not only insufficient but ultimately unnecessary for the making of a Christian marriage (as the example of infertility demonstrates), whereas friendship is indispensable (*On the Good of Marriage* 3.3); see Mark D. Jordan, *The Ethics of Sex* (Oxford: Blackwell, 2002), 108–13. As is frequently noted, "Augustine's position on marriage is not wholly without contradictions" (Willemien Otten, "Augustine on Marriage, Monasticism, and the Community of the Church," *Theological Studies* 59 [1998]: 399). Perhaps it is the very instability and contradiction of his views on marriage and friendship that allows him to remain suspended within a state of never-quite-sated desire, as Erin Sawyer hints ("Celibate Pleasures: Masculinity, Desire, and Asceticism in Augustine," *Journal of the History of Sexuality* 6, no. 1 [1995]: 3).

2. The Word, His Body

1. To call this an analogy is only part of the story. It is also a provocation—a jarring juxtaposition of opposites, around the oppositions both of creature/creator and of body/word. For inducement to reflect on it through these juxtapositions,

see Karmen MacKendrick, *Word Made Skin: Figuring Language at the Surface of Flesh* (New York: Fordham University Press, 2004), especially 25–47 and 161–73.

2. This is the hypothesis of Green on the basis of a very early manuscript, which includes *De doctrina* and the three earlier works of Augustine's episcopate. See William M. Green, "A Fourth Century Manuscript of St. Augustine," *Revue bénédictine* 69 (1959): 191–97. Using the same manuscript and other textual evidence, Martin argues that the prologue and the first two books were finished before April 4, 397; see Josef Martin, "Abfassung, Veröffentlichung und Überlieferung von Augustins Schrift 'De doctrina christiana,'" *Traditio* 18 (1962): 69–87.

3. Augustine does not explain his decision to stop writing the book. One specific hypothesis is that he knew he would have to make use of the *Rules* by the Donatist Tychonius in order to finish, but was reluctant to do so in the midst of the anti-Donatist campaign. See, among others, Charles Kannengiesser, "The Interrupted *De doctrina christiana*," in *De doctrina christiana: A Classic of Western Culture*, ed. Duane W. H. Arnold and Pamela Bright (Notre Dame, Ind.: University of Notre Dame Press, 1995), 3–13; and the introduction by Madeleine Moreau to *La doctrine chrétienne / De doctrina christiana* (Paris: Institut d'Études Augustiniennes, 1997), 9–51, at 10–12.

4. See, for example, A. Pincherle, "The Confessions of St. Augustine: A Reappraisal," *Augustinian Studies* 7 (1976): 119–33, at 125–26.

5. So too is this chapter, which is a thorough reversal of an essay one of us once wrote for Louis Mackey and then imprudently published as Jordan, "Words and Word: Incarnation and Signification in Augustine's *De doctrina christiana*," *Augustinian Studies* 11 (1980): 177–96.

6. We follow the Latin in *De doctrina christiana*, ed. R. P. H. Green (Oxford: Clarendon Press, 1995). Until otherwise indicated, parenthetical references are to this text.

7. We here infer the meaning of *doctrina* backward from notions of teaching in the text rather than from statistical or conceptual studies of the word's range in Augustine's whole corpus or in texts by others that he may have known. For a recent survey of such studies, see Karla Pollmann, *Doctrina Christiana: Untersuchungen zu den Anfängen der christlichen Hermeneutik unter besonderer Berücksichtigung von Augustinus, De doctrina christiana* (Freiburg: Universitätsverlag, 1996), 104–8.

8. David Dawson's often admirable reading of *De doctrina* alongside *Confessions* seems sometimes to forget that a proportion is not an identity. Augustine does not suggest that a single description could cover all the terms of the proportion or even that the relation of terms in any one pair is the same as that in the others. It is therefore unlikely that Augustine would have agreed to encompass all of the

relations under a single notion such as "self-transcending," much less that he would have risked equating human embodiment with divine—especially since divine embodiment is risky enough just on its own. Compare David Dawson, "Transcendence as Embodiment: Augustine's Domestication of Gnosis," *Modern Theology* 10 (1994): 1–26.

9. The term *figurata locutio* occurs here for the first time in the text, but then repeatedly up to the break in Book 3: 2.16.24, 2.30.47, 3.5.9, 3.10.14–15, 3.11.17, 3.15.23, 3.17.25, 3.24.34.

10. For a reading of this passage within a more encompassing Augustinian model of conversion, see J. Patout Burns, "Delighting the Spirit: Augustine's Practice of Figurative Interpretation," in Arnold and Bright, *De doctrina christiana*, 182–94, at 185–86.

11. Cicero often uses *suavis* or its siblings as interchangeable with *dulcis* in his descriptions of speeches. For the rhetorical sense here, see John C. Cavadini, "The Sweetness of the Word: Salvation and Rhetoric in Augustine's *De doctrina christiana*," in ibid., 164–81, at 165–68. But *suavia* are also erotic kisses as opposed to friendly or familial ones, and *suavis* is never the same metaphor as *dulcis*.

12. For the famous study of the criterion's genealogy, see Jean Pépin, "À propos de l'histoire de l'éxégèse allégorique: L'absurdité signe de l'allégorie," in *Studia Patristica* (Berlin: Akademie-Verlag, 1957), 1:395–413. Ronald Teske thinks that 3.19.14 offers "another [and ampler] criterion." See Ronald J. Teske, "Criteria for Figurative Interpretation in St. Augustine," in Arnold and Bright, *De doctrina christiana*, 109–22, at 110. There is only one criterion. Augustine's version of it would have been recognized by readers of the critique of the (lower) poets in Plato's *Republic*, which he (and we) will recall in *Confessions*.

13. Considering the last possibility need not reactivate certain clichéd questions about Augustine's conversion. The issue here is not his residual Platonism or his uncorrected Photinianism. Nor is the project to separate pure, autobiographical data from any overlay of later reflection, as in Marc Lods, "La personne du Christ dans la 'conversion' de saint Augustin," *Recherches augustiniennes* 11 (1976): 3–34, beginning on 3–4.

14. Pierre Klossowski, *Origines cultuelles et mythiques d'un certain comportement des dames romaines* (Ste-Croix-de-Quintillargues, France: Fata Morgana, 1968), 12.

15. Augustine uses *adumbrata* later within *Confessions* in tandem with *simulata* (6.7; compare *Contra academicos* 3.2.2). Elsewhere he uses it less pejoratively to refer to the way in which figures mean (*Quaestiones in Heptateuchum* 7 on Judges). Compare *On Christian Teaching* 2.26.40.

16. The allusion is to such passages as Cicero *Tusculan Disputations* 1.4.7.

17. On the formal arrangement of these contrasts, see Goulven Madec, "Une lecture des Confessions VII, ix, 13–xii, 27," *Revue des études augustiniennes* 16 (1970): 94–99.

18. *Poculum* is a good Ciceronian and Virgilian word that can mean not only "cup" or "drinking vessel," but also whatever is in them. It can thus function like the English "drink," but it often has a medicinal meaning that the English word does not carry. Since many ancient medicines were administered as liquids, *poculum* can be synonymous with the English "medicine" or even "prescription." We will return to what exactly it might mean in this passage of *Confessions*.

19. Athanasius *Vita Antonii* 2. The reference is to Matthew 19:21.

20. See Pierre Courcelle, *Recherches sur les Confessions de saint Augustin*, 2nd. ed. (Paris: Revue des Études Augustiniennes, 1968), 192 n. 2, and O'Donnell, *Confessions*, 3:53.

21. We would hesitate, though, to describe Continence as the madam of a rival bordello. Compare Maurice P. Cunningham, "*Casta dignitas continentiae* in Augustine's Confessions," *Classical Philology* 57, no. 4 (October 1962): 234–35.

22. In his reading of the rhetorical movements in *Confessions*, Kenneth Burke emphasizes that Continence is here and at once divine spouse, compassionate mother, and promised Spirit. See his *The Rhetoric of Religion: Studies in Logology* (Berkeley: University of California Press, 1970), 114–15.

23. The variant reading "*de divina domo*" may be recorded in a single manuscript, though see O'Donnell, *Confessions*, 3.62–63, on problems with that reading.

24. The version quoted by Augustine differs in one salient aspect from the main textual traditions of the Vulgate. Where Augustine ends with "*in concupiscentiis*," the main tradition has "*in desideriis*."

25. Roland Barthes, *Le plaisir du texte*, Oeuvres complètes (Paris: Seuil, 2002), 4:219.

26. The question of *Confessions* as parody of a theophanic narrative arises in relation not only to the gospels, but also to pagan texts, especially *The Golden Ass* by Apuleius, which might itself be a parody of Christianity or a parodic figuration of sublime mysteries. Read alongside that text, the form of *Confessions* may seem to be entirely preoccupied with the obscene and mortifying possibilities of endlessly readable divine appearance. For some of the implications, see Virginia Burrus, *The Sex Lives of Saints: An Erotics of Ancient Hagiography* (Philadelphia: University of Pennsylvania Press, 2004), 80–82.

27. Graham Ward, "The Displaced Body of Jesus Christ," in his *Cities of God* (Routledge 2000), 97–116, and "On the Politics of Embodiment and the Mystery of All Flesh," in *The Sexual Theologian*, ed. Marcella Althaus-Reid and Lisa Isherwood (London: T. & T. Clark, 2005), 71–85.

28. Compare O'Donnell's emphasis on antique cult and its secrecy (*Augustine: Confessions*, I:xxix).

29. If it is also true to say that Augustine "never describes or discusses the cult act that was the centre of his ordained ministry" (*Augustine: Confessions* I:xxix), then the description of communion here must be cleverly esoteric.

30. Louis Mackey would take this as a lesson about writing: "The nagging suspicion is that writing cannot recapture but only again represent the experience that prompts it. Because that suspicion cannot be silenced, the problem of the *Confessiones* becomes the problem of its own possibility. In the end that problem is never solved, and the possibility of a true writing—the writing of truth—is never confirmed. Necessarily, since the inscription of truth distances and defers the presence of truth that would confirm it. The moment of presence is lost as soon as it is written." See Mackey, *Peregrinations of the Word: Essays in Medieval Philosophy* (Ann Arbor: University of Michigan Press, 1997), 54.

31. Barthes, *Plaisir*, 4:223.

3. Freedom in Submission

1. Citations of the *Confessions* in this chapter follow the translation by Henry Chadwick (Oxford: Oxford University Press, 1991).

2. James Wetzel, "Pelagius Anticipated: Grace and Election in Augustine's *Ad Simplicianum*," in *Augustine: From Rhetor to Theologian*, ed. Joanne McWilliam (Ontario: Wilfrid Laurier Press, 1992), 121–32, at 129.

3. This excludes, of course, those schools of thought that hold all will, or any sense of either deliberation or freedom, to be an illusory byproduct of brain activity.

4. Risto Saarinen, *Weakness of the Will in Medieval Thought From Augustine to Buridan* (Leiden: E. J. Brill, 1994), 23. Saarinen cites G. O'Daly, "Predestination and Freedom in Augustine's Ethics," in *The Philosophy in Christianity*, ed. G. Vesey (Cambridge: Cambridge University Press, 1989), 89, and J. M. Rist, *Stoic Philosophy* (Cambridge: Cambridge University Press, 1969), 421.

5. Augustine, *On the Free Choice of the Will* (388), trans. Thomas Williams (Indianapolis: Hackett, 1993), 120: "Thus we see that the first man could have sinned even if he had been created wise; and since that sin would have been a matter of free choice, it would have been justly punished in accordance with the divine law." Though in his later work Augustine's view of original sin, and of the free choice making it possible, grows darker, he does not deny our choice to act. James Wetzel elegantly argues that Augustinian predestination, and particularly the doctrine of original sin, works as a theory of redemption, "the darkness of human desire for

God, to be broken by God alone," but "as a doctrine of reprobation, it is a thorough confusion of the laws of commerce, biology, and morality." Such a doctrine supposes that we can know desire for God without having it reciprocated: "it would be hell to desire God and never have that desire requited. No one comes to desire God, however, in the absence of God's love. Here, requital is intimated by the very presence of desire. According to Augustine's logic of predestination, there is no pain of separation from God that is wholly without its element of grace." James Wetzel, "Snares of Truth: Augustine on Free Will and Predestination," in *Augustine and His Critics: Essays in Honour of Gerald Bonner*, ed. Robert Dodaro and George Lawless (London: Routledge, 2000), 124–41, at 129–30.

6. James Bernauer, "Michel Foucault's Philosophy of Religion: An Introduction to the Non-Fascist Life," in *Michel Foucault and Theology: The Politics of Religious Experience*, ed. James Bernauer and Jeremy Carrette (Hampshire, UK: Ashgate Press, 2004), 77–97, at 78.

7. Thus cited in *St. Augustine on Marriage and Sexuality*, ed. Elizabeth A. Clark (Washington, D.C.: Catholic University of America Press, 1996), 85.

8. See note 2.

9. See Aristotle's discussion of habituation in *Nicomachean Ethics*, trans. Terence Irwin (Indianapolis: Hackett, 1999), Book 2.

10. Cf. Augustine, *Confessions* 8.10.22: "And so it was 'not I' that brought this about 'but sin which dwelt in me' (Rom. 7: 17, 20), sin resulting from the punishment of a more freely chosen sin, because I was a son of Adam."

11. Cf. Augustine, *Confessions* 7.3.5: "I saw that when I acted against my wishes, I was passive rather than active."

12. Augustine understands will as a motion of the soul, toward the desirable and away from the undesired. See, e.g., *City of God* 4.14.6, or *De Duabus Animabus* 14, thus cited (no further reference) in T. D. J. Chappell, *Aristotle and Augustine on Freedom* (New York: St. Martin's Press, 1999), 126.

13. In this, he is interestingly paralleled by Immanuel Kant, for whom freedom can only lead to morally good acts, since to act according to vice is always to act under the external influence of the harmful pleasure and not according to the rules one would rationally choose for oneself—thus, it is to act unfreely. See Immanuel Kant, *Groundwork of the Metaphysics of Morals* (1785), trans. Mary Gregor (Cambridge: Cambridge University Press, 1998).

14. Augustine, *City of God*, trans. Henry Bettenson (New York: Penguin Books, 1984), 4.13.14: "For we all were in that one man, since we all were that one man, who fell into sin by the woman who was made from him before the sin. For not yet was the particular form created and distributed to us, in which we as individuals

were to live, but already the seminal nature was there from which we were to be propagated; and this being vitiated by sin, and bound by the chain of death, and justly condemned, man could not be born of man in any other state. And thus, from the bad use of free will, there originated the whole train of evil." See also *City of God* 4.14.15.

15. Augustine suggests that it might not always have been so: "The man, then, would have sown the seed, and the woman received it, as need required, the generative organs being moved by the will, not excited by lust." *City of God* 4.14.24; see also 4.14.26. Geoffrey Galt Harpham notes that this notion of disobedient flesh was not universally accepted: "Origen glimpses a possibility for heresy in the interpretation that regards the flesh as an independent agent, a view which would imply that God had 'formed a nature hostile to Himself, which cannot be subject to Him or to His law.'" Geoffrey Galt Harpham, *The Ascetic Imperative in Culture and Criticism* (Chicago: University of Chicago Press, 1987), 41.

16. Cf. Augustine, *On Free Choice of the Will*, 17: "Surely the fact that inordinate desire (*libido*) rules the mind is itself no small punishment."

17. On this point Meister Eckhart is succinct: "There are some people who want to have their own will in everything; that is bad, and there is much harm in it. Those are a little better who do want what God wants, and want nothing contrary to his will; if they were sick, what they would wish would be for God's will to be for them to be well. So these people want God to want according to their will, not for themselves to want according to his will." German Sermon 6, "Justi vivent in aeternum," in *Meister Eckhart: The Essential Sermons, Commentaries, Treatises, and Defense*, trans. Edmund Colledge and Bernard McGinn (Mahwah, N.J.: Paulist Press, 1981), 185–89, at 186.

18. Joseph Delany, "Obedience," *Catholic Encyclopedia*, vol. 11 (New York: Appleton, 1911). Online edition at www.newadvent.org/cathen/11118c.htm.

19. Augustine, *Confessions* 2. 6.14: "Even by thus imitating you they acknowledge that you are the creator of all nature and so concede that there is no place where one can entirely escape from you. Therefore in that act of theft what was the object of my love, and in what way did I viciously and perversely imitate my Lord?"

20. At least according to Luke—Matthew and Mark have him prone upon the ground. Artists have generally preferred the kneeling version. Matthew 26:39, Mark 14:35, Luke 22:41, in *Oxford Catholic Study Bible* (New York: Oxford University Press, 1990).

21. Matthew 26:39, Mark 14:36, Luke 22:42, in ibid.

22. Joseph Cardinal Ratzinger, "The Theology of Kneeling," *Adoremus Bulletin*, 8, no. 8 (November 2002).

23. Ibid.

24. Cf. J. Joyce Schuld, *Foucault and Augustine: Reconsidering Power and Love* (Notre Dame, Ind.: University of Notre Dame Press, 2003), 119: "For Augustine, the whole weight of his critique [of classical pride] comes to rest on 'the shame of the cross'—its confounding wisdom, truths, virtues, and power. (*City of God* 10.28) The proud are unable to walk in its shadow, even if through such darkness, glory is revealed. . . . Augustine knows that for classical thinkers the narrative of Christ's passion and the symbolism of the cross upends their cultural traditions about wisdom, truth, and virtue: shame within a society of honor; humility in a community that seeks praise; lowliness for the spiritual who expect ascent; bodily sufferings that disrupt intellectual control and happiness; extremes of martyrdom in contrast to the proportionality of a well-balanced life."

25. Ratzinger, "The Theology of Kneeling."

26. Harpham, *The Ascetic Imperative*, 43.

27. See for example, John Cassian, *Conferences*, trans. Colm Luibheid (Mahwah, N.J.: Paulist Press, 1985), Conference 2, chap. 13.

28. Augustine, *The Rule of St. Augustine*, trans. Raymond Canning (London: Darton, Longman and Todd, 1984), 7.3: "Because of your esteem for him he shall be superior to you; because of his responsibility to God he shall realize that he is the very least of all the brethren."

29. Schuld, *Foucault and Augustine*, 11, citing Augustine: "Pride is not something wrong in the one who loves power, or in the power itself; the fault is in the soul which perversely loves its own power, and has no thought for the justice of the omnipotent" (*City of God*, 12.8).

30. For the paradigmatic discussion of the unethical element in this command, see Søren Kierkegaard, *Fear and Trembling*, trans. Alastair Hannay (New York: Penguin Books, 2006).

31. "[T]he greater or lesser excellence of a moral virtue is determined by the greater or lesser value of the object which it qualifies one to put aside in order to give oneself to God. Now . . . it is clear that the human will is the most intimately personal and most cherished of all. So it happens that obedience, which makes a man yield up the most dearly prized stronghold of the individual soul in order to do the good pleasure of his Creator, is accounted the greatest of the moral virtues. As to whom we are to obey, there can be no doubt that first we are bound to offer an unreserved service to Almighty God in all His commands." Delaney, "Obedience."

32. "On the other hand the obligation to obedience to superiors under God admits of limitations. We are not bound to obey a superior in a matter which does

not fall within the limits of his preceptive power. Thus for instance parents although entitled beyond question to the submission of their children until they become of age, have no right to command them to marry. Neither can a superior claim our obedience in contravention to the dispositions of higher authority. Hence, notably, we cannot heed the behests of any human power no matter how venerable or undisputed as against the ordinances of God." Ibid.

33. See especially Augustine, *Confessions*, Books 12 and 13.

34. John M. Rist draws attention to several similar passages: "We do not know our own hearts, which are an 'abyss' (*On Psalms* 42 (41).13); we are a 'great deep' (*Confessions* 4.14.22); 'The power of my understanding is actually unknown to me' (*The Nature and Origin of the Soul* 4.7.10); 'Practically no-one understands his own capacities' (*The Usefulness of Belief* 10.24)." John M. Rist, *Augustine: Ancient Thought Baptized* (Cambridge: Cambridge University Press, 1994), 37.

35. Leo C. Ferrari, "The Boyhood Beatings of Augustine," *Augustinian Studies* 5 (1974): 7. Ferrari documents helpfully the prevalence of references to the scourging God in *Confessions*. As Theodore De Bruyn demonstrates, a significant shift in representations of flogging is already evident in earlier fourth-century Latin Christian authors such as Ambrose: "The *flagellum* is no longer—or rather not merely—the cultural sign of servitude. It has become the cultural sign of sonship." De Bruyn notes further, "But, as so often with Augustine, ideas that are not in themselves unique are developed and articulated with an insistence that has not only caught the attention of modern scholars but also invited reaction from Augustine's contemporaries. These reactions—or what Augustine anticipates as reactions—are incorporated into Augustine's representation of paternal discipline" (Theodore de Bruyn, "Flogging a Son: The Emergence of the *Pater Flagellans* in Latin Christian Discourse," *Journal of Early Christian Studies* 7, no. 2 [1999]: 259, 264).

36. "Even those who did as the law commanded, without the help of the spirit of grace, did it through fear of punishment and not from love of righteousness. Thus in God's sight there was not in their will that obedience which to the sight of men appeared in their work; they were the rather held guilty for that which God knew they would have chosen to commit, if it could have been without penalty." Augustine, *The Spirit and the Letter*, 8, 13, trans. J. Burnaby, in *The Library of Christian Classics 8: Augustine, Later Works*, 182–250 (Philadelphia: Westminster Press, 1955). Thus cited in Saarinen, *Weakness of the Will*, 34. Saarinen notes, "Because Augustine regards consent as the source of merit and of sin, he naturally holds that only unrestricted consent counts as true merit." Ibid.

37. Harpham, *The Ascetic Imperative*, 45.

38. Schuld, *Foucault and Augustine*, 97. Schuld refers to Michel Foucault, *Politics, Philosophy, Culture* (New York: Routledge, Chapman and Hall, 1988), 118; *Power/*

Knowledge (New York: Pantheon Books, 1980), 92, 139ff.; and *History of Sexuality, Vol. 1* (New York: Vintage, 1990), 85. Cf. Harpham, *The Ascetic Imperative*, 233: "[Foucault] finds even in the fanaticism of the early Christians a more expansive economy than he had supposed when he wrote in the first volume that asceticism was marked by a 'renunciation of pleasure or a disqualification of the flesh' (*History of Sexuality*, vol. 1, 123); he now recognizes that each such renunciation or disqualification is attended by pleasure in another key."

39. See discussion of Freud's essay "Repression," in *General Psychological Theory: Papers on Metapsychology*, ed. Philip Rieff, trans. Cecil M. Baines (New York: Collier, 1963), 95–108, in Harpham, *The Ascetic Imperative*, 52.

40. Again, there is a Kantian parallel. For Kant, the grounds for moral behavior must be purely rational; it may be that a moral action is also one that will make us happy, but whenever happiness or pleasure enters the picture, we must be suspicious of our motivation. Kant, *Groundwork*. For an analysis of the paradoxes this creates, see Gilles Deleuze, *Kant's Critical Philosophy: The Doctrine of the Faculties*, trans. Hugh Tomlinson and Barbara Habberjam (Minneapolis: University of Minnesota Press, 1985).

41. Harpham, *The Ascetic Imperative*, 66, citing "Gerard the Great, Maximus the Confessor, Thomas à Kempis, and others."

42. Jeremy Carrette, "Beyond Theology and Sexuality: Foucault, the Self and the Que(e)rying of Monotheistic Truth," in *Michel Foucault and Theology*, 217–32, at 223.

43. Bernauer, "Michel Foucault's Philosophy of Religion," 81.

44. Michel Foucault, "On the Genealogy of Ethics," in *Michel Foucault: Beyond Structuralism and Hermeneutics*, ed. Hubert L Dreyfus and Paul Rabinow, 2nd ed. (Chicago: University of Chicago Press, 1983), 231–32: "My point is not that everything is bad, but that everything is dangerous, which is not exactly the same thing as bad."

45. On this claim, see Friedrich Nietzsche, *On the Genealogy of Morality*, trans. Maudemarie Clark and Alan J. Swensen (Indianapolis: Hackett, 1998), 67–118.

46. On faith as a seductive challenge, see Jean Baudrillard, *Seduction*, trans. Brian Singer (New York: St. Martin's Press, 1990), 142.

47. Augustine, *Confessions* 11.10.12: "Therefore God's will belongs to his very substance. If in the substance of God anything has come into being which was not present before, that substance cannot truthfully be called eternal."

48. Eckhart, *Essential Sermons*, 188. For a lucid analysis of this sermon, see Bruce Milem, *The Unspoken Word: Negative Theology in Meister Eckhart's German Sermons* (Washington, DC: Catholic University of America Press, 2003), 112ff.

49. Power as such, Foucault argues, does not exist; it is not a substantive but a relation. See Michel Foucault, *Power/Knowledge: Selected Interviews and Other Writings, 1972–1977*, ed. Colin Gordon (New York: Pantheon, 1980), 98. See also Michel Foucault, *Foucault Live: Interviews 1961–84*, ed. Sylvére Lotringer (New York: Semiotext(e), 1996), 187.

50. Harpham, *The Ascetic Imperative*, 231.

51. Ibid., 54. Cf. his observation of "a commonplace in ascetic writings, which teach that 'Man's life on earth is a temptation'; the ubiquity of resistance as a structuring principle intrinsic to desire rather than an alien element imposed from the outside." Ibid., xvi–xvii.

52. See Karmen MacKendrick, "Carthage Didn't Burn Hot Enough: Saint Augustine's Divine Seduction," in Virginia Burrus and Catherine Keller, eds., *Toward a Theology of Eros* (New York: Fordham University Press, 2006), 205–17.

53. Eckhart, *Essential Sermons*, 187.

54. Bernauer, "Michel Foucault's Philosophy of Religion," 87. Bernauer notes that Foucault's final lecture emphasized the element of obedience in Christian (and not in classical) asceticism, quoting Foucault as saying in his final lecture (March 28, 1984), "it is obedience to a god who is conceived of as a despot, a master for whom one is slave and servant. It is obedience to his will which is in the form of law; and it is obedience to those who represent the despot, master and lord, and who retain an authority to which submission must be total." Ibid., 85.

55. Ibid., 92.

56. See Augustine, *The Teacher*, in *Against the Academicians* and *The Teacher*, trans. Peter King (Indianapolis: Hackett, 1995). See also *De vera religione*, no. 39, as cited in Franco Pierini, "The Master in the Fathers and in Ecclesial Tradition (especially in *De Magistro*, by St. Augustine and St. Thomas Aquinas)," www.stpauls.it/studi/maestro/inglese/pierini/ingpie03.htm: "Do not go out, go back to yourself; it is in the inner man that truth resides. And if you shall have found your nature as changeable, transcend also yourself. But remember, when you transcend yourself, transcend a soul that reasons out. Lead yourself, therefore, to where the light of reason itself is put on." *Of True Religion*, trans. J. H. S. Burleigh (Chicago: Regnery, 1966).

57. Harpham, *The Ascetic Imperative*, 269.

58. The theme is recurrent throughout the *Confessions*, especially 7.9 and .10.

59. Louis Mackey, "From Autobiography to Theology: Augustine's *Confessiones*," in *Peregrinations of the Word* (Ann Arbor: University of Michigan Press, 1997), 7–55, at 25.

60. Indeed, as Mackey also notes, "Augustine's own pride and his commitment to serve the desires of the flesh obdurately resist the invitation to cast himself down on the lowliness of Christ." Ibid., 28, citing *Confessions* 7.18.

61. Ibid., 53: "Desiring incarnation but failing to find it even in his scriptural model, he settles for intertextuality. Throughout the *Confessions* Augustine's words are interlaced with passages from the Scriptures."

4. No Time for Sex

1. Elsewhere, MacKendrick refers to "the instant of rupture with duration, the return of the same without identity," suggesting that "[t]he instant intensified beyond the limits of the subject tears open time and saying, rips time from its trajectory to turn it back upon itself, forgets the orders of passage and endurance" (*Immemorial Silence* [Albany: SUNY Press, 2001], 109–10). See also Elliot R. Wolfson, *Alef, Mem, Tau: Kabbalistic Musings on Time, Truth, and Death* (Berkeley: University of California Press, 2006), 71: "a spontaneous flash, a crack in the spatial spread of the timeline, completely in and of the moment . . . a time so fully present it is devoid of (re)presentation, so binding it releases one from all causal links to past or future, a split second wherein and wherewith the superfluity of truth divests one of all memory and expectation."

2. MacKendrick (*Immemorial Silence*, 74, 78) speaks of "the disappearance of that present by infinite contraction or division," observing that "[m]emory can gather only when the present has withdrawn." There is a hint here of the resonance with the kabbalistic concept of divine contraction or withdrawal, which MacKendrick discusses in relation to Edmond Jabès (13–15, 49–53). For a more extensive meditation on kabbalistic understandings of time, see Wolfson, *Alef, Mem, Tau*, who makes explicit the link between the concepts of divine contraction and the temporalization of eternity.

3. We are not, however, convinced that Augustine's discovery in memory of "fabrication and habit, the constants of temptation," simply adds up to a "dismal coherence," as Geoffrey Harpham suggests, in an otherwise extremely illumining reading of Book 10 that places emphasis on the significance, for Augustine, of his own observation that he is able to remember forgetfulness (Geoffrey Galt Harpham, *The Ascetic Imperative in Culture and Criticism* [Chicago: University of Chicago Press, 1987], 115).

4. Cf. Jacques Derrida's complex attempt to "think together the machine *and* the event, a machinelike repetition *and* what happens," in the context of the archiving of confessions (Derrida, "Typewriter Ribbon: Limited Ink (2)," in *Without Alibi* [Stanford: Stanford University Press, 2002], 105).

5. Emmanuel Levinas observes, "Time means that the other is forever beyond me, irreducible to the synchrony of the same. The temporality of the interhuman opens up the meaning of otherness and the otherness of meaning" (*Face to Face with*

Levinas, ed. Richard A. Cohen [Albany: State University of New York Press, 1986], 21). Wolfson cites the text and glosses the point as follows: "The intrinsic linking of alterity and temporality underscores as well the texture of the erotic fabric that envelops time" (*Alef, Mem, Tau*, 52).

6. While endorsing her view that Augustine himself soars with joy in the last four books of his *Confessions*, we obviously cannot here agree with Margaret Miles's claim that "author's pleasure and reader's pleasure do not coincide" (Miles, *Desire and Delight: A New Reading of Augustine's Confessions* [New York: Crossroads, 1992], 129). As observed in the Introduction, some readers are more resistant, some more susceptible, than others, to the seductiveness of Augustine's more philosophical (less overtly autobiographical) flights of fancy.

7. See also MacKendrick, *Immemorial Silence*, 105: "Forgetfulness unremembered would be time's triumph against eternity, a finality of loss. Memory unforgotten would overcome absence."

8. Cf. ibid., 108: "memory does not reach back in time to an origin but outside of time to forgetting."

9. See also Karmen MacKendrick, "Carthage Didn't Burn Hot Enough: Saint Augustine's Divine Seduction," in *Toward a Theology of Eros: Transfiguring Passion at the Limits of Discipline*, ed. Virginia Burrus and Catherine Keller (New York: Fordham University Press, 2006), 205–17.

10. Michael Mendelson, "*Venter Animi/Distentio Animi*: Memory and Temporality in Augustine's *Confessions*," *Augustinian Studies* 31, no. 2 (2000): 140.

11. Silvia Magnavacca, "El pasaje de XI,29,39 en la estructura de las *Confessiones*," *Teologia y vida* 43 (2002): 269–84, makes a persuasive case for taking Augustine's articulation of the three movements of *distentio, intentio,* and *extentio* in 11.29 as a key to the structural unity of the text: on this reading, Book 10 is the pivot point of *intentio*, following the autobiographical performance of *distentio* in Books 1–9 and giving place to the exegetical *extentio* of Books 11–13.

12. See M. B. Pranger's discussion of "slippage," negativity, and simultaneity in Augustine's "plotless" notion of time and narrativity, positioned as a critical engagement of Paul Ricoeur's reading of Augustine ("Time and Narrative in Augustine's *Confessions*," *Journal of Religion* 81 [2001]: 391–93).

13. Ibid., 382.

14. Admittedly, others may merely feel harassed; see Miles, *Desire and Delight*, 130–31.

15. As Miles (ibid., 94–95) notes, "Augustine's metaphors of tumescence contribute to the cumulative connotations by which he establishes male sexuality as his model of scattered and wasted strength."

16. Charles T. Mathewes, "The Liberation of Questioning in Augustine's *Confessions*," *Journal of the American Academy of Religion* 70, no. 3 (2002): 542.

17. A particularly insightful and relevant reading, among the many available, of the *khora* of Plato's *Timaeus* can be found in John Sallis, *Chorology: On Beginning in Plato's Timaeus* (Bloomington: Indiana University Press, 1999).

18. Here, as Catherine Keller puts it, "a counter-ontology seems to emerge" (*The Face of the Deep: A Theology of Becoming* [London: Routledge, 2003], 75).

19. According to Augustine, the memory does not only store images of actual sensory perceptions; it is also the site of imaginative creativity, "either enlarging or diminishing or in any way varying what the senses have touched upon" (10.8). An excellent treatment of Augustine's understanding of the creative imagination is provided by Gerard O'Daly, *Augustine's Philosophy of Mind* (Berkeley: University of California Press, 1987), 108–11.

20. To cite but one example, this is how Miles reads him (*Desire and Delight*, 133): "Hierarchical order—everything in its place—has overcome the chaos in which the objects of lust restlessly butt against and displace each other, vying for priority."

21. The affinity, even near identity, of the figures of heaven and earth are brought out well—and humorously—in Keller's reading (*Face of the Deep*, 74–77).

22. Pranger refers to it as "curvilinear" ("Time and Narrative," 386). See also his discussion of the temporality of early medieval monastic literature: "the progressive concept of time is bent, so to speak, and made curvilinear" (M. B. Pranger, *The Artificiality of Christianity: Essays on the Poetics of Monasticism* [Stanford: Stanford University Press, 2003], 22). Writing in a different context, Wolfson, who coins the term "timeswerve," also captures the Augustinian movement well: "The sway of thought, like the trajectory of time at once circular and linear, seems always to lead one back to where one has not been, retracing steps yet to be imprinted" (Elliot R. Wolfson, *Language, Eros, Being: Kabbalistic Hermeneutics and Poetic Imagination* [New York: Fordham University Press, 2005], 372).

23. Augustine's reference to the figure of heaven of heaven as *mater carissima* in 12.16 creates a link with the figure of Monica, among others; see Keller, *Face of the Deep*, 76–77, and Virginia Burrus and Catherine Keller, "Confessing Monica," in *Feminist Interpretations of Augustine*, ed. Judith Chelius Stark (University Park: Pennsylvania State University Press, 2007), 119–45.

24. We find helpful John Norris's analysis of the significance of Augustine's exegesis of the *deep* of Genesis 1:2 in the latter books of *Confessions* for interpreting the autobiographical narrative of the earlier books, even if we cannot quite share his unambivalently negative reading of the Augustinian abyss ("Abyss: Cosmic

Darkness and Spiritual Depravity in the *Confessions*," in *Studia Patristica* 38 [Leuven: Peeters, 2001], 238–44).

25. M. B. Pranger, "Augustine and the Return of the Senses," in *Seeing the Invisible in Late Antiquity and the Early Middle Ages*, ed. Giselle de Nie, Karl F. Morrison, and Marco Mostert (Turnhout, Belgium: Brepols, 2005), 66–67.

26. Wolfson, *Alef, Mem, Tau*, 92. That only divine grace (as signified by the incarnation) can, in Augustine's view, inject *any* subjective or communal durability into creation's relentless temporality is an argument developed with great subtlety by M. B. Pranger, "Politics and Finitude: The Temporal Status of Augustine's *Civitas Permixta*," in *Political Theologies: Public Religions in a Post-Secular World*, ed. Hent de Vries and Lawrence E. Sullivan (New York: Fordham University Press, 2006), 113–21.

27. Citations from the *City of God* follow the translation of Henry Bettenson (New York: Penguin, 1984; original, 1972). Latin edition: Corpus Christianorum, Series Latina 47–48 (Turnhout, Belgium: Brepols, 1965).

28. See also Virginia Burrus, *Saving Shame: Martyrs, Saints, and Other Abject Subjects* (Philadelphia: University of Pennsylvania Press, 2008), 125–33.

29. Peter Brown is optimistic: "By contrast to the present, the married intercourse of Adam and Eve, had this occurred before the Fall, would have been an object lesson in the balanced rapture with which all human beings might have used the physical joys showered upon them by their Creator. The sweet attractive power of physical beauty and the delicious onset and sharp climax of sexual delight, traditionally associated with the act of conception, may not have been absent in Paradise; but, in Paradise, such delight would have coincided entirely with the will" (Brown, *The Body and Society: Men, Women, and Sexual Renunciation in Early Christianity* [New York: Columbia University Press, 1998], 407). We certainly find it possible to imagine that increased self-control could lead to increased pleasure, but only in a paradoxical way: at its limit, self-control undoes itself within abandonment. Brown's reading does not go that far, and probably rightly so. Augustine does not seem to know what to do with pleasure in Paradise.

30. Carol Harrison, *Beauty and Revelation in the Thought of St. Augustine* (Oxford: Clarendon, 1992), is a valuable study of the significant place of beauty in Augustine's theology that gives emphasis to his positive (and distinctly non-Platonic) evaluation of the material cosmos. We are attempting to press the argument a bit further, highlighting the ways in which his incarnationalism challenges formal concepts of beauty; this line of thought is also pursued in Virginia Burrus and Karmen MacKendrick, "Bodies without Wholes: Apophatic Excess and Fragmentation in Augustine's *City of God*," in *Apophatic Bodies*, ed. Chris Boesel and Catherine

Keller (New York: Fordham University Press, 2009), 79–93. See as well Ann Astell's evocative discussion of Augustine's treatment of the simultaneous beauty and ugliness of the crucified Christ (*Eating Beauty: The Eucharist and the Spiritual Arts of the Middle Ages* [Ithaca, N.Y.: Cornell University Press, 2006], 46–51).

31. Admittedly, it is highly doubtful that Augustine imagines a gender-neutral economy of reciprocal genital admiration. His perspective is thoroughgoingly androcentric, all the more so because often only implicitly so. Male genitals are shameful to view because their "movement" is visibly evident, female genitals because the sight of them might incite such movement. Nonetheless, some subversion of the masculinist economy is at work, perhaps, when female (rather than male) genitals are exposed not so as to be used but so as to be glorified for their beauty.

32. For a relatively recent discussion of the *uti* versus *frui* distinction as this applies to both *On Christian Teaching* and *City of God*, see Perry Cahall, "The Proper Order of Conjugal Love: The Relevance of St. Augustine's Insights," *Logos* 8, no. I (2005): 117–28.

33. Margaret R. Miles, "Sex and the City (of God): Is Sex Forfeited or Fulfilled in Augustine's Resurrection of Body?" *Journal of the American Academy of Religion* 73, no. 2 (2005): 323.

34. John Peter Kenney, *The Mysticism of Saint Augustine: Rereading the Confessions* (New York: Routledge, 2005), 89.

35. Ibid., 133.

36. Margaret R. Miles, "'Facie Ad Faciem': Visuality, Desire, and the Discourse of the Other," *Journal of Religion* 87, no. I (2007): 57.

37. "The epistemology for which the tradition is famous seems to begin by rejecting or transcending the sensible world of bodies and objects. But there is another, less noticed epistemology that originates in focused attentiveness to sensible objects" (ibid., 44). While emphasizing Augustine's continuities with both Plato and Plotinus in his development of the "other, less noticed" epistemology of vision, Miles also acknowledges that "Augustine's personal God, who addresses him intimately and forcefully *through his senses*, has no parallel in Plotinus" ("Who Are We Really? A Platonist's Contribution to Christianity," in *Rereading Historical Theology: Before, During, and After Augustine* [Eugene, Ore.: Cascade Books, 2008], 24). Note, however, that Pranger, considering the same problem of the status of the senses in Augustine's thought, warns that Platonism "should not be considered to constitute its infrastructure" ("Augustine and the Return of the Senses," 56).

38. See here Elliot Wolfson's distinction between the rejection of sensory perception characteristic of Neoplatonic contemplation as "imageless vision" and the centrality of image and the imagination in other strands of Western mysticism

(*Through a Speculum That Shines: Vision and Imagination in Medieval Jewish Mysticism* [Princeton: Princeton University Press, 1994], 58–67); in the latter case, "the symbolic vision bridges the gap between the invisible and the visible, the spiritual and the corporeal" (66). Note that Wolfson himself, like Kenney and others (and for similar good reasons), sees Augustine as predominately a proponent of the superiority of imageless vision.

39. Here, too, our reading diverges somewhat from that of Kenney, who finds in Augustine's eloquent descriptions of his contemplation of the beauty of the world a somewhat misleadingly conflated account of a "multi-staged transition" from sinful love of materiality to "interior love and enjoyment of God"; he notes further that Augustine's invocation of intensely sensory images to describe his "enjoyment of God" is "analogical" and thus finally has nothing to do with sensation (*Mysticism of Saint Augustine*, 99).

40. See Pranger, "Augustine and the Return of the Senses," 62–63, with emphasis on the significance of the displacement of vision by touch, which Pranger connects with the discussion of time in book 11 of *Confessions*: "Who will hold it and fix it [i.e., the volatile human heart], so that it is stable for a little while, and grasps for a little while the splendor of an always stable eternity" (11.11).

41. See, however, the contrasting emphasis of Virginia Burrus, "An Immoderate Feast: Augustine Reads John's Apocalypse," *Augustinian Studies* 30, no. 2 (1999): 183–94, as well as the sobering critique of the failures of Augustine's incarnationalism that run throughout chapter two of the present volume, in part echoing Mark D. Jordan, "Flesh in Confession: Alcibiades Beside Augustine," in Burrus and Keller, *Toward a Theology of Eros*, 32–37. It has seemed both unavoidable and necessary not only to read Augustine against himself at certain points but also to read ourselves against ourselves.

42. With regard to Augustine's curious description of the musical "harmony" revealed in the internal organs of resurrected bodies, Bruce Holsinger comments: "Body can no more be freed of its music than music itself can be unmarked by the bodies that produce and contain it, whether overflowing in psalmody or lying dead on an anatomist's table" (*Music, Body, and Desire in Medieval Culture: Hildegard of Bingen to Chaucer* [Stanford: Stanford University Press, 2001], 82).

43. Miles, "Sex and the City (of God)," 324. Miles here cites David Chidester, *Word and Light: Seeing, Hearing, and Religious Discourse* (Chicago: University of Chicago Press, 1992), 14.

44. This is not to deny Augustine's consistent preference for sight among the senses. Susan Harvey draws a telling contrast between the North African's "privileging of visuality" and Syriac theologian Ephrem's richly synesthetic descriptions

of the "sensory feast" anticipated in the resurrection (Susan Ashbrook Harvey, *Scenting Salvation: Ancient Christianity and the Olfactory Imagination* [Berkeley: University of California Press, 2006], 233–39).

45. As observed and discussed with particular acuity by Paul Ricoeur, *Time and Narrative*, trans. Kathleen McLaughlin and David Pellauer (Chicago: University of Chicago Press, 1984), 1:22–30.

Conclusion: Seductive Praises

1. Citations to the *Confessions* in this Conclusion are from Henry Chadwick's translation, unless otherwise noted.

2. Even maintaining it, he writes, "For he did not create and then depart; the things derived from him have their being in him" (4.12.18)—a philosophically complex formulation, to say the least, which some will read as implying a primal and eternal indistinction of God and creation (see especially Meister Eckhart, e.g., German Sermon 30, "*Praedica verbum, in omnibus labora*" [2 Tim 4:2], trans. Frank Tobin, in *Meister Eckhart: Teacher and Preacher*, ed. Bernard McGinn [Mahwah, N.J.: Paulist Press, 1986], 292–96, at 292).

3. In "The Unfathomability of Sincerity: On the Seriousness of Augustine's *Confessions*," *Actas do Congresso International As Confissoes de santo Agostinho 1600 Anos Depois: Presenca e Actualidade* (Lisbon: Universidade Catolica Editora, 2002), 193–242, M. B. Pranger persuasively argues that the prayerful prose of the *Confessions* entails the "arrogation of voice," a taking on of other, in this case scriptural, voices as one's own.

4. For some fairly clear examples, see John 20, throughout.

5. Augustine strongly rejects the idea of an incorporeal resurrection. See *Enchiridion on Faith, Hope and Love*, trans. J. B. Shaw (Washington, D.C.: Regnery, 1996), 84.

6. In his essay "Shattered Love," Jean-Luc Nancy epigraphically cites Lucretius: "So I say it again and again, pleasure is shared." In *The Inoperative Community*, ed. Peter Connor (Minneapolis: University of Minnesota Press, 1991), 82–109, at 99.

7. James O'Donnell emphasizes the peculiarity of this form in his commentary on the opening passages of the text: "There have been various attempts to find precedents for this form of opening, but in the history of Latin literature, its originality and oddity are clear." While emphasizing the uniqueness of the form among Augustine's works and in Latin literature generally, O'Donnell suggests that the closest resemblance might be the epistolary novel. James J. O'Donnell, *The Confessions of Augustine: An Electronic Edition*, http://ccat.sas.upenn.edu/jod/conf/

frames1.html. The document is an online reprint of James J. O'Donnell, *Augustine, Confessions: Text and Commentary* (Oxford: Oxford University Press, 1992).

8. She might, of course, feel *mis*addressed, but that is another matter. O'Donnell writes apropos the title, "God is ordinarily the addressee of [confessional] speech, but not exclusively." Ibid.

9. We are not suggesting slowness on the readers' part; silent reading, though not unknown in the late ancient world, would have been relatively uncommon.

10. Margaret R. Miles, *Desire and Delight: A New Reading of Augustine's Confessions* (New York: Crossroad, 1992), 64.

11. Jean-Louis Chrétien, "The Wounded Word: Phenomenology of Prayer," in Dominique Janicaud et al., eds., *Phenomenology and the "Theological Turn": The French Debate* (New York: Fordham University Press, 2000), 147–75, at 147.

12. Ibid.

13. On the nondiscursive function of praise, particularly in relation to eternity, see Karmen MacKendrick, "The Temporality of Praise," in Alice den Otter, ed., *Relocating Praise: Literary Modalities and Rhetorical Contexts* (Toronto: Canadian Scholars Press, 2000).

14. In *The Teacher*, Augustine sets forth the function of language as "teaching" or "learning"; pressed by Adeodatus, he adds "reminding." The particularly complicated case of prayer, which cannot function for its addressee in any of these ways, is distinguished by its attitude as well as its function. By it, we who speak are remembered or re-gathered, not for God but for ourselves and other people. *The Teacher*, trans. Peter King, in *Augustine: Against the Academicians and The Teacher* (Indianapolis: Hackett, 1995), I, 1 and 2; summarized in Chrétien, "The Wounded Word," 152–53.

15. Chrétien notes the inverse, too—that the revelation of God is also a revelation of humanity: "If [prayer] corresponds to a theophany, it is first of all an anthropophany. . . . The invisible before which man shows himself can range from the radical invisibility of the Spirit to the inward sacredness or power of a being visible by itself, like a mountain, a star, or a statue. This act of presence puts man thoroughly at stake. . . . It exposes him in every sense of the word *expose* and with nothing held back. It concerns our body, our bearing, our posture, our gestures." "Even he who turns toward the incorporeal does so corporeally, with all his body." "The Wounded Word," 149–50.

16. Pranger, "The Unfathomability of Sincerity," 224.

17. Johannes Tauler, *Sermons*, trans. Maria Shrady (Mahwah, N.J.: Paulist Press, 1985), 38. Cited in Merold Westphal, "Prayer as the Posture of the Decentered Self," in *The Phenomenology of Prayer*, ed. Bruce Ellis Benson and Norman Wirzba

(New York: Fordham University Press, 2005), 13–31, at 20. A note from Chrétien might complicate this idea: "The silence says *You*, beyond all names, like the opening of a gaze, but this gaze is open only through speech and remains that of speech. The silence of prayer is here a silence *heard* by God; it is still and always dialogue, and can be so only because a first silence, different and purely privative, was broken." "The Wounded Word," 160.

18. See Sermon 30 on the New Testament (Matt. 17:19), trans. R. G. Mac-Mullen, 2, *Patrologiae Latinae* 38 (Paris: J-P. Migne, 1844–49). In *Nicene and Post-Nicene Fathers*, ed. Philip Schaff (Buffalo, N.Y.: Christian Literature Publishing Co., 1888), vol. 6.

19. Cf. Meister Eckhart, who states that God "has never been named within time," German Sermon 38, "In illo tempore missus est angelus Gabriel a deo: ave gratia plena, dominus tecum" (Luke 1:26, 28), in *Meister Eckhart: Selected Writings*, ed. and trans. Oliver Davies (New York: Penguin Books, 1994), 112–18, at 117.

20. Chrétien, "The Wounded Word," 158. Cf. Jean-Luc Nancy: "As we have already seen, 'God!' only takes on 'sense' in calling, in being called, and even, if I may say so, in calling himself." *Dis-Enclosure: The Deconstruction of Christianity*, trans. Bettina Bergo, Gabriel Malenfant, and Michael B. Smith (New York: Fordham University Press, 2008), 118.

21. A point also made by O'Donnell in commenting on *Confessions* I.I.I: "He gestures in our direction and mentions us from time to time, but he *never addresses his readers.*"

22. Roland Barthes, *The Pleasure of the Text*, trans. Richard Miller (New York: Hill and Wang, 1975), 6.

23. "In all religions, it is asserted, however it might be interpreted, that the divine wants to be prayed to and wants to be addressed." Chrétien, "The Wounded Word," 161.

24. For a contemporary version of the essential connection of prayer to desire (and thus to will), see Denys Turner, "How Not to Pray," in *Faith Seeking* (London: SCM Press, 2002), 93–100 at 98. Explicitly invoking Augustine, Turner argues: "Prayer is an act of the will, not of thought or feeling, and we do not understand this because in our modern culture we have intellectually lost touch with any usable meaning of the word. . . . For the great spiritual writers of classical and premodern times meant by 'will' some thing more like our deepest desires. . . . And many of those desires lie very deep within us indeed, so that we do not know them, they do not fall within our experience. . . . Prayer is the process of discovering in ourselves that with which we can truly love God: that is our will, that is where our hearts are . . . . [For Augustine and Thomas] prayer is a kind of revelation to us of what our wills truly are, it is a kind of hermeneutic of the opaque text of desire."

25. Augustine, Sermon 30 on the New Testament, sec. 7.

26. Chrétien, "The Wounded Word," 174.

27. Ibid.

28. Chrétien attributes to the Platonic tradition a necessary association between the beautiful and that which calls. "[T]he Platonic tradition, from antiquity to the Renaissance, has thought beauty to be, in its very manifestation, a call, a vocation and provocation. Nor is calling superadded to beauty, as though accidental: things and forms do not beckon us because they are beautiful. . . . Rather, we call them beautiful precisely because they call us and recall us. Moreover, as soon as we are able to call them beautiful we must do so, in order to answer them." *The Call and the Response*, trans. Anne A. Davenport (New York: Fordham University Press, 2004), 3.

29. Augustine defines a sacrament as *"verbum visibile,"* the seeable word: "The word is added to the element, and there results the Sacrament, as if itself also a kind of visible word." Augustine, "Tractates on the Gospel of John," trans. John Gibb, Tractate 80, sec. 3 (John 15:1–3), in Schaff, *Nicene and Post-Nicene Fathers*, vol. 7.

30. See Karmen MacKendrick, *Word Made Skin* (New York: Fordham University Press, 2004), especially "Conclusion: Figures of Desire," 161–73.

31. Contra Miles, *Desire and Delight*, 129–30.

32. "Late have I loved you, beauty so old and so new: late have I loved you. And see, you were within and I was in the external world and sought you there, and in my unlovely state I plunged into those lovely created things which you made. You were with me, and I was not with you. . . . You called and cried out loud and shattered my deafness. You were radiant and resplendent, you put to flight my blindness. You were fragrant, and I drew in my breath and now pant after you. I tasted you, and I feel but hunger and thirst for you. You touched me, and I am set on fire to attain the peace which is yours" (*Confessions* 10.27.38). Lest the loveliness be thought an artifact of the translation: *"Sero te amavi, pulchritudo tam antiqua et tam nova, sero te amavi! Et ecce intus eras et ego foris, et ibi te quaerebam, et in ista formosa, quae fecisti, deformis inruebam. Mecum eras, et tecum non eram. Ea me tenebant longe a te, quae si in te non essent, non essent. Vocasti et clamasti et rupisti surditatem meam: coruscasti, splenduisti et fugasti caecitatem meam: fragrasti, et duxi spiritum, et anhelo tibi, gustavi et esurio et sitio, tetigisti me, et exarsi in pacem tuam."*

33. Henry Chadwick remarks in his translation, commenting on 10.6.8, "The mystical idea of five spiritual senses was developed already by Origen in the third century." Chadwick, 183.

34. We are, perhaps obviously, not among those who find pleasure to be missing in the last books of the *Confessions*.

35. Some of the reason for this development has to do with the historical development of iconic images; though he must certainly have considered the body of Christ, Augustine would not have meditated upon its image as crucifix; the earliest crucifixes postdated him slightly, probably appearing in the late fifth or early sixth centuries.

Works Cited

Aristotle. *Nicomachean Ethics*. Translated by Terence Irwin. Indianapolis: Hackett, 1999.

Arnold, Duane W. H., and Pamela Bright, eds. *De doctrina christiana: A Classic of Western Culture*. Notre Dame, Ind.: University of Notre Dame Press, 1995.

Asher, Lyell. "The Dangerous Fruit of Augustine's *Confessions*." *Journal of the American Academy of Religion* 66, no. 2 (1998): 227–55.

Astell, Ann W. *Eating Beauty: The Eucharist and the Spiritual Arts of the Middle Ages*. Ithaca, N.Y.: Cornell University Press, 2006.

Augustine. *Against Lying*. Translated by Rev. H. Browne. Grand Rapids, Mich.: Eerdmans, 1890. Latin edition: Corpus Scriptorum Ecclesiasticorum Latinorum 41. Vienna: F. Tempsky, 1900.

———. *City of God*. Translated by Henry Bettenson. New York: Penguin, 1984; original, 1972. Latin edition: Corpus Christianorum, Series Latina 47–48. Turnhout, Belgium: Brepols, 1965.

———. *Confessions*. Translated by Henry Chadwick. Oxford: Oxford University Press, 1991. Latin edition: James J. O'Donnell, *Augustine, Confessions: Text and Commentary*. Oxford: Clarendon Press, 1992.

———. *Enchiridion on Faith, Hope and Love*. Translated by J. B. Shaw. Washington, D.C.: Regnery, 1996. Latin edition: Corpus Christianorum, Series Latina 46. Turnhout, Belgium: Brepols, 1969.

————. *Literal Commentary on Genesis*. Translated by John H. Taylor. Ancient Christian Writers 41–42. New York: Newman Press, 1982. Latin edition: Corpus Scriptorum Ecclesiasticorum Latinorum 28.1. Vienna: F. Tempsky, 1894.

————. *On Christian Teaching*. Edited and translated by R. P. H. Green. Oxford Early Christian Studies. Oxford: Clarendon Press, 1995.

————. *On the Free Choice of the Will*. Translated by Thomas Williams. Fathers of the Church 59. Indianapolis: Hackett, 1993. Latin edition: Corpus Christianorum, Series Latina 29. Turnhout, Belgium: Brepols, 1970.

————. *On the Good of Marriage*. Translated by Charles T. Wilcox. Fathers of the Church 27. Washington, D.C.: Catholic University of America Press, 1955. Latin edition: Corpus Scriptorum Ecclesiasticorum Latinorum 41. Vienna: F. Tempsky, 1900.

————. *On True Religion*. Translated by J. H. S. Burleigh. In *Augustine: Earlier Writings*, 218–283. Library of Christian Classics 6. Philadelphia: Westminster Press, 1953. Latin edition: Corpus Christianorum, Series Latina 32. Turnhout, Belgium: Brepols, 1962.

————. *The Rule of Saint Augustine*. Translated by Raymond Canning. London: Darton, Longman and Todd, 1984. Latin edition: Patrologia Latina 32. Paris: J-P. Migne, 1845.

————. *Sermon 30 on the New Testament*. Translated by R. G. MacMullen. Nicene and Post-Nicene Fathers I.6. Buffalo, N.Y.: Christian Literature Publishing Co., 1888. Latin edition: Patrologia Latina 38. Paris: J-P. Migne, 1841.

————. *The Spirit and the Letter*. Translated by J. Burnaby. In *Augustine: Later Works*, 182–250. The Library of Christian Classics 8. Philadelphia: Westminster Press, 1955. Latin edition: Corpus Scriptorum Ecclesiasticorum Latinorum 60. Vienna: F. Tempsky, 1913.

————. *The Teacher*. Translated by Peter King. In *Augustine: Against the Academicians and The Teacher*. Indianapolis: Hackett, 1995. Latin edition: Corpus Christianorum, Series Latina 29. Turnhout, Belgium: Brepols, 1970.

————. *Tractate 80 on the Gospel of John*. Translated by John Gibb. Nicene and Post-Nicene Fathers I.7. Buffalo, N.Y.: Christian Literature Publishing Co., 1888. Latin edition: Corpus Christianorum, Series Latina 36. Turnhout, Belgium: Brepols, 1954.

Barthes, Roland. *The Pleasure of the Text*. Translated by Richard Miller. New York: Hill and Wang, 1975. French edition: *Le plaisir du texte*, in Roland Barthes, *Oeuvres complètes*, 4:217–64. Revised ed. Paris: Seuil, 2002.

Baudrillard, Jean. *Seduction*. Translated by Brian Singer. New York: St. Martin's Press, 1990. French edition: *De la seduction*. Paris: Editions Galilée, 1979.

Bernauer, James. "Michel Foucault's Philosophy of Religion: An Introduction to the Non-Fascist Life." In Bernauer and Carrette, *Michel Foucault and Theology*, 77–97.

Bernauer, James, and Jeremy Carrette, eds. *Michel Foucault and Theology: The Politics of Religious Experience*. Hampshire, UK: Ashgate Press, 2004.

Brown, Peter. *The Body and Society: Men, Women, and Sexual Renunciation in Early Christianity*. New York: Columbia University Press, 1988.

Burke, Kenneth. *The Rhetoric of Religion: Studies in Logology*. Berkeley: University of California Press, 1970.

Burns, J. Patout. "Delighting the Spirit: Augustine's Practice of Figurative Interpretation." In Arnold and Bright, *De doctrina christiana*, 182–94.

Burrus, Virginia. "An Immoderate Feast: Augustine Reads John's Apocalypse." *Augustinian Studies* 30, no. 2 (1999): 183–94.

———. *Saving Shame: Martyrs, Saints, and Other Abject Subjects*. Philadelphia: University of Pennsylvania Press, 2008.

———. *The Sex Lives of Saints: An Erotics of Ancient Hagiography*. Philadelphia: University of Pennsylvania Press, 2004.

Burrus, Virginia, and Catherine Keller. "Confessing Monica." In *Feminist Interpretations of Augustine*, edited by Judith Chelius Stark, 119–45. University Park: Pennsylvania State University Press, 2007.

Burrus, Virginia, and Catherine Keller, eds. *Toward a Theology of Eros: Transfiguring Passion at the Limits of Discipline*. New York: Fordham University Press, 2006.

Burrus, Virginia, and Karmen MacKendrick. "Bodies without Wholes: Apophatic Excess and Fragmentation in Augustine's *City of God*." In *Apophatic Bodies*, edited by Chris Boesel and Catherine Keller, 79–93. New York: Fordham University Press, 2009.

Cahall, Perry. "The Proper Order of Conjugal Love: The Relevance of St. Augustine's Insights." *Logos* 8, no. 1 (2005): 117–28.

Carrette, Jeremy. "Beyond Theology and Sexuality: Foucault, the Self and the Que(e)rying of Monotheistic Truth." In Bernauer and Carrette, *Michel Foucault and Theology*, 217–32.

Cassian, John. *Conferences*. Translated by Colm Luibheid. Mahwah, N.J.: Paulist Press, 1985.

Cavadini, John C. "The Sweetness of the Word: Salvation and Rhetoric in Augustine's *De doctrina christiana*." In Arnold and Bright, *De doctrina christiana*, 164–81.

Chappell, T. D. J. *Aristotle and Augustine on Freedom*. New York: St. Martin's Press, 1999.

Chrétien, Jean-Louis. *The Call and the Response*. Translated by Anne A. Davenport. New York: Fordham University Press, 2004. French edition: *L'Appel et la réponse*. Paris: Editions de Minuit, 1992.

————. "The Wounded Word: Phenomenology of Prayer." In Dominique Janicaud et al., *Phenomenology and the "Theological Turn": The French Debate*, 147–75. New York: Fordham University Press, 2000.

Clark, Elizabeth A., ed. *St. Augustine on Marriage and Sexuality.* Washington, D.C.: Catholic University of America Press, 1996.

Coetzee, J. M. "Confession and Double Thoughts: Tolstoy, Rousseau, Dostoevsky." In *Doubling the Point: Essays and Interviews*, edited by David Atwell, 251–93. Cambridge, Mass.: Harvard University Press, 1992.

Courcelle, Pierre. *Recherches sur les Confessions de saint Augustin.* 2nd ed. Paris: Revue des Études Augustiniennes, 1968.

Cunningham, Maurice P. "*Casta dignitas continentiae* in Augustine's *Confessions.*" *Classical Philology* 57, no. 4 (1962): 234–35.

Dawson, David. "Transcendence as Embodiment: Augustine's Domestication of Gnosis." *Modern Theology* 10 (1994): 1–26.

De Bruyn, Theodore. "Flogging a Son: The Emergence of the *Pater Flagellans* in Latin Christian Discourse." *Journal of Early Christian Studies* 7, no. 2 (1999): 249–90.

Delaney, Joseph. "Obedience." In *The Catholic Encyclopedia*, vol. 11. New York: Appleton, 1911.

Deleuze, Gilles. *Kant's Critical Philosophy: The Doctrine of the Faculties.* Translated by Hugh Tomlinson and Barbara Habberjam. Minneapolis: University of Minnesota Press, 1985. French edition: *La Philosophie critique de Kant.* Paris: Presses Universitaires de France, 1963.

Derrida, Jacques. "Circumfession." In Geoffrey Bennington and Jacques Derrida, *Jacques Derrida*, 3–315. Chicago: University of Chicago Press, 1993.

————. "Composing 'Circumfession.'" In *Augustine and Postmodernism: Confessions and Circumfession*, edited by John D. Caputo and Michael J. Scanlon, 19–27. Bloomington: Indiana University Press, 2005.

————. *Demeure: Fiction and Testimony.* Translated by Elizabeth Rottenberg. Stanford: Stanford University Press, 2000.

————. *Geneses, Genealogies, Genres, and Genius: The Secrets of the Archive.* Translated by Beverley Bie Brahic. New York: Columbia University Press, 2006.

————. *On the Name.* Translated by David Wood, John P. Leavey, and Ian McLeod. Stanford: Stanford University Press, 1995.

————. *Without Alibi.* Edited and translated by Peggy Kamuf. Stanford: Stanford University Press, 2002.

Eckhart, Meister Johannes. "In illo tempore missus est angelus Gabriel a deo: ave gratia plena, dominus tecum (Luke 1:26, 28)." In *Meister Eckhart: Selected Writings*,

112–18. Translated and edited by Oliver Davies. New York: Penguin Books, 1994.

———. "Justi vivent in aeternum." In *Meister Eckhart: The Essential Sermons, Commentaries, Treatises, and Defense*, 185–89. Translated by Edmund Colledge and Bernard McGinn. Mahwah, N.J.: Paulist Press, 1981.

———. "Praedica verbum, in omnibus labora." In *Meister Eckhart: Teacher and Preacher*, 292–96. Translated by Frank Tobin. Mahwah, N.J.: Paulist Press, 1986.

Ferrari, Leo C. "The Boyhood Beatings of Augustine." *Augustinian Studies* 5 (1974): 1–14.

———. "The Pear-theft in Augustine's 'Confessions.'" *Revue des études augustiniennes* 16 (1970): 233–42.

Foucault, Michel. "About the Beginning of the Hermeneutics of the Self." In *Religion and Culture: Michel Foucault*, edited by Jeremy R. Carrette, 158–81. New York: Routledge, 1999.

———. *History of Sexuality, Vol. 1*. New York: Vintage, 1990.

———. "On the Genealogy of Ethics." In *Michel Foucault: Beyond Structuralism and Hermeneutics*, 2nd ed., edited by Hubert L. Dreyfus and Paul Rabinow, 229–52. Chicago: University of Chicago Press, 1983.

———. "Power and Sex." In *Politics, Philosophy, Culture*, edited by Lawrence D. Kritzman, 110–24. New York: Routledge, Chapman and Hall, 1988.

———. "Sade, Sargeant of Sex." In *Foucault Live: Interviews 1961–84*, 2nd ed., edited by Sylvére Lotringer, 186–89. New York: Semiotext(e), 1996.

———. "Two Lectures." In *Power/Knowledge: Selected Interviews and Other Writings, 1972–1977*, edited by Colin Gordon, 78–108. New York: Pantheon, 1980.

Freud, Sigmund. "Repression." In *General Psychological Theory: Papers on Metapsychology*, edited by Philip Rieff, 104–15. New York: Collier, 1963.

Green, R. P. H., ed. *De doctrina christiana*. Oxford: Clarendon Press, 1995.

Green, William M. "A Fourth Century Manuscript of St. Augustine." *Revue bénédictine* 69 (1959): 191–97.

Griffiths, Paul J. *Lying: An Augustinian Theology of Duplicity*. Grand Rapids, Mich.: Brazos Press, 2004.

Harpham, Geoffrey Galt. *The Ascetic Imperative in Culture and Criticism*. Chicago: University of Chicago Press, 1987.

Harrison, Carol. *Beauty and Revelation in the Thought of St. Augustine*. Oxford: Clarendon, 1992.

———. *Rethinking Augustine's Early Theology: An Argument for Continuity*. Oxford: Oxford University Press, 2006.

Harvey, Susan Ashbrook. *Scenting Salvation: Ancient Christianity and the Olfactory Imagination*. Berkeley: University of California Press, 2006.

Holsinger, Bruce W. *Music, Body, and Desire in Medieval Culture: Hildegard of Bingen to Chaucer*. Stanford: Stanford University Press, 2001.

Hunter, David G. "Augustine and the Making of Marriage in Roman North Africa." *Journal of Early Christian Studies* 11, no. 1 (2003): 63–85.

———. "Augustinian Pessimism? A New Look at Augustine's Teaching on Sex, Celibacy, and Marriage." *Augustinian Studies* 25 (1994): 153–77.

Irigaray, Luce. *This Sex Which Is Not One*. Translated by Catherine Porter and Carolyn Burke. Ithaca, N.Y.: Cornell University Press, 1985.

Jordan, Mark D. *The Ethics of Sex*. Oxford: Blackwell, 2002.

———. "Flesh in Confession: Alcibiades Beside Augustine." In Burrus and Keller, *Toward a Theology of Eros*, 23–37.

———. "Words and Word: Incarnation and Signification in Augustine's *De doctrina christiana*." *Augustinian Studies* 11 (1980): 177–196.

Kannengiesser, Charles. "The Interrupted *De doctrina christiana*." In Arnold and Bright, *De doctrina christiana*, 3–13.

Kant, Immanuel. *Groundwork of the Metaphysics of Morals*. Translated by Mary Gregor. Cambridge: Cambridge University Press, 1998.

Keller, Catherine. *The Face of the Deep: A Theology of Becoming*. London: Routledge, 2003.

Kenney, John Peter. *The Mysticism of Saint Augustine: Rereading the Confessions*. New York: Routledge, 2005.

Kierkegaard, Søren. *Fear and Trembling*. Translated by Alastair Hannay. New York: Penguin Books, 2006.

Klossowski, Pierre. *Diana at Her Bath, and The Women of Rome*. Translated by Stephen Sartarelli and Sophie Hawkes. Boston: Eridanos, 1990. French edition: *Le bain de Diane*. Paris: NRF/Gallimard, 1980.

———. *Origines cultuelles et mythiques d'un certain comportement des dames romains*. Ste-Croix-de-Quintillargues, France: Fata Morgana, 1968.

Lods, Marc. "La personne du Christ dans la 'conversion' de saint Augustin." *Recherches augustiniennes* 11 (1976): 3–34.

MacKendrick, Karmen. "Carthage Didn't Burn Hot Enough: Saint Augustine's Divine Seduction." In Burrus and Keller, *Toward a Theology of Eros*, 205–17.

———. *Immemorial Silence*. Albany: SUNY Press, 2001.

———. "The Temporality of Praise." In *Relocating Praise: Literary Modalities and Rhetorical Contexts*, edited by Alice den Otter, 19–32. Toronto: Canadian Scholars Press, 2000.

————. *Word Made Skin: Figuring Language at the Surface of Flesh*. New York: Fordham University Press, 2004.

Mackey, Louis. *Peregrinations of the Word*. Ann Arbor: University of Michigan Press, 1997.

Madec, Goulven. "Une lecture des Confessions VII, ix, 13—xii, 27." *Revue des études augustiniennes* 16 (1970): 94–99.

Magnavacca, Silvia. "El pasaje de XI,29,39 en la estructura de las *Confessiones*." *Teología y vida* 43 (2002): 269–84.

Martin, Josef. "Abfassung, Veröffentlichung und Überlieferung von Augustins Schrift 'De doctrina christiana.'" *Traditio* 18 (1962): 69–87.

Mathewes, Charles T. "The Liberation of Questioning in Augustine's *Confessions*." *Journal of the American Academy of Religion* 70, no. 3 (2002): 539–60.

Mendelson, Michael. "*Venter animi distentio animi*: Memory and Temporality in Augustine's *Confessions*." *Augustinian Studies* 31, no. 2 (2000): 137–63.

Milem, Bruce. *The Unspoken Word: Negative Theology in Meister Eckhart's German Sermons*. Washington, D.C.: Catholic University of America Press, 2003.

Miles, Margaret R. *Desire and Delight: A New Reading of Augustine's Confessions*. New York: Crossroad, 1992.

————. "'*Facie ad faciem*': Visuality, Desire, and the Discourse of the Other." *Journal of Religion* 87, no. 1 (2007): 43–58.

————. "Not Nameless but Unnamed: The Woman Torn from Augustine's Side." In *Feminist Interpretations of Augustine*, edited by Judith Chelius Stark, 167–88. University Park: Pennsylvania State University Press, 2007.

————. "Sex and the City (of God): Is Sex Forfeited or Fulfilled in Augustine's Resurrection of Body?" *Journal of the American Academy of Religion* 73, no. 2 (2005): 307–27.

————. "Who Are We Really? A Platonist's Contribution to Christianity." In *Rereading Historical Theology: Before, During, and After Augustine*, 20–33. Eugene, Ore.: Cascade Books, 2008.

Miller, Patricia Cox. "Pleasure of the Text, Text of Pleasure: Eros and Language in Origen's Commentary on the Song of Songs." *Journal of the American Academy of Religion* 54 (1986): 241–53.

Moreau, Madeleine. "Introduction." *La doctrine chrétienne / De doctrina christiana*. Paris: Institut d'Études Augustiniennes, 1997.

Nancy, Jean-Luc. *Dis-Enclosure: The Deconstruction of Christianity*. Translated by Bettina Bergo, Gabriel Malenfant, and Michael B. Smith. New York: Fordham University Press, 2008. French edition: *La déclosion (Déconstruction du christianisme, 1)*. Paris: Editions Galilée, 2005.

————. "Shattered Love." In *The Inoperative Community*, edited by Peter Connor, translated by Peter Connor, Lisa Garbus, Michael Holland and Simona Sawhney, 82–109. Minneapolis: University of Minnesota Press, 1991.

Nietzsche, Friedrich. *On the Genealogy of Morals*. Translated by Maudemarie Clark and Alan J. Swensen. Indianapolis: Hackett, 1998.

Norris, John M. "Abyss: Cosmic Darkness and Spiritual Depravity in the *Confessions*." In *Studia Patristica: Papers Presented at the 13th International Conference of Patristic Studies*, 38:238–44. Leuven: Peeters, 2001.

O'Connell, Robert J. *Images of Conversion in St. Augustine's Confessions*. New York: Fordham University Press, 1996.

O'Daly, Gerard. *Augustine's Philosophy of Mind*. Berkeley: University of California Press, 1987.

————. "Predestination and Freedom in Augustine's Ethics." In *The Philosophy in Christianity*, edited by G. Vesey, 85–97. Cambridge: Cambridge University Press, 1989.

O'Donnell, James J. *Augustine, Confessions: Text and Commentary*. Oxford: Clarendon Press, 1992.

Otten, Willemien. "Augustine on Marriage, Monasticism, and the Community of the Church." *Theological Studies* 59 (1998): 385–405.

Oxford Catholic Study Bible. New York: Oxford University Press, 1990.

Pépin, Jean. "À propos de l'histoire de l'éxégèse allégorique: L'absurdité signe de l'allégorie." In *Studia Patristica: Papers Presented at the 2nd International Conference of Patristic Studies*, 1:395–413. Berlin: Akademie-Verlag, 1957.

Pincherle, A. "The Confessions of St. Augustine: A Reappraisal." *Augustinian Studies* 7 (1976): 119–133.

Plant, Sadie. "Baudrillard's Woman: The Eve of Seduction." In *Forget Baudrillard?*, edited by Chris Rojek and Bryan S. Turner, 88–106. London: Routledge, 1993.

Pollmann, Karla. *Doctrina Christiana: Untersuchungen zu den Anfängen der christlichen Hermeneutik unter besonderer Berücksichtigung von Augustinus, De doctrina Christiana*. Freiburg: Universitätsverlag, 1996.

Power, Kim. *Veiled Desire: Augustine on Women*. New York: Continuum, 1996.

Pranger, M. B. *The Artificiality of Christianity: Essays on the Poetics of Monasticism*. Stanford: Stanford University Press, 2003.

————. "Augustine and the Return of the Senses." In *Seeing the Invisible in Late Antiquity and the Early Middle Ages*, edited by Giselle de Nie, Karl F. Morrison, and Marco Mostert, 53–67. Turnhout, Belgium: Brepols, 2005.

————. "Politics and Finitude: The Temporal Status of Augustine's *Civitas Permixta*." In *Political Theologies: Public Religions in a Post-Secular World*, edited by Hent de Vries and Lawrence E. Sullivan, 113–21. New York: Fordham University Press, 2006.

———. "Time and Narrative in Augustine's *Confessions*." *Journal of Religion* 81 (2001): 377–93.

———. "The Unfathomability of Sincerity: On the Seriousness of Augustine's *Confessions*." *Actas do Congresso International As Confissoes de santo Agostinho 1600 Anos Depois: Presenca e Actualidade*, 193–242. Lisbon: Universidade Catolica Editora, 2002.

Ranke-Heinemann, Ute. *Eunuchs for the Kingdom of God: Women, Sexuality, and the Catholic Church*. Translated by Peter Heinegg. New York: Doubleday, 1990.

Ratzinger, Joseph. "The Theology of Kneeling." *Adoremus Bulletin* 8, no. 8 (November 2002).

Ricoeur, Paul. *Time and Narrative*. Translated by Kathleen McLaughlin and David Pellauer. Chicago: University of Chicago Press, 1984.

Rist, John M. *Augustine: Ancient Thought Baptized*. Cambridge: Cambridge University Press, 1994.

———. *Stoic Philosophy*. Cambridge: Cambridge University Press, 1969.

Saarinen, Risto. *Weakness of the Will in Medieval Thought from Augustine to Buridan*. Leiden: E. J. Brill, 1994.

Sallis, John. *Chorology: On Beginning in Plato's Timaeus*. Bloomington: Indiana University Press, 1999.

Sawyer, Erin. "Celibate Pleasures: Masculinity, Desire, and Asceticism in Augustine." *Journal of the History of Sexuality* 6, no. 1 (1995): 1–29.

Schlabach, Gerald W. "Friendship as Adultery: Social Reality and Sexual Metaphor in Augustine's Doctrine of Original Sin." *Augustinian Studies* 23 (1992): 125–47.

———. "'Love Is the Hand of the Soul': The Grammar of Continence in Augustine's Doctrine of Christian Love." *Journal of Early Christian Studies* 6, no. 1 (1998): 59–92.

Schuld, J. Joyce. *Foucault and Augustine: Reconsidering Power and Love*. Notre Dame, Ind.: University of Notre Dame Press, 2003.

Shanzer, Danuta. "*Avulsa a latere meo*: Augustine's Spare Rib: *Confessions* 6.15.25." *Journal of Roman Studies* 92 (2002): 157–76.

———. "Latent Narrative Patterns, Allegorical Choices, and Literary Unity in Augustine's Confessions." *Vigiliae Christianae* 46, no. 1 (1992): 40–56.

———. "Pears Before Swine: Augustine, *Confessions* 2.4.9." *Revue des études augustiniennes* 42 (1996): 45–55.

Soble, Alan G. "Correcting Some Misconceptions About St. Augustine's Sex Life." *Journal of the History of Sexuality* 11, no. 4 (2002): 545–69.

Tauler, Johannes. *Sermons*. Translated by Maria Shrady. Mahwah, N.J.: Paulist Press, 1985.

Teske, Ronald J. "Criteria for Figurative Interpretation in St. Augustine." In Arnold and Bright, *De doctrina christiana*, 109–122.

Turner, Denys. "How Not to Pray." In *Faith Seeking*, 93–100. London: SCM Press, 2002.

Ward, Graham. *Cities of God*. New York: Routledge, 2000.

———. "On the Politics of Embodiment and the Mystery of All Flesh." In *The Sexual Theologian*, edited by Marcella Althaus-Reid and Lisa Isherwood, 71–85. London: T&T Clark, 2005.

Westphal, Merold. "Prayer as the Posture of the Decentered Self." In *The Phenomenology of Prayer*, edited by Bruce Ellis Benson and Norman Wirzba, 13–31. New York: Fordham University Press, 2005.

Wetzel, James. "Pelagius Anticipated: Grace and Election in Augustine's *Ad Simplicianum*." In *Augustine: From Rhetor to Theologian*, edited by Joanne McWilliam, 121–32. Ontario: Wilfrid Laurier Press, 1992.

———. "Snares of Truth: Augustine on Free Will and Predestination." In *Augustine and His Critics: Essays in Honour of Gerald Bonner*, edited by Robert Dodaro and George Lawless, 124–41. London: Routledge, 2000.

Wolfson, Elliot R. *Alef, Mem, Tau: Kabbalistic Musings on Time, Truth, and Death*. Berkeley: University of California Press, 2006.

———. *Language, Eros, Being: Kabbalistic Hermeneutics and Poetic Imagination*. New York: Fordham University Press, 2005.

———. *Through a Speculum That Shines: Vision and Imagination in Medieval Jewish Mysticism*. Princeton: Princeton University Press, 1994.

Index

distension, 96, 97, 106, 112–13; and desire, 86, 93, 94, 95, 98
distentio, 93–94, 97
divinity, 31, 97, 110, 117; body and, 46,
52, 60, 84; of Christ, 30; and evil, 68;
and figuration, 39; flesh and, 34, 83
domination, 62, 63, 66, 75, 76, 77

earth, 95–96, 97, 98
Eckhart, Meister, 79, 81, 141*n*17, 154*n*19
ecstasy, 50, 51, 56
Eden, 53–59. *See also* garden; heaven;
Paradise
elusion, 116
embodiment, 117, 126
emotions, 23, 47, 81, 100–1; and memory,
89
eros, 6, 81, 82, 86, 115
erotic cosmology, 97
erotic desire, 49, 55–56
eroticism, 8, 15, 28, 30, 61, 85, 86, 103,
115–16; and asceticism, 3, 81; of obedience, 64, 81–84
erotic secrets, 14
erotic text, 2–3, 5
erotic touch, 39–40
eternal life, 26, 118
eternity, 2, 8, 22, 93, 97, 107, 118; body
and, 50, 65, 105, 106, 114; of God's
love, 85; and senses, 111; time and, 3,
86–90, 94–96, 99, 112–14
ethics, 58, 73, 82
Eucharist, 45, 60
Eve, 2, 21, 29, 99–100, 101, 102
evil, 68, 79, 116, 141*n*14
The Excellence of Widowhood (Augustine), 66
existence, 81, 92, 107, 112, 118
extension, 93
extentio, 94, 97

faith, 42, 43, 45–46, 59, 75–76, 79; and
obedience, 80; and will, 74
faithfulness, 97
fantasy, 94, 113
fascism, 66, 82
Faustus (Manichee bishop), 49

fear, 100–1
females. *See* women
feminine, 19, 24, 96
femininity, 7, 18, 24, 56
Ferrari, Leo, 75
fiction, 13–14, 17, 27, 29, 99, 103; and
poetry, 46, 90. *See also* literature
figuration, 18, 24, 39, 41, 55
figures, 39–44, 50, 57, 89, 95; female, 18–
19, 22–25, 55
flesh, 32, 116, 117, 118, 124, 126; divine,
34, 83; and The Word, 49–52, 72, 83–
84, 116–17, 124, 125; and words, 8,
116, 124, 125. *See also* body
flogging, 143*n*35. *See also* punishment
Folly, 23, 24
forgetfulness, 86, 88–92, 102. *See also*
remembering
fornication, 12, 14, 17, 18, 47
Foucault, Michel, 14, 66, 77, 78, 79,
145*n*54
freedom, 17, 31, 43, 140*n*13; divine, 16,
71; and obedience, 66, 71; in submission, 62–84; and truth, 69; and will,
65–66, 70, 71
friendship, 15–18, 31; between men, 30; of
mortal things, 25–30
fruit, 15, 17, 24, 25, 26, 88. *See also* pears
future, 87, 88, 92, 99, 112, 113

garden: of Augustine's conversion, 1–2, 49,
50, 52, 53–59, 60, 61, 76, 117
gender, 4, 7, 29, 45, 57, 58, 96
Gervasius, 104
Gethsemane, 54
gifts, 14, 27, 50, 66
God, 14, 63, 69, 80–81, 98–112; Adam
and Eve and, 21–22; body and, 38, 44,
46, 50, 65, 109; and Continence, 54,
56; and conversion, 31; and desire, 69,
97, 102, 140*n*5; enjoyment of, 36; forgetting of, 90–91, 92; and humility, 74;
and incarnation, 60; infallibility of, 73;
love and, 27–28, 39, 66, 67, 81, 85, 87,
91, 101, 110; and memory, 91, 92; and
obedience, 64, 65, 71, 73–74, 82, 83;

God, 45; reader's, 5, 147*n*6; of reading, 50, 57, 59; and resistance, 80; of responsibility, 64, 66, 82; in rhetorical figures, 39; sensual, 5; sexual, 15, 86, 109, 113–14; of submission, 64; and text, 3, 5, 6, 43, 83; and will, 103

The Pleasure of the Text (Barthes), 3, 59

Plotinus, 150*n*37

poculum, 51, 138*n*18

poetry, 46–47, 50, 125

politics, 4, 6, 7

Ponticianus, 53, 54, 57

pornography, 18, 59

Porphyry, 110

"the potion of our price," 59–61

power, 38, 71, 77, 78, 79–80; of Christ, 30; of creation, 111; of friendship, 29; of God, 44, 118; love of, 73; of poetry, 46; and responsibility, 73; of the will, 67

praise, 45, 108, 112, 115–27

Pranger, M. B., 9, 94, 98, 121, 148*n*22

prayer, 119, 121, 122, 124, 153*n*14, 153*n*15

preaching, 34, 45

predestination, 139*n*5

presence, 85, 98; divine, 97; and memory, 86–87, 88; and remembering, 90, 91; and scripture, 35; and time, 112, 113

present, 93, 94, 99, 108, 112, 113, 121

pride, 83, 117, 118; and humility, 70–76

procrastination, 92, 94

procreation, 2, 29, 56, 99, 101, 108, 135*n*48

promiscuity, 22, 28, 31, 56

prostitutes, 56

Protasius, 104

Protreptic (Aristotle), 48, 55

Psyche, 41

punishment, 75, 100, 108

Pylades, 27

Ranke-Heinemann, Ute, 2

Ratzinger, Joseph (Cardinal), 71. *See also* Benedict XVI, Pope

readers, 5, 7, 31, 88, 123, 147*n*6

reading, 35, 36, 52, 58, 61, 63, 76; erotics of, 7; and God, 88, 120; pleasure of, 50, 57, 59

redemption, 71, 102, 117

religion, 19, 66

remembering, 87, 89, 90, 92, 93. *See also* memory

renunciation, 2, 78

repression, 77–78, 80; sexual, 5, 6

resistance, 6, 7, 64, 65, 69, 74, 125, 127; and asceticism, 82; and pleasure, 80; to seduction, 4–5; and submission, 4, 76–81

responsibility, 68, 80; and obedience, 64, 66; pleasure of, 64, 66, 82; and power, 73. *See also* irresponsibility

resurrection, 88, 105, 108, 113, 152*n*5; and desire, 107; Jesus', 43; and vision, 110. *See also* bodies: resurrected

Retractations (Augustine), 9

rhetoric, 35, 37, 43, 44, 45, 47–48, 50, 52, 54, 56

rites, 41, 43, 44, 60

sacrament, 43, 125. *See also* Eucharist

sacrifice, 14, 78

saints, 39, 61, 108–9, 111

salvation, 8, 18, 31, 71, 100

Sapientia, 134*n*40

satisfaction, 8, 78, 107, 111

Schlabach, Gerald, 135*n*43

Schuld, Joyce, 77

scopophilia, 108

scripture, 17, 34–35, 38, 59, 95, 97, 123; Augustine's reading of, 48–54, 57, 58, 98, 117; and Continence, 56; figural language and, 42; and figures, 39, 44; and God's will, 75; and Jesus' body, 41; miracles in, 104; secrecy of, 87; and signs, 36–37

Scripture (as female figure), 23, 24, 56

secrecy, 11–32, 61, 102; and exposure, 3; of memory, 89; of scripture, 87

Seduction (Baudrillard), 11

self, 81, 121; and asceticism, 80; and desire, 87, 112; and lust, 102; and memory, 88, 93; and will, 64, 78, 79

Seneca, 49

senses, 4, 92, 96, 109, 110–12, 117, 126, 150n37

sex, 2, 19, 24, 31, 85–114, 116; in heaven, 98–112; and joy, 31, 99, 109; in Paradise, 2, 88, 105, 107, 113; truth of, 15, 17

sexual desire, 92, 101

sexual difference, 29, 105

sexuality, 9, 102; of Augustine, 1–6, 8, 13, 15, 17, 29, 31, 47, 131n1; male, 4, 7, 147n15

sexual pleasure, 15, 86, 109, 113–14

sexual repression, 5, 6

shame, 16, 100, 102

Shanzer, Danuta, 21

Shepherd of Hermas, 55

signification, 24, 37, 38, 40, 120

signs, 39, 41, 42, 48, 59, 60; bodily, 40, 50; economy of, 46, 60; morality of, 34–38; and rhetoric, 44; and scripture, 36–37; and words, 40

silence, 4, 60, 61, 121

sin, 21, 46, 69, 70, 73, 102, 108, 118, 140n10; Augustine's, 16, 19, 21, 22; and lies, 13; original, 2, 18, 66, 69, 70, 99–100; and salvation, 8

skin, 38, 44, 46, 58, 61, 117

Soble, Alan, 29

Socrates, 49

Song of Songs, 39–40, 56

souls, 30, 36–42, 70, 99, 100, 101, 109–10, 140n12

spectacles, 33, 43, 46, 58, 76. *See also* performances

speech, 12, 34, 41, 46, 47, 49, 60, 124

spirituality, 4, 83

stealing. *See* theft

submission, 62–84, 103; and resistance, 4, 76–81; to seduction, 30–32. *See also* obedience

subordination: of figures, 43; hierarchical, 38; of will, 71–73

Tauler, Johannes, 121

teaching, 34, 35. See also *On Christian Teaching* (Augustine)

temporality, 10, 65, 85–87, 94, 98–99, 107, 126, 146n5; and eternity, 95, 112, 114; and forgetfulness, 90. *See also* time

temptation, 22, 66, 77, 78, 81, 92, 126; and resistance, 3, 4, 7

terra, 95–96, 97

text, 8, 53–54, 83, 88, 125–26; body and, 84; Platonic, 117; and pleasure, 3, 5, 6, 43, 83; as prayer, 124; and reader, 7; scriptural, 35, 52, 56, 75

textual erotics, 3, 4, 7. *See also* language

Thagaste, 26

theft: of pears, 14, 15–18, 31, 54, 64

theology, 9, 31, 60, 115, 116, 117; of Foucault, 66

things, 12, 25–30, 36–39, 43, 93, 96

time, 9, 65, 126, 127; and desire, 93–98, 112–14; and eternity, 3, 86–90, 94–96, 99, 112–14; and sex, 85–114; and truth, 87, 91. *See also* temporality

transcendence, 28, 95, 98, 126

transformation, 1, 90, 110, 127

transience, 27, 28, 96, 97, 98, 109, 118

truth, 5, 7, 31, 91, 120, 123, 124, 139n30; and Adam and Eve, 99; of Christianity, 34; of confession, 13–14; of faith, 42; and freedom, 69; and language, 18; and Platonism, 50, 51; and scripture, 24, 97; and seduction, 11, 14; of sex, 15, 17; and time, 87, 91

Turner, Denys, 154n24

veils, 14, 18, 23, 25, 102, 122, 127

vice, 16, 67, 140n13

violence, 2, 40, 46, 76

Virgil, 47

virtue, 16, 22, 50, 69, 73, 80, 118

vision, 109, 110–11